25 Glorious Years

25 GLORIOUS YEARS

XXV

BY PETER HAINING

Published by arrangement with BBC Books,
a division of BBC Enterprises Ltd

This book is published by arrangements with BBC Books, a division of BBC Enterprises Ltd.
Doctor Who is a registered trademark of The British Broadcasting Corporation.

Set in 9/15 Optima Medium by Phoenix Photosetting, Chatham, Kent
Printed and bound in Great Britain by Mackays of Chatham PLC, Chatham, Kent for the publishers WH Allen & Co Plc
338 Ladbroke Grove, London W10 5AH

First published 1988
Reprinted, November 1988
This edition published 1990

Designed by Osborn & Stephens
Additional research David Howe

ISBN 0 86369 324 5

ACKNOWLEDGEMENTS

The author and publishers are grateful to the following for their help and supply of photographs and illustrative material for use in this book: the BBC and BBC Enterprises; John Nathan-Turner, the late Heather Hartnell, the late Patrick Troughton, Jon Pertwee, Tom Baker, Peter Davison, Colin Baker and Sylvester McCoy; Jeremy Bentham, Ray Cusick, Peter Brachaki, John Wood, Spencer Chapman, Peter Kindred, Derek Dodd, Michael Ferguson, Roger Murray-Leach, Forest J. Ackerman, Colin Howard; The Pearson Publishing Group, the *Listener*, *Radio Times*, *Private Eye*, *The Times*, *Daily Mail*, the *Mail on Sunday*, Solo Syndication & Literary Agency, the *Observer*, *Evening Standard*, Marvel Comics, Hammer Pictures and Lion International Films.

CONTENTS

THE LEGEND BEGINS...

MUM'S THE WORD FOR *DOCTOR WHO*

'**Television history** will be made on Saturday when the BBC launch the first programme of a year-long series, *Doctor Who*. Never before has a series been guaranteed such a long run.

TV planners usually work in batches of 13 weeks or less. *Emergency Ward Ten* was first designed as a six-week show.

Ask anybody in the BBC about *Doctor Who* and you will get an unhelpful reply. After one or two leaks from the cast, security was clamped down and mum's the official word.

But there's no doubt the programme chiefs will be disappointed if the show doesn't strike high into the ratings, dislodging many followers from ITV's serials for the young in heart.

This much I can tell you: the show will roam about the centuries in a new kind of time machine – and it will land its occupants at any time, past or future, at any spot on this globe – or elsewhere.

Where history is involved, accuracy is the keyword. Settings, costumes and manners will be perfect for the time.

"It's an absolutely perfect chance for an actress," said Carole Ann Ford, the rumple-haired brunette who is one of only four artists destined to stay with the show from beginning to end.

"There's no chance of getting stale – as one sometimes does in a long serial – because we shall be changing period and even nationality.

"I nearly didn't go for the interview for the job because I was fed up with playing children. It's because I'm so small, I suppose – only five feet. I have to buy boys' shirts and trousers and things, because I can never find anything else to fit me!"

This bubbling little elf, who plays Dr. Who's 15-year-old grand-daughter, has been married four years and has a three-year-old daughter. At 22, she has already been featured in several films – recently as Adam Faith's girl friend in *Mix Me a Person*.

While we talked in a Shepherd's Bush pub, she was eagerly awaiting a second-hand car she had just bought – one specially chosen so that she could reach the pedals!

The rest of us are eagerly awaiting the first transmission of *Doctor Who* at the peak family viewing time of 5.25 p.m. on Saturday, when for the Doctor (William Hartnell) and his gang it will be *First Stop – The Stone Age!*'

David Hunn, Show Piece
Tit-Bits Magazine, 23 November 1963

Below: Brunette Carole Ann Ford, who played the Doctor's first companion, Susan, in 1963.

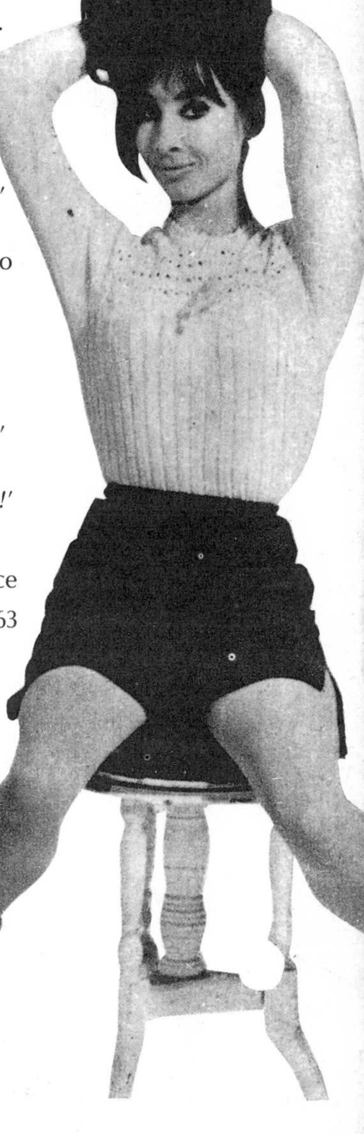

Opposite top: The Doctor (William Hartnell) and Susan get their first sight of their most famous enemy in 'The Daleks' (1963).

Opposite bottom: The creation that launched a series – Terry Nation's Dalek, designed and made by Ray Cusick.

'He seemed to see the threads that bind the universe together, and have the ability to mend them when they break.' – The Doctor in his fourth regeneration, played by Tom Baker.

INTRODUCTION

THE WORLD'S LONGEST RUNNING TV SCIENCE FICTION SERIES

During the course of one of the Doctor's dramatic adventures, set on the planet Tigella where once again he found himself busy saving a civilisation from extinction, a most perceptive remark was made about the Time Lord and his one-man mission in space and time.

'Some fifty years ago,' said Zastor, the leader of the beleaguered planet, 'I knew a man who solved the insoluble by the strangest means. He seemed to see the threads that bind the universe together, and have the ability to mend them when they break.'

Perhaps understandably puzzled by this remark, one of the ruler's lieutenants enquired whether this person was a 'wise man . . . Or a mystic,' he asked further, 'like Lexa here and her acolytes?'

For those fans who had watched *Doctor Who* since it started, this was a moment of pure magic. For not only did Zastor's statement neatly encapsulate everything the Doctor stood for, but the reference to Lexa was, by a curious twist of fate, a link to the series' very beginnings.

The story was 'Meglos' by John Flanagan and Andrew McCulloch, screened in September 1980. The Doctor was then played by Tom Baker, and appearing as the mystic, Lexa, was Jacqueline Hill, who seventeen years earlier had helped launch the series by playing the Doctor's first companion, schoolteacher Barbara Wright!

If the time scale of Zastor's quote about the Doctor were reduced from fifty years to twenty-five, it could just as easily represent our current view of the amazing Time Lord from Gallifrey and his quarter of a century of adventuring across our television screens – and what decades they have been!

From its very modest beginnings as an early Saturday evening television series for children, *Doctor Who* has become a national institution and an international success story almost unparalleled in the history of entertainment. Certainly it is the longest-running TV science fiction series in the world, and one around which has grown a mythology of astonishing complexity as well as a multi-million-pound merchandising operation again unmatched in media history.

The show which began in November 1963 as a 25-minute black and white series with a budget of £2500 per episode, now twenty-five years later can claim over 110 million viewers in sixty countries, all enjoying the best in

Above: 'A national institution and an international success story' – a cartoon from *The Listener*, 8 December 1983 to mark the twentieth anniversary of *Doctor Who*.

special effects, lavish costuming and technical expertise that the BBC now gives to what is without doubt one of their flagship productions in the world-wide market place.

Doctor Who is a series that has generated both passionate support and strong condemnation over the years. Each of the six Doctors who have followed the originator of the role, William Hartnell, has had his supporters and his detractors. Some have been criticised for their personalities, some attacked for the so-called violence of their stories. Never at any time in its history, however, has *Doctor Who* been ignored, as the bulging files of newspaper reports and magazine articles – not forgetting cartoons – which pack the show's Production Office in London bear ample witness.

Though the series is widely admired within the genre of science fiction from which it sprang, there have been those who have hated it. Nigel Kneale, creator of the legendary *Quatermass* TV stories and one of the most respected figures in the field, is among the foremost of these. 'I was actually asked to write some scripts for *Doctor Who* when it was first being planned,' Kneale said recently. 'But it seemed to be such a rotten idea that I said I wouldn't do it. It was meant to be an adventure series with a central character who was able to dodge about in time and space, which seemed to be a typical crummy producer's idea. It certainly wasn't the sort of thing that would ever be a writer's idea. It was the sort of idea one had sitting in the bath, and you say "Oh, no!" and you turn the tap off. "How ghastly!" And you forget it

Chicago Tribune Wednesday, July 14, 1982 Section 2

Tempo

A hero for all ages, 'Dr. Who' is just out of this world

By Clarence Petersen

WHO IS THIS fellow with the Harpo Marx grin, the seven-color 15-foot knitted scarf, the Edwardian coat and the 10-gallon fedora?

Who is this fellow in whose breast beat two hearts, who admits to 750 years of age, who travels through time and space in a London police call box to battle the forces of evil, invariably keeping his head when all about him are losing theirs?

Yes, Who. Dr. Who, that is. He is all of those things, and lately he has become the focus of a cult known as Who-ites.

Who-ites represent none of the perils to American youth that parents associate with the Unification Church or Hari Krishna. Who-ites do not spirit away impressionable teenagers, brainwash them and hide them from their parents.

Who-ites actually do little except sit before the television set [at 11 p.m. Sundays] and watch reruns of reruns of the 19-year-old BBC science-fiction series, "Dr. Who," which debuted on Chicago's WTTW-Ch. 11 in 1975.

Some Who-ites also collect "Dr. Who" comic books and paperback novelizations, listen to "Dr. Who" records, play "Dr. Who" board games, wear "Dr. Who" T-shirts, drink from "Dr. Who" coffee mugs, knit "Dr. Who" scarves, toss "Dr. Who" Frisbees and test their memories with "Dr. Who" trivia quizzes.

Although the first American Who-ites were discovered in Los Angeles, they are believed to be more numerous in Chicago. No one has taken a census, but television ratings indicate nearly 250,000 of them watch the series every week. Chicago's Dr. Who Fan Club, a correspondence club operated by Cynthia Guido of 2970 N. Sheridan Rd., has more than 200 members.

AS A RESULT, Chicago has attracted the attention of the North American Dr. Who Appreciation Society, formed in Van Nuys, Calif., as the official branch of the British Dr. Who fan club. The second annual Dr. Who convention will be held Friday through Sunday at Chicago's Americana-Congress Hotel, 520 S. Michigan Ave.

The Dr. Who convention will be part of the seventh annual Chicago Comicon [comics convention], which last year attracted 7,000 one-day admissions, said Larry Charet of Larry's Book Store, 1219 W. Devon Ave., who organized both conventions. Largely because of Dr. Who events, advance admissions this year [$5 a day] are running well ahead of 1981.

It takes an extraordinary man to attract such devotion, and, indeed, Dr. Who is extraordinary even among spacemen.

A Time Lord, one of an elite group of scholars from the planet Gallifrey in a galaxy beyond the reach of today's most sophisticated telescopes, Dr. Who transports himself from period to period, place to place, adventure to adventure in a remarkable vehicle called a Tardis. He acquired the Tardis years ago while it was in London for repairs, and it has since retained its original form as a police call box.

Dr. Who, in contrast, has changed appearance five times since 1963. William Hartnell originated the title role; Patrick Troughton took over in 1966, Jon Pertwee in 1970, Tom Baker in 1974 and Peter Davison [costar of "All Creatures Great and Small"] last fall. Americans have seen only the Pertwee and Baker episodes. They will get their first look at some Davison episodes at the convention.

OVER THE YEARS, Dr. Who has traveled with an assortment of companions: Leela, the alien warrior; Romanadvoratrelunder, whom Dr. Who insists on calling simply Romana ["It's either that or Fred," he tells her]; K-9, the computerized wonder dog; and, in the episodes currently being aired, Sarah Jane Smith, a beautiful English journalist [played by Elisabeth Sladen, who will attend the convention together with producer John Nathan-Turner and writer Terry Nation]; and Harry Sullivan [Ian Marter], a naval doctor who in some episodes is bright and capable and in others something of a nerd. Despite their diverse planetary origins, they all speak with Earthly English accents.

Dr. Who carries an odd assortment of tools in his pockets, including a sonar screwdriver, handy for getting into locked buildings and spacecraft and for dismantling enemy hardware. He also carries a Yo-Yo, useful, he explains with a sheepish grin, for taking gravity readings. "Dr. Who" is not a series that takes itself too seriously.

Tom Baker as Dr. Who: Quirks, gadgets and adult fans.

Wherever the Tardis takes Dr. Who, he encounters villainy of such enormity that should any example of it triumph, it could peril the destiny of the universe forever.

Among Dr. Who's most persistent foes are the dreaded Daleks, which look like nothing so much as 5-foot salt shakers on wheels, but instead of salt, they emit deathrays.

In a recent episode, "The Genesis of the Daleks," newcomers learned that the Daleks are a malevolent hybrid species, part robot and part mutated organic life, created by

Continued on page 4

Above: Doctor Who is also a cult figure in America – a typical newspaper story from the *Chicago Tribune* of 14 July 1982.

The Daleks have long been favourites with the cartoonists, as these two typical examples demonstrate. Right: Ian Dicks for *Radio Times*, 3–9 March 1984. Below right: Barry Fantoni in *The Times*, 1 March 1985.

as quickly as possible and try to think of something good.'

Such a view, though it may have been possible to understand at the time – and in fact *was* shared by others – has not subsequently been borne out. Indeed,

LOOK DOCTOR! THERE GO THE DALEKS DEALING OUT DEATH AND DESTRUCTION AS USUAL
20 GASPO CIGS
·DICKS·

Doctor Who has spiritedly overcome any shortcomings in its conception, and now enjoys the admiration of some of the leading writers of SF: in particular Britain's Brian Aldiss and America's *enfant terrible*, Harlan Ellison.

'I think *Doctor Who* is very British in its characteristics and derives from a long tradition of lovable, fallible and resourceful central characters in adventure fiction,' Brian Aldiss maintains. 'The series has always retained warmth and wit, while the Doctor through all his avatars has remained a credible and amusing figure. To my mind there is no disputing that *Doctor Who* is streets ahead of *Star Trek*: the American series may have had more money and more special effects lavished upon it, but at the expense of the dehumanisation of the characters. *Star Trek* is a synthetic package, reduced to its own constricted formula.'

Such words might sound like heresy to most American ears – but not so to Harlan Ellison, who was first introduced to the series in 1975 by another British fantasy writer and enthusiast of the programme, Michael Moorcock. So captivated was he by what he saw that on his return to the States, Harlan astounded a 1500-strong convention of science fiction fans – many of them wearing the costumes of their heroes – with this typically outrageous statement. '*Star Wars* is adolescent nonsense!' he thundered from the podium, '*Close Encounters* is obscurantist drivel! *Star Trek* can turn your brains to purée of bat guano! The greatest science fiction series of all time is *Doctor Who*! And I'll take you all on, one by one, or all in a bunch, to back it up!'

BARRY FANTONI

'Dalek, you were wonderful'

Such a deliberately inflammatory statement can be seen with hindsight to have had two dramatic effects. It not only aroused passionate emotions among Harlan Ellison's listeners, but also sent many of them away to discover just *what* the programme was that he was raving about. The result has been the development of one of the biggest and most fervent followings of the show to be found anywhere in the world. The audience for *Doctor Who* is undoubtedly large and faithful in Britain, but not on the same scale as that across the Atlantic. The Doctor may be British in his characteristics, as Brian Aldiss says, but the Americans have found him universal in his appeal.

Harlan Ellison has also underlined his admiration of *Doctor Who* in an enthusiastic introduction to the novelisations of his adventures published in America. Writing of the Doctor as 'my hero', he has urged his readers to discover both on TV and in print 'the one and only, the incomparable, the bemusing and bewildering *Doctor Who*!'

And if such an exhortation is not sufficient, he adds in equally flamboyant terms: 'What I'm saying here, in case you're a *yotz* who needs things codified simply and directly, is that *Doctor Who* is the apex, the pinnacle, the tops, the Louvre museum, the tops, the Colosseum, and other *et cetera*.'

Harlan Ellison has, quite correctly I think, compared the Doctor to three other fictional characters who have universal appeal: Sherlock Holmes, Tarzan and Superman. What he also shares with them is the fact that all four have been portrayed by different

Foot is new Dr Who

by Our Political Correspondent T.V. TIMES

The 67-year-old Michael Foot is to be the new Dr Who, it was revealed today.

The part of the eccentric doctor who spends his life in another world was left vacant when James Callaghan decided last month that he had "had enough".

Tardis & Emotional

Said Foot, 67, "I am over the moon. It is a part I have always coveted and it is a great honour to be chosen."

In his first series Foot, 67, will do battle with the ruler of the dreaded Tory Party, the extraordinary so-called Leaderene, a statuesque blonde with staring blue eyes and high-pitched mechanical voice.

"I haven't seen the script yet," said the Doctor-elect, "but I know the character is in for a hard time."

Hello, Dalek!

Meanwhile a searing question-mark hangs over the dog-like robot K-Benn, which has proved an especially unpopular feature of the story.

"We shall just have to see," said Mr Foot, putting on his long scarf and disappearing into the Tardis.

Michael Foot is 81.

actors both on TV and in films with the complete acceptance – though not always total admiration – of their audiences.

In this, the twenty-fifth year of the crusading through the galaxies of space and time, he is currently being portrayed by Sylvester McCoy, the seventh actor to have donned the mantle. Yet, while the latest incumbent is markedly different to each of his predecessors, so also is he somehow essentially *like* them. Such, in fact, has been the fate of all the Doctors, from Colin Baker, Peter Davison, Tom Baker, Jon Pertwee, Patrick Troughton, right back to the first of their number, William Hartnell. Only he was wholly original. Yet all the actors have left their own special mark on the Doctor – enlarged his character, defined his motivation, broadened his appeal.

Despite all this, the Doctor is still the enigmatic figure he was when first sighted: a mysterious being we now know to be a Time Lord from the planet Gallifrey, over 900 years old, with a body temperature of 60 degrees and two hearts. All of which adds up to the fact that he is an alien – yet somehow one who still believes in the human race despite its fallibility and readiness to fall back into the darkest recesses of its nature. In a way, he is our *conscience*.

In making such a comment, it is easy to see how one can lose track of the fact that *Doctor Who* is, after all, just a television programme. It has its history and mythology, to be sure, but its essential point is to entertain, which it does superbly despite being subject to enormous and varied pressures.

The reason for its success is the mixture of a sound basic concept (despite what Mr Kneale may say), some imaginative storytelling, and excellent production standards – all of which have stood up to the challenge of changing attitudes and tastes. Equally important has been the hard work of seven very different and highly individual actors in the central role – not forgetting some interesting and varied companions who have followed the Doctor, Watson-like, on his adventures; and the many ingenious villains (The Master, The Rani, *et al.*) and monsters (from the Daleks onwards) who have crossed his path with fearsome inevitability.

The timing of the screening of the programme has also played a major part in its success – as the much-debated recent change away from the traditional Saturday evening spot has demonstrated. I was strikingly reminded of this fact when reading a recent study about watching habits among TV viewers conducted by Laurie Taylor and Bob Mullan and reported in their book, *Uninvited Guests: The Intimate Secrets of TV & Radio*, published in 1986. I found the following passage very revealing:

'The timing of the programme was probably also important. In the early years of mass television, it was much more customary for the set to be switched on for general viewing at certain times rather than left flickering constantly in the corner.

John (37): "Yes, we used to religiously watch Dixon of Dock Green."

Reggie (42): "Every Saturday evening, wasn't it?"

The fame of *Doctor Who* has even embraced the British political scene! (Opposite) a news item from the satirical magazine, *Private Eye*, proposing Labour MP, Michael Foot, as the new Doctor in November 1980; and (below) Prime Minister Thatcher with 'companion', Chancellor Nigel Lawson, from an article by Marcia Falkender, 'Maggie is out of this World!', *The Mail on Sunday*, 13 October 1985.

John: "Either after or before *Doctor Who*."'

Any television programme as firmly entrenched in the subconscious as that has undoubtedly achieved a fame which far transcends its mere contents!

In general terms, though, the flexibility of the programme has to be seen as its greatest strength. For it is not only the Doctors that change regularly, but also his companions, the producers, the script writers and so on through all the other personnel who put together this now very complex and highly technical series. Its history is undoubtedly important, but in our world where science is constantly making great new discoveries and inexorably pushing back the frontiers of space, *Doctor Who* has no chance for complacency, no chance to stand still.

Indeed, part of the magic is that none of us – even those most closely associated with the programme – can know for *certain* what will happen next. For at the very heart of everything lies the unpredictability of the Doctor and of his time machine, the TARDIS. Only the human imagination, it would seem, places any limitation on *Doctor Who*.

In BBC terms, of course, the programme has to justify its worth in the size of the audiences it attracts, and though it has far outlasted most other shows on television, its future has been the subject of much debate in recent years and, indeed, still remains so. (Michael Grade, the recently departed Director of Programmes for Television, under whose authority lay the future of *Doctor Who*, replied, perhaps understandably, to my invitation to contribute to this book, 'I regret I am unable to help you, but thank you for asking.')

So, with a quarter of a century gone, and another season marking the twenty-fifth anniversary just ahead as I write these words, the Doctor prepares for yet more galactic endeavours. I am sure all of us wish him well – just as do those who have been associated with the programme over the years. Almost without exception, they have carried away with them a little of its magic, as you will discover in their anecdotes and memories which fill the pages that follow. Twenty-five years may be only a blink in eternity for a Time Lord, but it is a major achievement in television.

A few years back I recall hearing on a late-night TV chat show the following exchange between the host and a guest. (I believe it was *The David Frost Show*.) The topic was yet another addition to the already considerable number of series being shown on television about hospitals and doctors. The guest enquired of Frost at one stage: 'Who is the most interesting doctor on television?' To which David Frost replied instantly and with a smile: 'Correct!'

I very much hope that when the fiftieth anniversary of *Doctor Who* is being commemorated, everyone will be able wholeheartedly to echo that sentiment!

PETER HAINING
December 1987

Opposite: Illustration by Virgil Finlay for H. G. Wells's story, *The Time Machine*.

THE GREAT WHOVIAN MYSTERY

Virgil Finlay

Right: Sydney Newman (inset) and an illustration by Johan Briedé of the Dalek-like invaders in H. G. Wells's other classic SF story, *War of the Worlds*.

Like the personality of the Doctor himself – his very appellation being a question rather than a name – there is an intriguing mystery about his creation: namely, precisely *where* and *when* he came into being. There is no disputing that he was the brain-child of TV programme wizard Sydney Newman – it merely remains to establish just where Who was conceived. The evidence falls into two distinct parts, but first some basic information on 'Mr Who', Sydney Newman.

Sydney, who was born in Canada in 1915, joined the BBC in December 1962 as Head of Drama, following a mercurial rise in the world of television. He had first set out to become an artist in his native Canada, but during World War II found his true métier when he entered the world of film-making at the Canadian National Film Board. In 1946, he was sent to spend a year at NBC TV in New York where he gained a grounding in all aspects of television production, and this proved invaluable when he was invited to cross the Atlantic in 1958 by ABC TV (the forerunner of today's Thames Television) to become Producer of *Armchair Theatre*, which has since been described by TV historian Leslie Halliwell as 'the first drama series in Britain to achieve a personality of its own'.

He quickly built a formidable reputation with the series, which concentrated on contemporary plays about contemporary topics, earning this praise from television critic Philip Purser, in 1963:

'Newman is a tough supervisor of talents. He will humour the sensitive writer, the temperamental actor, the raging director, but in the end he gets his own way as surely as (at ABC, anyway) his name took the final credit on the screen after every drama show – "Producer: Sydney Newman". His interest starts with the initial script – or even before, for his policy, through his story editors, has always been to commission in advance. Many an *Armchair Theatre* play started with a half-formulated idea mentioned by a despairing author at the end of an interview in which all his more cherished projects had been dashed down. "It's like trying to sell the telephone to Alexander Graham Bell," complained one writer.'

Philip Purser added even more revealingly of the man, 'Casting, set design, first rehearsals of the show – Newman keeps an eye on them all, though his directors say he doesn't interfere with their technical handling of the piece. Once the production moves into the studio he is rarely seen, preferring to watch run-throughs on a closed-circuit screen in his office.'

Sydney's outstanding success in this position – he was also responsible for the creation of another classic series, *The Avengers*, with Patrick MacNee (which had actually evolved from his earlier drama serial *Police Surgeon* (1960) starring Ian Hendry) – resulted in him being offered the prestigious post of Head of Drama at the BBC in 1962. It was there, a year later, that he launched *Doctor Who* on what has become a quarter-of-a-century journey of entertainment for millions of people around the world. (By a curious twist of fate, while *Doctor Who* was leaping up the ratings chart in 1964, *Armchair*

Theatre scored one of its biggest post-Newman successes with a drama entitled 'The Trial of Dr Fancy', about an enigmatic scientist!)

But with the debut of *Doctor Who* under Sydney Newman's auspices, the question that demands an answer is *when* the idea evolved. Was it freshly minted, or had he been pondering it for some time? Howard Thomas, the much respected former BBC radio producer and creator of the *Brains Trust*, who later became Managing Director of ABC, has written in his autobiography, *With an Independent Air* (1977), that the idea was known to him while Sydney Newman was still at ABC. During the course of writing about some studies made by ABC into the needs of its viewers, Mr Thomas says:

'We made an interesting experiment with children's programmes to find out reactions to a series of half-hour science fiction serials. I had asked Sydney Newman if his drama department could produce these programmes for children, and their range stretched from "Valley of the Monsters" to "Pathfinders to Venus". However, many parents, critics and ITA representatives had expressed concern to the effect that such entertainment might disturb children.

'As so little practical research was available, I asked our children's programme consultant, Mary Field, if she would work on this with Professor Arnold Lloyd, Head of the Department of Education at Cambridge. I remember the infra-red photographs Mary Field had taken at children's Saturday morning film shows to capture their

POLICE

Above: The Doctor's remarkable time machine, the TARDIS, designed by Peter Brachaki in 1963; and (opposite top) its two Console rooms – the older one (opposite bottom) is now generally considered redundant.

reactions. We decided to apply a similar method to television viewing. It was impractical to put film or television cameras into an ordinary home to record children's normal responses, so we decided the next best method was to reconstruct a home in a studio and hope that children would behave naturally even though in a contrived situation.

'With the co-operation of the Middlesex Education Authority, three boys and five girls (three aged ten and five aged thirteen) were invited on a Saturday afternoon to the ABC studios at Teddington, ostensibly for a demonstration of a television camera. Whilst one group toured the premises, the others were asked to wait their turn and sit in a small studio, where they could spend the time watching a recorded programme. I quote from Sydney Newman's observations, written for an illustrated booklet we published at the time of the experiment:

"What a humiliating, funny, illuminating and humble-making experience this experiment on children's reactions was for us, the makers of this programme. For about eighteen of the twenty-five minutes of the running time, the thirteen-year-old test group paid no attention to the programme whatsoever! To what we thought was terrifying footage of primeval monsters trying to kill one another, a ten-year-old exclaimed, 'Oh, they're models!' However, we learnt many things."

'The footnote to this was that we were then considering a programme called "Dr Who". But we came to the conclusion that the Authority would never allow us to broadcast it. When Sydney Newman joined the BBC he took "Dr Who" with him.'

Such is the recollection of Howard Thomas, enshrined in print. But Sydney Newman does not concur with this memory. Though he admits to a lifelong love of science fiction – and in particular H. G. Wells's famous novel, *The Time Machine*, which he first read as a young boy – and agrees that this was influential in his creation of *Doctor Who*, he insists that the idea first germinated in his mind *after* he had joined the BBC. In an in-depth conversation with Gary Levy, editor of the *Doctor Who Bulletin*, he said that the idea was 'a residue' from earlier SF productions he had been involved in right from his earliest days in Canada, but still insisted:

'No, it [*Doctor Who*] was definitely not brought over from ABC. At ABC we did a series called *Pathfinders in Space* which was about a girl and her father and a mad scientist, the latter played by that wonderful actor George Coulouris.

'Knowing my audiences, I was always a great believer in points of identification and, therefore, if you are doing a series for kids you have to have a child in it, so we had a 14-year-old girl. You wanted adult viewers, too, so we had two adult teachers as well, with a potential for love interest. And for the grandparents and older viewers there was this irascible old man. These are just practical, ordinary showbiz notions if you've got a feeling for your audience.

'But the central character was going to be Doctor Who. That, I think, grew out of "What are we going to call this old guy?" and since the question was always "Who was he and where did he come from?", it was obvious to call it *Doctor Who*.'

Whichever view the reader may choose to accept, what remains beyond doubt is that Sydney Newman had the vision, and the vision became fact at the BBC early in the winter of 1963. Also beyond question – and readily acknowledged by Sydney Newman – was that it was the team of people, under his choice of Producer, the youthful Verity Lambert, that made *Doctor Who* a reality. As a man who has always believed in the importance of team-work in the creative process, he was lucky indeed in those who translated his basic concept into a weekly series.

Initially, Sydney Newman believes, he was fortunate in getting the unqualified backing of Hugh Greene, the Director General of the BBC, and Huw Weldon, the Managing Director. These two senior BBC men were anxious to fight back against commercial television's domination in the popular areas of programming, and saw Sydney Newman with his insider's experience of ABC as the right man to lead the attack. With their support, Sydney felt free to pick the people *he* wanted to turn his many and varied ideas into reality.

In the case of *Doctor Who*, however, he took a real gamble where one crucial appointment was concerned. Instead of selecting a producer with a proven track record, he brought over from ABC one of his former young production assistants on *Armchair Theatre*, 28-year-old Verity Lambert. Not surprisingly, she was delighted to accept his offer – and on arriving found a back-up team already being assembled. This pool of professional TV makers were 'The Original Whovians'.

Sydney's basic concept for the programme was outlined in a one-page memo. It was an idea both simple and potentially limitless. In essence, he wanted an early Saturday evening series in which an erratic alien in a rather commonplace spacecraft moved about in space and time. The space traveller was to be a 760-year-old man, partially senile, who had fled from his own far-distant planet because it had been taken over by enemies. Because of his feeble state of mind, however, he was not able to operate his machine properly, and instead of getting back home – which was his main objective – he landed on Earth instead. From there, his blundering attempts to return home were to transport him through various periods of the Earth's history. The old man's machine, Sydney said, had to be something that any viewer could identify with: an old car was one example he cited. But what he was absolutely insistent upon was that this space vehicle had to be much bigger on the inside than out.

It was from these basic guidelines that Verity Lambert and her team built *Doctor Who*. 'What Sydney asked me for was a series that was both exciting and educational,' says Verity Lambert, now one of the most respected figures in British television, and still deeply involved with programme-making at Euston Films. 'He wanted to use a time machine as the means of going back into history and allowing contemporary characters to observe critical changes in the world. He said the children's interests must always come first and that there should be no bug-eyed monsters. It was a concept that I found very exciting.'

The first person with whom the new Producer came into contact at the BBC was Donald Wilson, the highly capable Head of Serials, who had for years been in charge of the Corporation's script department. A reserved, pipe-smoking Scotsman in his early fifties with a love of the classics and a dry sense of humour, he provided an admirable foil to the quicksilver young Verity. His dedication to the art of broadcasting as a means of informing audiences and his knowledge of the tricky business of successful script creation were also of paramount importance.

According to contemporaries at the BBC in the 'sixties, what started out as a rather uncertain relationship between the old professional and the ambitious young Producer soon blossomed into one of mutual respect. Donald Wilson, who now lives in retirement on the outskirts of London, recalls *Doctor Who* as just one of many programmes that Sydney Newman and he were involved in. But of Verity Lambert he says, 'She knew what she wanted and after a while I thought it best to let her get on with it. There was really nothing more to it than that. She and Sydney deserve the credit.'

There are others, however, who believe that Donald Wilson's contribution was much more extensive than has generally been appreciated. Among these is one of the first of the script writers on the series, John Lucarotti, now living in Corsica where he continues to write as well as running a successful restaurant. (Early in his career, John had been associated with Sydney at ABC writing for both *The Avengers* and a children's SF series called *City Beneath the Sea*.) 'Donald was a writer himself and I think Sydney got him involved because he knew that the quality of the scripts was going to be very important in making *Doctor Who* work,' John says. 'Certainly, Donald discussed the series with a number of writers he had used in earlier productions, and I'm sure he was responsible for bringing in several of the show's most innovative ideas during those early discussions between Sydney, himself and Verity Lambert.'

According to John, Donald was responsible for resolving many of the behind-the-scenes problems during the early years of the series, as well as taking the decisions about replacing people when they left the *Doctor Who* team. (If the extent of Donald Wilson's contribution to *Doctor Who* has not been fully appreciated until now, his work in the field of TV drama, where he produced many highly successful serials, certainly has. In 1967 he was given the BAFTA Award for his production of the critically acclaimed and highly popular series *The Forsyte Saga*.)

Donald Wilson was also responsible for appointing the first of the now long line of *Doctor Who* script editors, David Whitaker, another intensely dedicated and hard-

working professional, who died in 1980. David, a former actor, with experience as a director and producer, had turned to script writing for the BBC in 1957 and was then made a script editor in the early 1960s. His knowledge of the workings of television plus his wide contacts among writers were of enormous value to both Verity Lambert and the embryonic show. It was he, on the recommendation of Donald Wilson, who decided to commission an Australian-born writer, Anthony Coburn, then working at the BBC, to script not one, but the first two stories for *Doctor Who*, thereby providing a template for all later writers for the series.

Anthony Coburn is also now dead – he died in 1978 – but his widow told me that he had been enormously proud about the part he had played in launching *Doctor Who* in 'An Unearthly Child' (which he initially called 'Doctor Who and the Tribe of Gum'). Equally, he had been sad and rather angry about the way in which he was dropped from the series. At her home in Herne Bay, Kent, Mrs Joan Coburn said:

'Although Tony had to work very closely with David Whitaker in devising the introduction of the Doctor and his companions, the idea of the space machine in which they travelled, the TARDIS, was very much his. I remember him coming home after a walk when he had been thinking about

Above: The junk yard in Totters Lane, where the Doctor first appeared in the story of 'An Unearthly Child' in 1963 – designed by Peter Brachaki.

Above: Jacqueline Hill and William Russell, as schoolteachers Barbara and Ian, make an unusual discovery in the junkyard in 'An Unearthly Child'.

the script. In Australia things like police boxes were unknown, but he had suddenly come across one while he was out. "They want something unusual for this old man to travel in," he said to me. "What about a police box?" I thought straight away what a novel idea, and so did everyone at the BBC. Tony even gave it the name. He thought it could change its appearance in every location it went into, but that would have cost too much.

'My husband had been very interested in the Stone Age for years, and he liked the idea of the contrast of twentieth-century people meeting their savage ancestors. He was, though, bothered by the thought of a young girl travelling around with an old man, and decided that Susan should be his grand-daughter. I know some people might think that a bit old-fashioned, but *Doctor Who was* supposed to be a children's show and people were not as broad-minded as they are now.'

Having sent the Doctor into the distant past, Anthony Coburn was next asked by David Whitaker to take him into the far-flung future in the second story, thereby demonstrating to young viewers that the scope of his adventures would range from history to science fiction.

Mrs Coburn continued the story:

'Tony had been reading some reports about computers, which were just starting to be used in industry, and this gave him the idea for a story he called "The Robots". It was set on Earth in the thirtieth century when mankind had become extinct because of atomic warfare. Robots under the leadership of a super robot had taken their place. The Doctor and his companions were going to put the process into reverse in the hope that life might be regenerated on Earth just as it had begun at the dawn of time.

'Well, when David Whitaker saw the script he decided he didn't like the idea. Even though Tony offered to rewrite parts of it, he wouldn't change his mind. Instead, they got Terry Nation's story about the Daleks, and if *they* aren't robots I don't know what is! Anyhow, Tony decided he would never write for *Doctor Who* again, and that was that. He never regretted his decision, but I do think he deserves more credit in the creation of the series than he has been given.'

In fact, Verity Lambert was quick to acknowledge Anthony Coburn's contribution when I mentioned his widow's comments to her. 'I liked Tony's work very much indeed,' she said. 'He had style, invention and knew how to use dialogue. But I just don't think he was a natural *Doctor Who* writer. He had very definite ideas about the sort of stories he thought should be in the series, but they were not the same as David Whitaker's and mine. But this should not be allowed to detract in any way from the importance of his work for the show.'

Although David Whitaker failed to build a lasting partnership with Anthony Coburn, this did not shake his belief in the importance of bringing together writers capable of working as a team for the creation of *Doctor Who* adventures. And in addition to John Lucarotti, he also signed up the versatile Dennis Spooner, who had worked with Sydney Newman at ABC on *The Avengers*; a second BBC staff writer, Louis Marks; Peter R. Newman, a writer of screenplays for Hammer Films; and another Australian, Bill Strutton. He even wrote three stories himself for the first two seasons.

With their understanding of each other's work, plus their ability to alternate between historical and science fiction storylines, these were the men who, under Whitaker's guidance, provided the episodes which launched the Doctor on his 25-year odyssey – with one major addition to their ranks, of course – Terry Nation, formerly the script writer for comedian Tony Hancock, who dreamed up the immortal Daleks.

For technical guidance on the scientific elements of the series, a knowledgeable expert named Mervyn Pinfield was added to the 'Whovians' as Associate Producer. He came to *Doctor Who* fresh from directing a science fiction serial for the BBC entitled *The Monsters*. His brief was to help the production team make full use of the rapidly developing capabilities of television; and one of his enduring legacies to the programme were the swirling electronic patterns which made up the title sequence to *Doctor Who*. Tragically, Mervyn Pinfield was another of the original team who did not live long enough to see the show become a world-wide success with over 100 million viewers.

Opposite top: The first Doctor, William Hartnell, with William Russell on the set of 'The Web Planet' (1965).

Opposite bottom: The secret of the Daleks – two operators, actors Robert Jewell and John Scott Martin, on the set of 'Power of the Daleks' (1966).

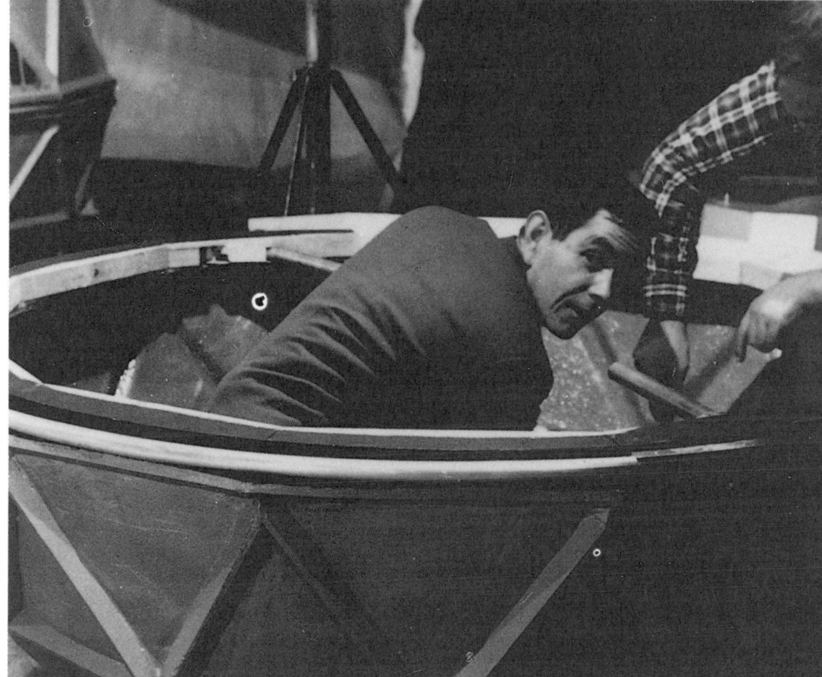

The last of the members of the behind-the-scenes team was a 25-year-old Anglo-Indian director named Waris Hussein, into whose care Verity Lambert entrusted the job of filming the very first story. Because she herself had been given a major opportunity to advance her career at a very tender age, Verity in turn decided to recruit new talent for *Doctor Who*.

In the autumn of 1963, Waris Hussein's only substantial television work had been directing a number of episodes of the twice-weekly BBC soap opera series about a woman's magazine, called *Compact*, which had begun in 1962. From this modest beginning – by way of *Doctor Who* – he was to go on to become one of the most stylish of modern directors, widely admired for many of his productions, in particular films such as the supernatural thriller *The Possession of Joel Delaney* (1972) and the historical drama *The Six Wives of Henry VIII*, made that same year.

But Waris's early work on *Doctor Who* did not initially bode well for his future. The pilot version of 'An Unearthly Child', which he directed in September 1963, to give Sydney Newman and Donald Wilson a flavour of what was to come, was given an emphatic thumbs-down. Newman thought the production was substandard and that the Doctor came across as a positively evil character, so he ordered the story to be remade. Waris comments:

'I am afraid my memory of *Doctor Who* is rather cloudy today, but I do remember there were a number of production changes as far as that first Stone Age story ("An Unearthly Child") was concerned. We had a lot of

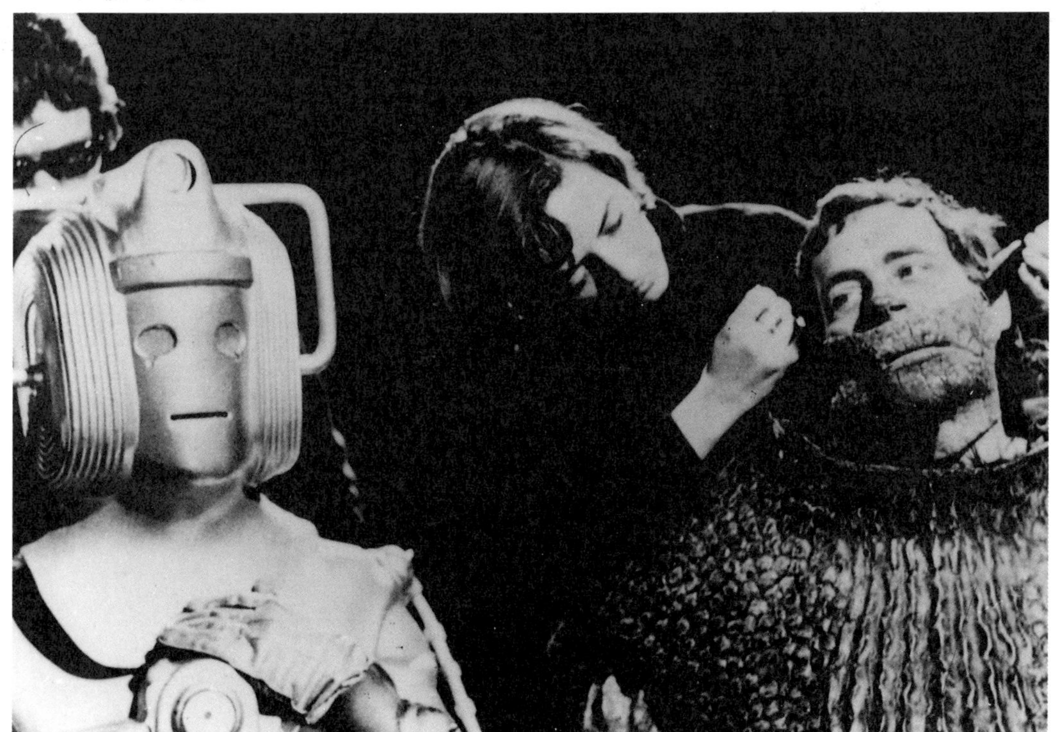

Opposite page and below: Another revealing set of photographs taken on the set of Terry Nation's story, 'The Chase' [1965], in which it was hoped the Mechonoids would rival the popularity of the Daleks.

Left: Making-up two of the most popular of the Doctor's humanoid enemies, a Cyberman and an Ice Warrior.

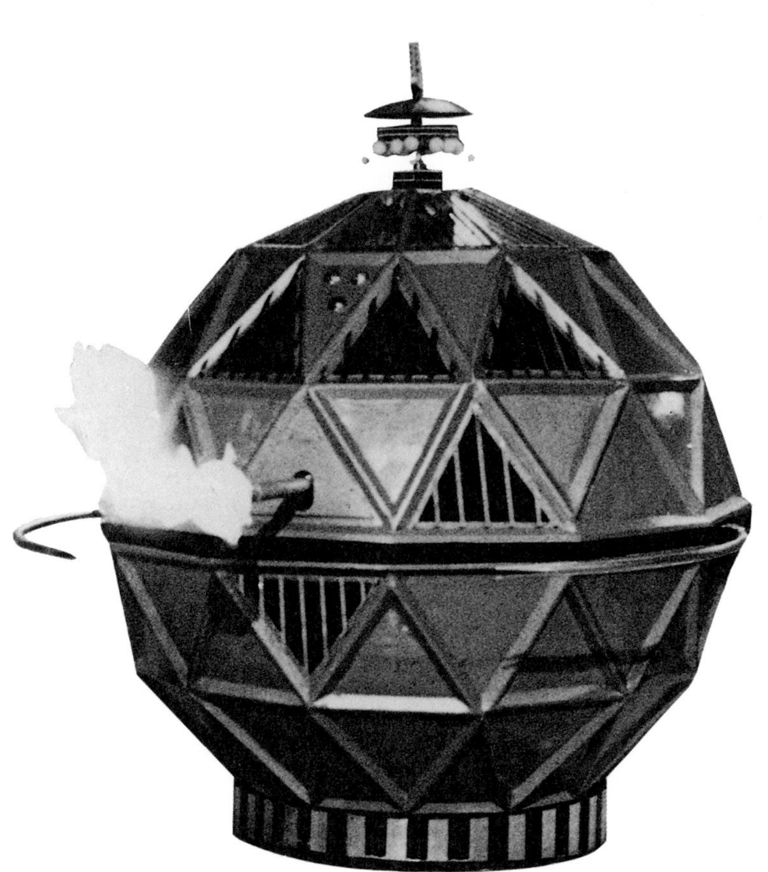

accidents on the set with cameras and scenery which showed up in the pilot. Verity Lambert was a very supportive producer, though, and I think she only cut one scene from the finished story – a scene where one of the cave men hit another on the head with a rock. She didn't like the fact that I had added the noise of a cabbage being squashed to the sound track!

'By the time I did my second story, the adventure about Marco Polo, the characters and the style were much more definitely established.'

In fact, Waris himself must take a good deal of the credit for establishing these elements. He softened the Doctor's initial disagreeable and selfish nature into that of a man whose apparent anger was more due to his frustration at not being able to control his space machine than to irritability with his human companions. He also devised the process by which the TARDIS was seen dematerialising on the prehistoric Earth landscape.

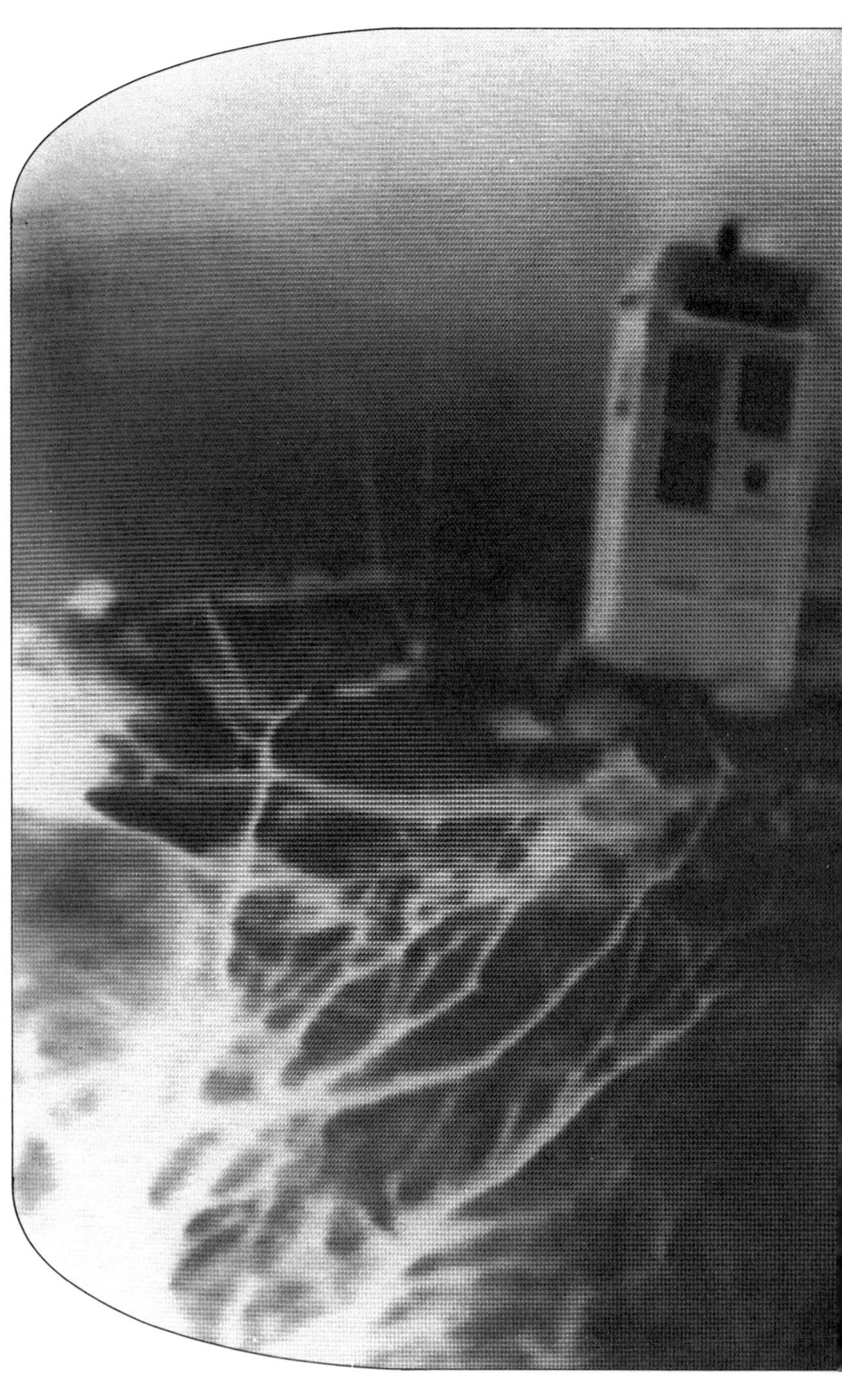

Interestingly, Waris Hussein's Production Assistant at this time was a young man named Douglas Camfield, who was destined to have a lengthy association with the series from 1963 to 1976, during which time he directed what have since become some of the best-remembered stories. Camfield was a man of enormous energy with a lively sense of humour, which he matched with great technical expertise. His death in 1984 was yet another major loss to the series.

Of his early days with *Doctor Who*, Douglas has been quoted as saying: 'The series was always intended as a bit of fun, escapism, amusement. It was never meant to be taken seriously. It's grown up a lot since I started, of course, but the series still sometimes produces the wondrous idea or the intriguing concept.'

Douglas Camfield was always quick to admit that his association with *Doctor Who* had been of enormous help in his career – as had working with Waris Hussein and Verity Lambert. 'They were both caught up in the excitement of doing something that was really new in television, and some of that rubbed off on me,' he said.

The final piece in the jigsaw of creating *Doctor Who* was, of course, the casting of William Hartnell as the Doctor – a choice made wholly by Verity Lambert, but enthusiastically supported by Sydney Newman who, once he viewed Hartnell on the screen, finally saw brought to life the figure that had haunted his imagination.

As soon as *Doctor Who* was established on television, Sydney Newman took his usual

(Opposite) Doctor Who – the figure that had haunted Sydney Newman's imagination – brought to television life by William Hartnell, complete with his travel machine, the TARDIS (above), as first seen in 'An Unearthly Child'.

course of leaving the 'Whovians' to get on with producing the show. He was now convinced he had put his idea in the right hands, and quickly turned his mind to the hundred and one other ideas and projects that demanded his attention. To him, it was now just a show in the BBC's armoury to wrest viewers away from the commercial stations. It could be argued that nothing else he created achieved that objective quite so successfully – though Sydney insists on seeing it as just one of his contributions to television, by no means as high in his estimation as, say, *Armchair Theatre*.

Indeed, a quarter of a century after he dreamed up *Doctor Who*, Sydney Newman still bubbles with ideas for television. He has no real regrets about having left the BBC at the end of his five-year contract in order to take charge of production for the Associated British Pictures Corporation at Elstree Studios. None, that is, except that when EMI took over ABPC not long afterwards, Sydney's department was closed down and he found himself on his way back to Canada. His rich and varied life on this side of the Atlantic had come full circle.

However, one strange irony links the close of Sydney Newman's working career in England with the famous show he gave to television. For the man who was responsible for closing down his department at ABPC was Lord Grade, uncle of Michael Grade, the former BBC Controller of Programmes and now Head of Channel 4, who, in 1985, also very nearly ended the Doctor's wanderings in space and time!

THE SILVER DECADE

A QUARTER OF A CENTURY OF *DOCTOR WHO* IN PERSPECTIVE

On the bleak winter evening of Saturday, 23 November 1963 when *Doctor Who* was launched on BBC Television, the greyness of the first images it presented on the tiny screens of the nation's TV sets of a darkness-shrouded junk yard seemed somehow to match the mood of the times. For the previous day, American President John F. Kennedy, the great youthful hope for the future, had been gunned down in Dallas, and the whole free world lay sunk in depression.

Yet 1963 had been a momentous year in other quite different ways – just as in its own way *Doctor Who* was to prove a milestone in television history which is now being marked a whole quarter of a century later. The Russians, for example, had launched the first woman into space, Valentina Tereshkova, while fan worship of The Beatles – headlined 'Beatlemania' – was making the British world leaders in popular music.

It was also the year of the Great Train Robbery in England, when over £2.5 million was stolen (and that is another serial which is still going on, of course!), and when unemployment rose to 815,000, the highest total since 1947! As far as the cost of living was concerned, the average wage was £1000 per year; a typical three-bedroom semi-detached house in Twickenham cost £6250; a new car under £800; a washing machine around £80 and a bottle of whisky £2. A television set would set a purchaser back £150.

The first *Doctor Who* episode, 'An Unearthly Child', was screened after the afternoon *Grandstand* sports programme and at that moment broke once and for all the mould of the usual Saturday evening offerings for children. It achieved this because, despite its early time slot, it was a fully fledged Drama Department programme (instead of having originated from the Children's Department) and offered high standards of script writing, good production standards, a strong cast – including an inspired choice of Doctor in William Hartnell – and what gave every indication of being promising special effects to emphasise the 'out of this world' qualities of its storyline.

The dramatic appearance of *Doctor Who* on BBC undoubtedly caught the opposing channel, ITV, by surprise, and their only alternative for viewers was an unlikely-sounding variety show called *Emerald Soup!* Ironically, it was this network that the creator of *Doctor Who*, Sydney Newman, had left to join the BBC the previous December. There, while working at ABC TV (part of the ITV group), he had utilised his love of science fiction stories to produce a kind of 'dry run' for *Doctor Who* with a series for children under the title *Pathfinders in Space*, which ran for three seasons.

In the week just prior to Christmas 1963, the second *Doctor Who* story introduced the now infamous Daleks and overnight not only established the show but turned it into one of the most talked about programmes on television.

Within days of the appearance of Terry Nation's evil creations, the British national press began its fascinated preoccupation with *Doctor Who*, which has not diminished to

Below: One of the Doctor's early trips back into history, 12th-century Palestine, for the story of 'The Crusade' (1965), where he met the noble lady Joanna (Jean Marsh).

this day. Though other monsters, such as the Voord and the Sensorites, were well received during 1964, it was the Daleks which most attracted the attention of the young viewers who were growing up amid the gadgetry of what was aptly called Prime Minister Harold Wilson's 'Technological Revolution'. Other favourites of the time were James Bond's Aston Martin, the Gemini space capsule and Gerry Anderson's super-submarine *Stingray*. Amidst all these wonders, too, the BBC launched its second channel, BBC 2, in the spring.

The faith and hard work of the *Doctor Who* production team, under Verity Lambert, were more than justified when, just a year after its launching, the tenth serial story, 'The Dalek Invasion of Earth', took the show into the Top Ten ratings chart in November 1964. It was evident, too, that the show was attracting not only children but often whole families of viewers, united in a blend of apprehension and fascination.

The Dalek boom, accompanied by merchandise of all kinds from toys to comic strips (see separate sections '*Doctor Who* and the Merchandisers' and 'The Doctor in the Comics'), not to mention the first of two films and a stage play, continued throughout 1965. The year also saw the arrival of *Doctor Who*'s first serious rival on ITV, Gerry Anderson's *Thunderbirds*, with its miniature figures and inventive special effects. When several ITV stations deliberately screened *Thunderbirds* at the same time as *Doctor Who*, the time traveller managed to win the ratings battle only thanks to an epic, twelve-episode serial, 'The Dalek Masterplan', which ran from November to January.

The year 1966, however, saw the first setbacks in the programme's so-far successful life span. The 'Swinging 'Sixties', as these years were to be known, were throwing up a constant stream of new fads to catch public interest, and other television series such as *The Avengers* and the American-made *The Man From U.N.C.L.E.* and *Batman* began to make *Doctor Who* look rather dated. When Verity Lambert retired from her job as Producer of the show, she was clearly aware of this trend, for she swiftly created *Adam Adamant Lives*, a weekly, 60-minute show in which Gerald Harper played a period hero thawed out in the twentieth century to pit his wits against modern evils. Its introduction of mini-skirted girls, souped-up Mini Coopers, and an evil masked super-villain was very much of the moment.

Right: A publicity photograph for the second Dalek story, 'The Dalek Invasion of Earth' (1964).

John Wiles, who succeeded Verity Lambert as *Doctor Who*'s Producer in the autumn of 1965, attempted to update the show's image by putting more serious science fiction into it on rather the same lines as the then popular BBC 2 series *Out of the Unknown*, masterminded by another of Sydney Newman's discoveries, Irene Shubik.

But *Doctor Who* had unquestionably first gained favour because of its originality, and when a third Producer, Innes Lloyd, took over in early 1966, he changed the Doctor's companions into contemporary young people and – because of the declining health of William Hartnell in the title role (he was suffering from multiple sclerosis) – supervised his replacement with an also younger, livelier, more mischievous and witty time traveller in the shape of Patrick Troughton.

In 1967, the historical stories which had predominated in the Hartnell era made way

for more monster stories, and the year became – in many viewers' estimation – a golden age for things that loomed and menaced. The Daleks reappeared once more, but it was creatures such as the Yeti, the Ice Warriors and most memorable of all, the Cybermen, who combined to restore the show's audience figures. It has been argued that as Hammer Films were then in the midst of producing their string of hugely popular 'monster movies' for the cinema, *Doctor Who* was really just copying this success – but the programme was nothing if not original in the kind of creatures it offered its wide-eyed audience.

Thanks to the efforts of Troughton, Lloyd, and his successor, Peter Bryant, *Doctor Who* was now well prepared to take on the various American science fiction series which were being aired by ITV – though rarely in direct opposition. Among these were three from the prolific Irwin Allen: *Voyage to the Bottom of the Sea* (1964–7), about an atomic submarine encountering underwater monsters; *Lost in*

Opposite: Patrick Troughton, a prisoner of two Gellguards in the story of 'The Three Doctors', screened in 1973 to mark the tenth anniversary of the programme.

Above: The second Doctor, Patrick Troughton, with his popular young companion, Jamie (Frazer Hines).

Right: The arrival of the Cybermen at the BBC Studios, for the filming of 'The Moonbase' by Kit Pedler, in 1967.

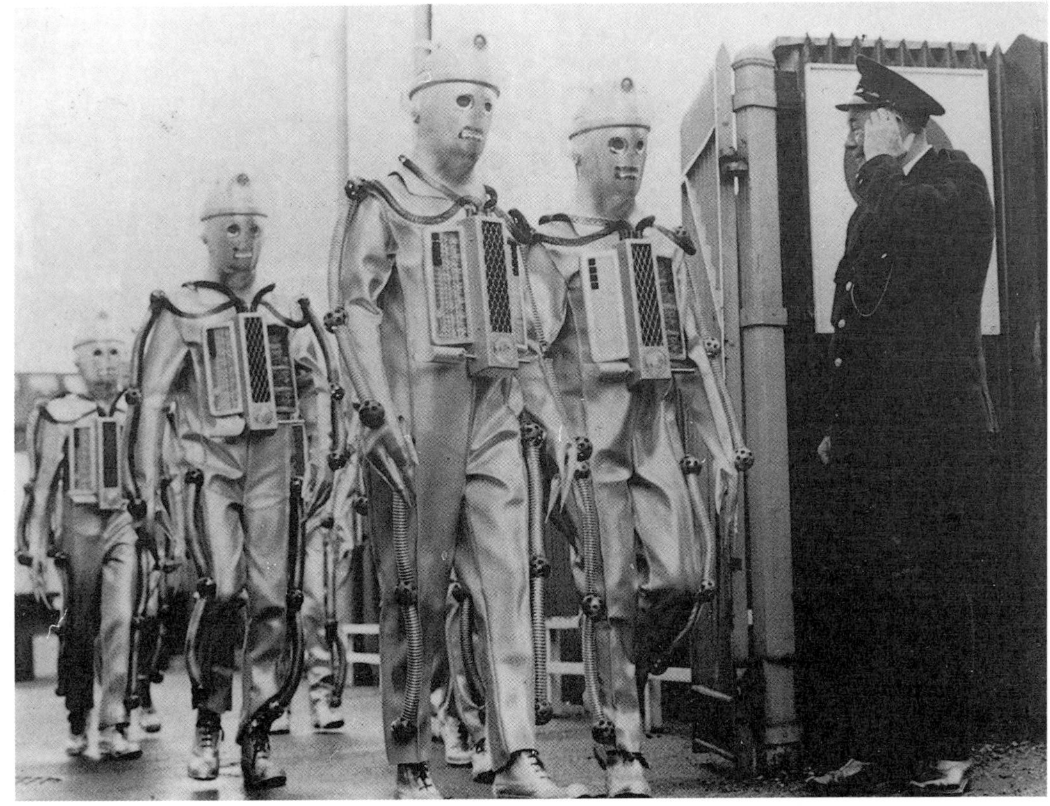

Space (1965–7), featuring a family shipwrecked in space; and *Land of the Giants* (1968–9), which employed skilful trick photography to record the adventures of the crew of a rocket ship which had crashed on a planet of giants.

Because of the considerable amount of finance available to them, these American productions could indulge in lavish special effects and expensive model sequences in a way that *Doctor Who*, on its far more modest budget, could never hope to match. Though how they tried when the occasion arose!

So, in order to husband their resources, Peter Bryant and his successor, Derrick Sherwin, opted to set more of the Doctor's adventures on present-day Earth, which allowed them not only to use suitably dramatic locations but also to place the most popular monsters in settings at once familiar and therefore more frightening to viewers. All the time, however, the cost of these creations was growing inexorably.

The year 1969 is remembered by long-time fans of *Doctor Who* as that in which the programme came within a hair's breadth of total cancellation. To add to the problems of mounting inflation, Bryant was suddenly faced with the loss of three stories which fell through at the scripting stage. And while this was going on, department heads at the BBC began to look for a possible replacement for what they saw as a waning programme.

According to popular lore, a number of science fiction ideas were considered. One plan was to adapt a number of the classic SF novels into serials. Less straightforward was an idea for a Jules Verne-type series about a wealthy Edwardian scientist/adventurer journeying into strange and mysterious events, and, later, a pilot for this programme was made under the title 'The Incredible Robert Baldick', which was written by Terry Nation and produced by Anthony Coburn!

Despite all the head-scratching that went on, no one could come up with an alternative that was either better or cheaper to produce than *Doctor Who*. What probably most saved the show was its flexibility, and so Peter Bryant and Derrick Sherwin set out to restructure it completely. Firstly, it was decided that the show would run for only six months rather than all year round, and secondly, the Doctor would be entirely confined to the Earth in his activities. By a curious twist of fate, when *Doctor Who* went off the air in June 1969 it was replaced by another SF series that was destined for cult-status – *Star Trek*.

When, much to the fans' relief, *Doctor Who* returned to the screens of Britain on 3 January 1970, it was flush with new innovations. After six years of being made in black and white at the BBC's cramped Lime Grove studios, it returned in full colour from the spacious new Television Centre. There was a new Doctor, too, in the person of the flamboyant and crusading Jon Pertwee, as well as the creation of the UNIT organisation as a home base for the grounded Time Lord.

Advances in optical and electronic effects at the BBC as well as bigger and better-equipped studios gave greater scope to the show's designers and resulted in some

Jon Pertwee, the third Doctor, with (opposite top) his veteran roadster 'Bessie' and first companion, Liz Shaw (Caroline John), in 'The Ambassadors of Death' (1970); and (opposite bottom) the futuristic 'Whomobile' and modern young assistant, Sarah Jane (Elisabeth Sladen), in 'The Planet of the Spiders' (1974).

impressive sets representing industrial complexes, space mission control centres and even an entire underground city.

Because the stories were set on Earth, there was every opportunity for dramatic battles between monsters and the UNIT soldiers, and the BBC hired a regular stunt team named HAVOC, whose special set pieces became a hallmark of many of the Pertwee episodes. The star himself soon won the approval of the fans through his dramatic interpretation of the role when many had expected him to adopt one of his numerous comic disguises.

A new Producer and Script Editor, Barry Letts and Terrance Dicks, were installed when the now revitalised programme moved into the seventies. Both men were keen on strong storylines and substantial characters rather than endless action scenes, but with their drive for realism the show not long afterwards generated one unfortunate side-effect when complaints of excessive violence were brought against it. After years of general praise, such a charge stung like a douche of cold water.

The attack came from the National Viewers' and Listeners' Association, whose President was the formidable Mrs Mary Whitehouse. On behalf of her members, Mrs Whitehouse criticised the programme for its violent content, singling out 'Terror of the Autons' with its army of killer shop dummies, murderous plastic daffodils and a lethal child's doll, as being quite unsuitable viewing for children.

Both the Producer and the BBC accepted some of the complaints levelled against *Doctor Who*, and the show was moved from its traditional 5.15 Saturday evening spot to close to six o'clock when – it was argued – children's hour was effectively over. None the less, viewers of all ages were still obviously more than happy with the Doctor's exploits, as the increased ratings throughout the year powerfully underlined. A not altogether surprising result of this popularity surge was the decision to begin editing some of the best-received serials together to be shown as 'TV movies' at Christmas, the first of these being *The Daemons*, which Barry Letts himself had written under the pen-name of Guy Leopold.

Another highlight of the year was unquestionably the introduction of The Master, played with great panache by Roger Delgado – Moriarty to the Doctor's Sherlock Holmes, and at one stage even threatening to overtake the popularity of the Doctor himself!

The production team opened the new 1972 season in January with a return for the first time in five years of the Daleks. (In the interim, Terry Nation had been trying unsuccessfully to launch the evil creatures in America.) That their appeal had not diminished was evidenced by figures collected by the BBC's Audience Research Unit that the show was now attracting eight million viewers a week. Perhaps even more striking was the fact that of these eight million people, 60 per cent were adults and only 40 per cent children, indicating a major swing from the early days of the programme when the young made up the major part of its audience.

Right: The Master – 'Moriarty to the Doctor's Sherlock Holmes' – as first played by Roger Delgado in 'The Claws of Axos' (1971).

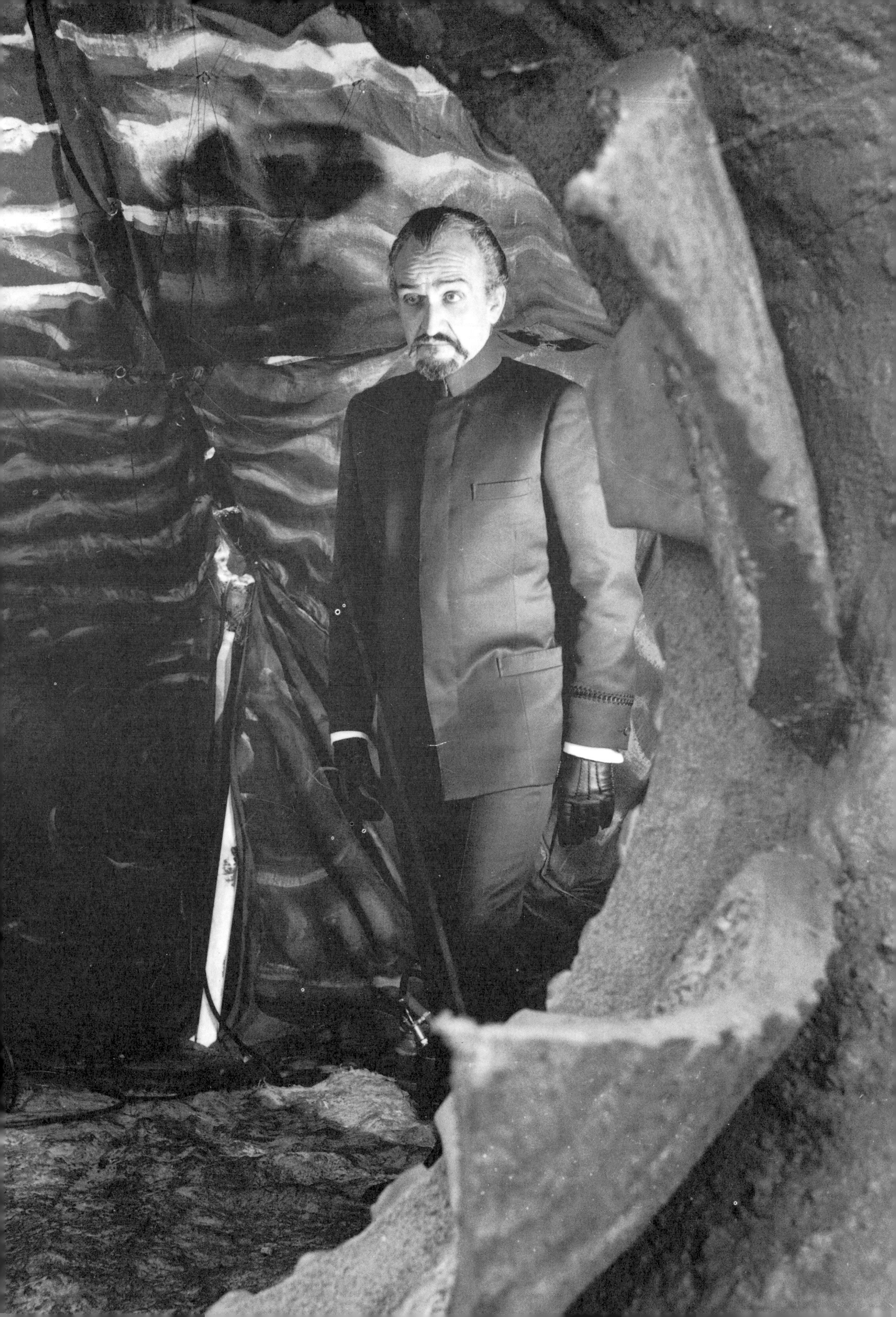

25 GLORIOUS YEARS

Unlike his predecessor, Jon Pertwee promoted *Doctor Who* wherever and whenever he could, his public appearances attracting huge crowds, especially when he arrived in the old roadster car he had had specially made for the show and nicknamed 'Bessie'.

At the turn of the year, Barry Letts decided to mark the tenth anniversary of Sydney Newman's idea with a special four-episode series bringing all the incumbents of the main role together in a story appropriately called 'The Three Doctors'. As always throughout his life, Patrick Troughton was happy to be reunited with the show for a special occasion, but sadly William Hartnell's fast declining health allowed him only the briefest of time in the studio, and his contribution to the story had to be confined to an appearance in a cameo role on the TARDIS scanner and on a screen before the Time Lords on their home planet of Gallifrey.

The story of 'The Three Doctors', which was broadcast from the end of December 1972 to January 1973, also marked the end of the Doctor's exile on Earth, the Time Lords (aka the BBC chiefs) allowing him once again to travel the far reaches of time and space now that his health (in terms of budgeting) and strength (in rating terms) had been fully restored. *Doctor Who* was also now firmly established as the world's longest running science fiction serial.

The anniversary was also marked by extensive newspaper and magazine publicity (not a little of it expressing surprise that a 'children's programme' should have endured so long), a special exhibition at the Science Museum in London, the launching of the first of now over one hundred novelisations of the Doctor's adventures by Target Books, and a feature on the BBC's *Blue Peter* children's programme showing clips from the past ten years and an interview with Jon Pertwee during which he unveiled his new 'flying saucer' type motor vehicle, the 'Whomobile'.

Only one sad note was struck in this year – and with hindsight it can be seen as a harbinger of the changes that were soon to come once again to the series. On 18 June, while filming in Turkey, Roger Delgado's taxi ran into a ravine and he was killed. Though his passing was much mourned, his role did not die with him, for so strong had it become that in 1980 it was revived in a new regeneration with the equally saturnine-looking and skilled actor Anthony Ainley now playing the Doctor's arch-enemy.

The tragedy seemed like an omen, however, and when Barry Letts and Terrance Dicks decided to move on from the series, Jon Pertwee similarly announced that he was giving up the role of the Doctor. Before he left, Barry Letts picked out Tom Baker, a comparatively unknown character actor, to become the fourth Time Lord, thereafter handing the series over to a new Producer, Philip Hinchcliffe, and also a new Script Editor, Robert Holmes – though as a writer, Holmes, with his wicked sense of humour, had already penned a number of memorable stories for *Doctor Who*.

The future of the show was not in doubt, however, for the BBC was now selling the

Below: Tom Baker, pictured below in 'The Armageddon Factor', attracted a record audience in excess of 14 million for 'The Ark in Space', in 1975.

series to many countries around the world – including places as far flung as Canada, New Zealand and Uganda – and were negotiating what would amount to the biggest breakthrough of all: entry into the vast USA market via the Public Broadcasting Service. When this was achieved with thirteen Jon Pertwee stories it was to prove a major step towards placing *Doctor Who* at the forefront of the world's science fiction TV series.

Tom Baker's larger-than-life interpretation of the Doctor as an anti-hero made him a public celebrity and earned the series whopping audience figures. It also brought from the Hinchcliffe–Holmes partnership three years of tough, uncompromising suspense and horror stories that not surprisingly attracted diametrically opposing viewpoints. Typifying this new wave of storytelling was one of Robert Holmes's own serials, 'The Ark in Space', which in January–February 1975 attracted viewing figures in excess of 14 million. This trend was maintained for the rest of the year and brought the programme back into the Top Ten ratings for the first time since the Dalek epics of the 'sixties.

The strength of the show and its invigorated new Doctor also proved more than enough to see off the challenge for viewers from two American-made series, *Planet of the Apes* (1974), based on the enormously successful movie of the same title, and *The Six Million Dollar Man* (1972–8), in which Lee Majors starred as a superhuman bionic spy. Even a new LWT multi-million-pound Gerry Anderson series called *Space*

Tom Baker in 'The Brain of Morbius' in January 1976, which also generated strong criticism from Mrs Mary Whitehouse.

1999 (1975–6), about a breakaway space station travelling through the universe and encountering alien civilisations, could not dislodge the Doctor from his Saturday evening TV pinnacle.

All this success meant that there was to be no six-month respite for *Doctor Who* that year. Philip Hinchcliffe was instructed by his peers to keep the momentum going by starting Tom Baker's second season not in January – as had been the case for some years now – but in August, making it one of the major programmes in the battle to attract viewers to the whole new autumn season of viewing on BBC TV.

The autumn of 1976 brought another record for *Doctor Who* when the third episode of Robert Holmes's 'The Deadly Assassin', screened in November, earned the highest ever viewing figures for a single episode. It also brought the strongest possible complaints from Mrs Mary Whitehouse about the drowning sequence featuring the Doctor which climaxed the episode. Nor was the President of the National Viewers' and Listeners' Association alone in her protest, for several newspapers also ran front-page stories declaring that the violence in the show was now becoming excessive. Such was the outcry that it promoted a response from none other than Sir Charles Curran, the Director General of the BBC, who defended the show but conceded that the story in question had gone a little too far. Though no one knew it at the time, there were to be further repercussions from this development in the following year.

Such complaints notwithstanding, there was clearly an enormous and enthusiastic audience for Tom Baker's colourful adventures. He himself enjoyed the limelight and became the focus of innumerable feature articles in magazines and newspapers which underlined his eccentric style and passionate zest for life. Recalling this period of his tenure as the Doctor, Baker was to remark later that perhaps the oddest accolade paid to him was the invitation he received from BBC 2 to appear on an edition of the panel show *Call My Bluff*, which had once been described by *Punch* as the 'lexical trivia quiz for oddballs'!

In 1977, because of the amount of criticism that had been levelled at *Doctor Who*, changes were instituted by the BBC. The programme was moved to a slot further into the evening, closer to 6.30, and Philip Hinchcliffe was transferred to produce a new tough police series, *Target*, which, it was felt, would benefit from his hard-hitting style. In his place as Producer came Graham Williams, whose first instructions from his superiors were to remove the violence from the series.

This, Williams felt, would take away one of the show's major strengths – and he said as much at the world's first *Doctor Who* convention, which was held in August 1977 in Battersea. It was this very adult-appeal in the programme which had brought the Doctor Who Appreciation Society into being, and its members at that gathering were fervent in their suggestions for the future of the series.

Humour was one obvious element that could be brought back, because of Tom Baker's facility for comedy. And sensing the appeal to the public of robots, which had been generated in the recently released American movie *Star Wars*, Graham Williams invested time and money in the construction

Below: A publicity shot of Tom Baker and his robot pet K9, devised by Bob Baker and Dave Martin, and introduced in 'The Invisible Enemy' in 1977.

of a robot dog, K9, made by the BBC Visual Effects Department and introduced in the Bob Baker and Dave Martin story 'The Invisible Enemy' in October. The sometimes wayward pet at once caught the imagination of viewers, and in due course was even considered for a series of his own.

November 1978 saw the fifteenth anniversary of *Doctor Who*, and during that month the one hundredth serial conveniently arrived in the shape of 'The Stones of Blood', written by David Fisher. This milestone was marked by the BBC with a party at Television Centre which brought together past and present Doctors, their companions and many other actors and technicians who had worked on either side of the cameras over the years.

On television, the programme once more had very real competition from a new SF series, *Blake's 7*, created by Terry Nation and starring Paul Darrow and Michael Keating. In time, the show attracted audience figures in excess of 10 miliion, and like *Doctor Who* found favour in 25 overseas countries as well as generating a fan club and its own magazines. The one major advantage *Blake's 7* enjoyed over *Doctor Who* was its screening time of 8 p.m. which enabled it to tackle stronger and potentially more controversial themes. This said, though, no one was quite prepared for the finale which wiped out Blake and his compatriots just before Christmas 1981.

The *Doctor Who* fan network was at this time growing apace, and in 1978 launched a campaign that is still continuing to try to recover the earlier episodes of the series that had either been lost or were thought to have been destroyed by the BBC. (See separate section 'The Lost Stories of *Doctor Who*'.) Pressure was also exerted by this group on the Corporation to repeat some of the classic shows from the past for the benefit of long-time fans as well as newcomers.

Despite the restrictions which had been placed on him, Graham Williams, aided by his script editors – initially Robert Holmes and then Anthony Read and Douglas Adams – introduced a number of fresh and innovative ideas into the show as compensation for its inability to compete with the other expensive hardware-orientated SF productions that could be seen in the cinema or on TV. Among these were the introduction of an excellent villain, The Black Guardian (played with chilling menace by Valentine Dyall) and further fascinating information about the Doctor's background as a Gallifreyan Time Lord.

The year 1979 went down as that in which *Doctor Who* took the USA by storm. Although some of the Jon Pertwee stories had been screened in a number of American states, it was the signing by the BBC of a contract with Time/Life Television that guaranteed nationwide exposure for Tom Baker's Doctor. The star himself turned up in front of the American embassy in Grosvenor Square, London, to mark the 'invasion', and was supported by an escort of Daleks, Zygons, Sontarans and Wirrn which generated huge publicity for both the show and its American 'coup'.

The impact of Baker's Doctor on American

PETER DAVISON © BBC Enterprises, Ltd

The fifth Doctor, Peter Davison, will go down in Doctor Who history as having reigned as the renegade Time Lord in the least number of stories produced. He will have completed only seventy-four half-hour episodes. After March of 1984 (in England), his Doctor Who will only be seen in reruns! The sixth Doctor (played by Colin Baker) will take over the TARDIS control panel in March, 1984. The following, however, is the chronology of Peter's Doctor Who.

Doctor number five's first full story is appropriately named "Castrovalva". Having struggled with the Master at Earth's Pharos Project, the Doctor would find this regeneration the most difficult one yet. To make matters worse, the Master forced Adric to lay in co-ordinates for the TARDIS to speed backwards in Time to Event One: the creation of the universe . . . the Big Bang! The Doctor's mind was so erratic, fluttering back and forth from past regenerations, he was "almost" no help at all to Tegan and Nyssa. Finally, however, his wits returned just in time to save them from imminent disaster. Part of the TARDIS had to be jettisoned to avoid direct collision with the hydrogen inrush that lay ahead of them. Unfortunately, it was the TARDIS zero room that was lost. The zero room was a sort of neutral environment; an isolated space, cut off from the rest of the universe. It "was" the place where the Doctor had planned to regenerate!

After the time travellers seemed out of danger, the TARDIS sped off to Castrovalva where the Doctor would rest. Unfortunately, the Master had captured Adric and, coupled with Adric's computations and the Master's mental powers, he put them all in a perilous Space/Time trap: recursive occlusion! The whole of Castrovalva was caught in a mess of illogical geography, moving up, down and side to side in various dimensions of kaleidoscopic gyrations! Only an act of supreme self-sacrifice enabled them to escape.

"Castrovalva" is the third and final story in a Doctor-Master trilogy. It began in the Tom Baker era with "Keeper of Traken" and followed with "Logopolis". "Castrovalva" sets the tone of Davison's Doctor as a more vulnerable, even "skittish" hero. It would take time for the new Doctor to settle into his new role.

audiences was immediate and overwhelming – and within months fan clubs and conventions began to mushroom across the nation. Tom Baker and Graham Williams were invited to the first major US convention in California and found themselves swamped by admirers whose enthusiasm for the Doctor bordered on that normally reserved for rock superstars!

In Britain, however, the year ended on a sad note for *Doctor Who*. A series of industrial disputes among technicians at both the BBC and ITV badly affected programmes, though for two months the BBC – and *Doctor Who* – benefited from a complete shutdown of the ITV network. Then, just before Christmas, the BBC's Television Centre was also brought to a standstill, and filming had to be abandoned on what Graham Williams had hoped would be one of his most ambitious *Doctor Who* stories, a six-part adventure called 'Shada', written by his Script Editor, Douglas Adams. (Adams's disappointment at the loss of his story was to be somewhat assuaged, of course, when his radio series *The Hitch-Hiker's Guide to the Galaxy* put him firmly on the road to fame and riches.)

The cancellation of 'Shada' also marked the rather unsatisfactory end to Graham Williams's three-year stint as Producer of *Doctor Who*, for 1980 saw the arrival of the current man in charge, John Nathan-Turner, also with a new Script Editor, Christopher H. Bidmead.

John Nathan-Turner saw his arrival as a very opportune moment to move *Doctor Who* into the new decade with a new look. The series had benefited from radical changes in the 'sixties and 'seventies, so why not in the 'eighties, too?

In a far-ranging sweep of changes, the series was given a new title sequence, new theme music, and the Doctor himself appeared in a restyled costume. There was also to be greater reliance on video and visual effects; slicker, glossier production techniques; and a renewed emphasis on guest stars. The BBC also gave the new Producer an additional two episodes for his schedule.

When the first of these new-look stories, 'The Leisure Hive' by David Fisher, went out on 30 August 1980, *Doctor Who* once again found itself with stiff opposition from ITV in the form of a new American-made series, *Buck Rogers in the 25th Century*, based on the 'pulp magazine' hero, and starring Gil Gerard. The series was stylishly made with some excellent special effects, but undoubtedly its most appealing feature was a robot named 'Twiki', acted by Felix Silla and spoken by that man of a million voices, Mel Blanc. Unbiased observers felt that there was little difference between the sizes of the audiences attracted to the two series.

The major news of the year, however, was the announcement by Tom Baker on 23 October that he was to leave the series after playing the Doctor for a record seven years. The story not only made the front pages of the national papers but was even featured in the BBC's main news programme, *The Nine O'Clock News*. Tom Baker, with typical mischievous delight, even suggested that his successor could be a woman!

A second surprise was John Nathan-Turner's announcement that K9 was to be phased out of the series – a statement that prompted a considerable backlash from the robot dog's many devoted young fans.

March 1981 saw Tom Baker's exit from the series that he had played a major part in making an international success, in the dramatic story of 'Logopolis' which Christopher Bidmead himself wrote. The return of The Master, played by Anthony Ainley, was used as the plot device to cause the death of the Doctor when he fell off the top of a radio telescope and regenerated into the fifth Doctor, the youthful Peter Davison.

The Master had, in fact, been seen twice in the interim played by two other actors. Following Delgado's tragic accident, the evil Time Lord had re-appeared hideously decayed in 'The Deadly Assassin' (1976) played by Peter Pratt in what was said to be his twelfth regeneration. And he was in the same unpleasant state – portrayed this time by Geoffrey Beevers – in 'The Keeper of Traken' just prior to assuming the body of Anthony Ainley.

Following a BBC decision to return *Doctor Who* to its January to June run, John Nathan-Turner was now faced with a nine-month gap before Peter Davison could begin his own series of adventures as the Doctor. This he adroitly bridged by organising a season of repeats of classic *Doctor Who* stories under the generic title 'The Five Faces of Doctor Who', including the very first William Hartnell adventure, 'An Unearthly Child'. The selected

Below: The fifth Doctor, the youthful Peter Davison, who made his debut in January 1982 in 'Castrovalva', with his companion Nyssa (Sarah Sutton).

Right: Peter Davison with the Doctor's ill-fated young companion, Adric, played by Matthew Waterhouse.

repeats were shown from Mondays to Thursdays for five weeks in November and December and were so well received as to climb into the BBC 2 Top Ten listing.

The stories shown were: William Hartnell's pioneer tale from 1963; Patrick Troughton's 'The Krotons' (1968), Jon Pertwee's 'Carnival of Monsters' (1973); the trio adventure 'The Three Doctors' (1973) and, lastly, the Baker–Davison 'Logopolis' which gained excellent publicity in preparation for the new Doctor's first complete-story appearance in January 1982.

Christmas that year also gave *Doctor Who* fans an extra present with the movie-length 'K9 and Company' starring the fourth Doctor's companion, Elizabeth Sladen, and the smart robot dog. The show had been made partly in response to the outcry over K9's axing from *Doctor Who* and partly as a pilot for a possible series which, unhappily, did not materialise.

The appearance of Peter Davison in January 1982 as the fifth Doctor in 'Castrovalva' was so unlike that of any of his older predecessors as to surprise most viewers. But it was not, perhaps, as big a surprise as the BBC's decision to move *Doctor Who* from the traditional Saturday night spot that it had enjoyed for almost twenty years to a 7 p.m. screening on Monday and Tuesday evenings. This decision, made by the Controller of BBC 1, Alasdair Milne, brought an outcry from some fans – many of whom said they could not get home from work in time to see their favourite series – but nevertheless the audience figures almost doubled.

Peter Davison soon proved himself a fresh and likable new Time Lord, and in March he became the second Doctor (Jon Pertwee had been the other) to be the subject of a *This Is Your Life* programme, when he was confronted by Eamonn Andrews while filming with some Daleks and Cybermen in Trafalgar Square in the heart of London!

The twentieth anniversary of *Doctor Who*, which fell in the winter of 1983, was preceded by a number of small disasters. Firstly, a lengthy electricians' strike at the Television Centre caused the cancellation of the season's big climactic story, a four-part adventure with the Daleks written by the new Script Editor, Eric Saward. Then, when work was well advanced on a 90-minute special anniversary adventure to feature all the surviving Doctors, Tom Baker decided he would not appear. The former Script Editor, Terrance Dicks, who had been brought in to write the special, then had speedily to make a number of major changes to the story – although a way of ingeniously including the reluctant fourth Doctor was found by using an extract featuring him from the unshown Douglas Adams story 'Shada'.

At Easter, BBC Enterprises organised a special weekend at Longleat in Wiltshire called 'Twenty Years of a Time Lord', which brought 35,000 visitors to the two-day event. Tom Baker did, this time, join Patrick Troughton, Jon Pertwee and Peter Davison at the event, which was rightly described in the extensive newspaper coverage which followed as the most successful *Doctor Who* convention ever staged.

Not to be outdone, however, the American *Doctor Who* fans also put on a multi-thousand dollar convention in Chicago which was heralded as 'The Ultimate Celebration'. These lucky enthusiasts were the first actually to see 'The Five Doctors', which was shown to them on the precise day of the show's anniversary, 23 November – two days before British viewers got to see it as part of the 'Children in Need' charity telethon. A remarkable performance by Richard Hurndall looking and sounding uncannily like the first Doctor was widely regarded as a highlight of the production.

With the celebrations hardly over, 1984 started with the news that Peter Davison was leaving the series after having won over legions of young, new viewers to the programme. His successor proved an even greater surprise than he had been – the chunky, rather pugnacious Colin Baker, who was normally associated with villainous roles and who had been the 'man-you-love-to-hate', Paul Merroney, in the BBC serial *The Brothers*.

Producer John Nathan-Turner decided to break with precedent with the sixth Doctor, and instead of introducing him in the last of the season's stories as was usual, brought him into the penultimate adventure, 'The Caves of Androzani' by Robert Holmes. This explosive end to Peter Davison's tenure grabbed eight million viewers and also allowed them to have an entire story, 'The Twin Dilemma', with the new Doctor before the nine-month break to the next season.

Opposite: Colin Baker, whose troubled regeneration as the sixth Doctor only lasted from 1984 to 1986, with his companion Peri (Nicola Bryant).

If there had been startling developments in 1984, however, they were as nothing compared to the news which broke in February 1985. Just when fans were enjoying the return of *Doctor Who* to its traditional Saturday evening slot, and with episodes lasting 45 minutes instead of 25, it was announced that the series was to be rested.

This decision had been taken by the recently appointed Controller of BBC 1, Michael Grade, who was reportedly unhappy about a number of aspects of the series including the levels of blood and gore, its increased costs, sinking ratings and general format. The reaction to this news was instantaneous and amazing. The story made front-page news, the BBC switchboard was jammed with callers expressing their anger at the decision, and overseas fans – particularly those in America – offered to raise funds to keep the series going.

The result of the outcry was a statement from the BBC that *Doctor Who* was not being cancelled but merely postponed for a 'rest and reassessment'. The Time Lord would be back, they insisted – but not before eighteen months had elapsed.

The year 1986 was a bleak one for fans of the world's longest running science fiction serial as they waited patiently for it to return. When it did, on Saturday, 6 September, it was in the form of a 14-part epic consisting of 25-minute episodes suitably entitled (most newspapers and a lot of people agreed) 'The Trial of a Time Lord'. Though 14 episodes was a third of the total averaged by William Hartnell and half the number allocated to

25 GLORIOUS YEARS

Tom Baker in his last season, some Doctor on television was better than no Doctor at all. And the fact that five of the episodes had been written by Robert Holmes was a bonus in itself. Sadly, these proved to be Holmes's last contribution to the series to which he had given some of the finest fruits of his imagination and writing talent, for he died suddenly while work on the programme was under way.

Although the outcome of 'The Trial of a Time Lord' led to acquittal for the Doctor – when some fans had feared he might be heading for the final curtain – the case for Colin Baker was not good in ratings terms. In December, Michael Grade issued instructions that the actor was not to be re-engaged for the next season.

Hard on the heels of Colin Baker's axing came the tragic news of Patrick Troughton's death in February while he was visiting America talking to fans about his role in the series. Tributes to his work were paid by many fans and a number of fellow actors, notably Jon Pertwee, now the elder statesman of the surviving Doctors.

Jon himself received some cheering news a little later when BBC Enterprises put on sale the video of his 'Death to the Daleks' adventure from 1974 and it sold so well as to become one of the most popular BBC pre-recorded tapes ever released. The advent of 'Superchannel', the nationwide cable television channel in Britain, also pleased those fans with access to it when the programmers began broadcasting re-runs of some of the Tom Baker *Doctor Who* stories.

In March, the seventh Doctor was finally announced after yet another period in which rumours abounded about who might get the coveted role. In any event, the part went to Sylvester McCoy, a veteran of children's TV with experience of all kinds of acting, including the National Theatre, who it was felt could combine drama with eccentricity in a manner not unlike his idol, Patrick Troughton. To underpin Sylvester's debut as the new Doctor, John Nathan-Turner signed up several leading actors for the twenty-fourth season including Ken Dodd, Hugh Lloyd and Richard Briers – the last appearing as a Hitler-like figure in Stephen Wyatt's 'Paradise Towers'!

For the first time in its history, *Doctor Who* was also deliberately lined up against an established TV favourite when it returned to the nation's screens on Monday evenings in September. Instead of looking over his shoulder to see what new offering ITV might put up to oppose him (most recently it had been the all-action *The A-Team*), the Doctor was slotted into Monday evenings against the veteran soap serial, *Coronation Street*. The choice for viewers was the gossip and intrigue of back-street Manchester or the far-flung excitement of time travel.

Somehow, though, despite the obvious drawbacks of this juxtaposition, it seemed curiously appropriate that, in its silver anniversary year, *Doctor Who* should be screened side by side with the *only* other programme on television that could match its longevity. . . .

Opposite: The seventh and most recent Doctor, Sylvester McCoy, with Mel, played by Bonnie Langford.

BOX
HOME SWEET HOME.

INSIDE THE WORLD OF *DOCTOR WHO*

The centre of the world of *Doctor Who* is a compact set of offices to be found in the heart of the huge BBC building called Union House, facing tree-lined Shepherd's Bush Green in London. The cluster of rooms is on the third floor amongst a warren of similar offices and corridors as easy for the visitor to get lost in as the Doctor's TARDIS.

This is the core of the small empire which not only generates the Time Lord's adventures in space and time as seen on television, but is also the focal point of a host of associated enterprises which have sprung up over the 25 years that *Doctor Who* has grown from being a children's TV show to an international cult programme and certainly one of the most famous small-screen serials in the world. The Doctor's magical and mystical tours of the galaxy may be filmed in the BBC's more glamorous Television Centre or on specially selected locations throughout the country (occasionally even more exotic ones abroad), but it all begins in Room 303 – the Producer's Office.

The current occupant of this prestigious chair, the ninth to hold the job, is John Nathan-Turner, a stocky figure of engaging good humour with a liking for wildly coloured shirts and filter-tipped cigarettes. A *Doctor Who* enthusiast through and through, he has a passionate commitment to the show as well as to the many actors who have appeared – and appear – in it. Having been associated with the show for eleven years (and been its Producer for nine) and having worked with all but one of the Doctors, John possesses a unique overview of the series and its astonishing success.

Much of *Doctor Who*'s development in the 'eighties has been as a result of John Nathan-Turner's work; and though the show has suffered its swings of fortune, his show – unlike others which have fallen by the wayside – has gone on constantly keeping abreast of trends and the latest developments in science and television technology. Which makes his achievement no small one for a man who professes he was never a science fiction fan as a child!

John was born in Birmingham in 1947, but forsook a university career to go on the stage where, he confesses, he endured three very hard years in repertory before realising he was not a very good actor! In 1968, he joined the BBC and worked as a floor assistant on a number of programmes including *Doctor Who* and *The Morecambe and Wise Show*, and then as an assistant floor manager on *Z-Cars*, as a production assistant on *Barlow at Large*, and as a production unit manager on *All Creatures Great and Small* and *Doctor Who*. All these earlier experiences were to have varying influences on his work with the SF serial.

John talks easily and engagingly about his job and never allows the listener to forget completely that though there are people who treat the Doctor and his adventures as being almost real, to him *Doctor Who* is primarily a show to provide viewers of all ages with a good story, a little science and technology, a helping of drama and high adventure, but above all else excitement and entertainment. His office is almost a showplace for *Doctor*

Opposite: John Nathan-Turner, the ninth producer of *Doctor Who*.

Who: photographs of his years in the show adorn one wall; a cupboard bulging with souvenirs and merchandise fills another; while beside him is a wall chart plotting the progress of future stories of *Doctor Who*. Behind his chair is a large picture window which looks out – most appropriately – across west London towards the old Lime Grove studios where the show he now runs was first brought to life all those years ago. Indeed, one can almost imagine Sydney Newman and Verity Lambert discussing that first season of stories in just such an office. John himself is a showman somewhat in the Sydney Newman mould, and certainly shares Verity Lambert's drive to make *Doctor Who* a pace-setter in modern television. His knowledge of the history of the series is also unrivalled.

'Yes, I'm afraid I have to own up that I was never a science fiction fan,' John says. 'When I was very young I enjoyed the Walt Disney pictures, but I used to hate cowboy films. What excited me were the stories of Ivanhoe, William Tell and Robin Hood – not Sword and Sorcery, but Sword and Sword! The versions that were done on television were really very good considering all the limitations they worked under.' John was an avid collector of autographed stars' photographs and wrote off to many film and TV studios in search of these souvenirs. He amassed a huge collection which he now regrets he has lost track of!

'Despite the fact SF did not appeal to me, I did see *Doctor Who* right from the beginning,' he continues. 'I was not an aficionado, but I did watch it regularly. I suppose I stopped watching at about the end of the Hartnell era or just when Pat Troughton took over. That was when I went into the theatre and I was usually doing a Saturday afternoon matinee at the time the programme went out.'

John smiles with amusement and shakes his head at a question as to whether he ever watched *Doctor Who* and dreamed that one day he might be involved with the programme. He does, though, vividly remember the first Doctor. 'I think there is no doubt that the memory can play tricks when we think back to the past, you know, when people keep harping back to the "halcyon

Above: 'William Hartnell created a memorable Doctor, and put his own stamp on the series right from the beginning,' says John Nathan-Turner.

Above: 'There was a very jolly atmosphere about everything Patrick Troughton did in the series,' according to John, who worked with the second Doctor on 'The Space Pirates' in 1969.

days",' John continues. 'Some of those early *Doctor Who* shows *were* undoubtedly marvellous, but there were others that were rather poor. Of all of them, the one that is still fascinating and intriguing and stands up as a good example of television is that first episode of "An Unearthly Child". William Hartnell certainly created a memorable Doctor. He was very much a professional who knew what he wanted and put his own stamp on the series right from the beginning. I suspect he must have been a challenge for any producer and director to work with!'

It was in early 1969 that John himself got his first insight into *Doctor Who* when he was floor assistant on the six-episode Patrick Troughton story 'The Space Pirates', written by Robert Holmes, in which the Doctor was plunged into some nefarious activities taking place on a navigation beacon in deep space.

John waves a hand towards the window and the buildings to the west. 'We made "The Space Pirates" at Lime Grove studios over there. The actual studio was on the fourth floor and the dressing rooms were on the ground floor and in the basement. There was just one minute old lift with metal gates linking the floors and I seemed to spend my entire time running up and down the four flights of stairs fetching people!

'Sadly, much of that story doesn't exist any more, but I also remember it entailed the actors doing an awful lot of crawling around through tunnels which were set up on rostrums – and I kept wondering to myself why they weren't on the floor. Of course, now I know that there were no low-angle cameras then and they had to be built up so that the existing cameras could see the people crawling!

'There was a very jolly atmosphere about making that story, something which Pat Troughton helped create and which was a hallmark about everything he did in the series. There was also a wonderful cast including Donald Gee, George Layton, Dudley Foster, Lisa Daniely and Gordon Gostelow.'

The ease with which he rolled off the

names of this cast from a story made almost twenty years ago is indicative of his recall of information about the series. Indeed, his knowledge of *Doctor Who*'s past has shaped his strong belief in continuity – that new stories should acknowledge what has happened in the past and that the Doctor's history should be carefully adhered to wherever possible. He does not like change for change's sake, and when he is not absolutely certain about something from memory will consult the library of cassettes or scripts he has available on past serials, or consult with leading aficionados.

'It is a tragedy that part of *Doctor Who*'s history is missing because earlier shows were junked,' he says, 'and it is always very good news when a copy of an old show turns up from somewhere or other.' (This intriguing facet of the show's history is dealt with more fully in the section entitled 'The Lost Stories of *Doctor Who*'.)

John carried away happy memories of his work with Patrick Troughton and had no reservations about returning to *Doctor Who* during the third Doctor's era. Indeed, he worked as floor assistant on two of Jon Pertwee's adventures, 'The Ambassadors of Death' by David Whitaker in 1970 and 'Colony in Space' by Malcolm Hulke the following year. John recalls:

'Although many of Jon's stories were filmed on location, I was only involved in the studio sessions. "Ambassadors" was an excellent story by the programme's first script editor, while "Colony in Space" was the Doctor's first journey away from Earth in over a year and had a marvellous performance by Roger Delgado as the original Master. I'll never forget the impact of the character, and it was one of the reasons why I later brought it back after Roger's death.

'My strongest recollection of Jon Pertwee was how fascinated he was by gadgets. He was forever bringing in things he wanted to use in the series. I suppose what everyone remembers best are the old car, "Bessie", and the "Whomobile".

'Jon has since done a lot of promotion for the series, and in fact he's the keenest of all the Doctors to put on his costume and perform. Whenever he turns up at a convention he always starts his appearance with the words "*I* am the Doctor!"'

It was with the fifteenth season of *Doctor Who*, which started in September 1977 with the transmission of 'Horror of Fang Rock' by Terrance Dicks, that John began the full-time association with the show which has lasted until this year. The Producer of the show at that time was Graham Williams, and Tom Baker was the Doctor.

Above: 'Jon Pertwee was fascinated by gadgets,' recalls John, who worked with the third Doctor on location for 'The Ambassadors of Death' in 1970.

John's function as the permanent Production Unit Manager was to work as general and financial adviser to Graham Williams. 'I had three years in that job before I took over as Producer in November 1979, so I had a really good grounding in the finances of the show, the kind of day-to-day problems that can arise, as well as working with Tom,' John recalls. He admits that the fourth Doctor left a lasting impression on him.

'Tom was *so* inventive. I know it is awful to have to say "enough is enough", but he was the kind of actor who would try right up until the moment of a take to come up with a better way to play the scene. Quite often there were ways to do the things he wanted to introduce, but if occasionally it meant having to reshoot a whole scene then it became impossible if the clock was against us. But always he had this constant feeling that he could do better – which was exhilarating and remarkable from someone who had been playing the part for so long. And he was still like it at the end of seven years – his enthusiasm never waned.'

Off camera, John found Tom Baker equally dedicated to his role and the Doctor's image. 'As is generally known,' he says, 'Tom likes a drink and he likes a cigarette. But if ever he saw any children about he would always immediately switch to orange juice and stop smoking. He was absolutely meticulous about that.'

In 1980, Tom Baker took off his flamboyant hat, scarf and coat for the last time, and John cast in his place the youthful Peter Davison

Below: 'Tom Baker was *so* inventive – he always had this constant feeling that he could do better,' recalls John, seen here on location on Brighton beach in 1980.

Below: 'Peter Davison had a wonderful cool quality and helped take the series in new directions.' John is pictured with the fifth Doctor and his companions, Tegan (Janet Fielding) and Nyssa (Sarah Sutton), while filming 'Time-Flight' on location at London's Heathrow Airport in 1982.

with whom he had worked on the series *All Creatures Great and Small*.

'Peter provided a complete contrast to Tom, which is what I wanted after the fourth Doctor had become so firmly entrenched in viewers' minds after all that time. Peter helped take the show in a new direction and with all the problems such a transition created we couldn't have had a better person.

'What I remember most about Peter was his wonderful cool quality. You know, things can get very fraught making a series like *Doctor Who* – running out of time, sets needing changing, all that sort of thing. But Peter was always cool – his youthful appearance belied an enormous professionalism.

'You always felt that if you had to say to Peter that everything had to be changed – could he do all his moves backwards and even speak his dialogue backwards – he would just do it!'

Then, following the announcement of Peter Davison's departure, John had to start the search for a new Doctor all over again – eventually settling in August 1983 for the robust, even brusque Colin Baker who had made his name as the villain in the TV series *The Brothers*. It was to be a stormy tenure for the sixth Doctor both on screen and off, yet none of these upsets has changed John's view of Colin Baker. 'I think in friendship terms I was closer to Colin than any of the other Doctors,' he says quite candidly. 'We have a similar wicked sense of humour and I was happy to be in his company for hours because he could make me laugh constantly.' He pauses and then adds, 'I have no wish to

Above: John with the outstanding cast he assembled for the 20th anniversary special, 'The Five Doctors' in 1983 – including a wax model of Tom Baker, who declined to appear in the programme.

get into a heated debate about him going and the reasons for this – they have been aired fully and mostly incorrectly in the press. But I think – and still think today – that he was a terrific Doctor and should have continued.'

The result of Colin Baker's unexpected exit from *Doctor Who* put John for the third time in the position of having to select a new Doctor – something none of his predecessors had ever had to do. It was not a new process for him, but none the less a tough one with fans and the media anxious to influence his decision and more than likely criticise his choice. He recalls with candour how he came to select the seventh Doctor.

'I had endless lists of possible Doctors,' he says, shuffling a pile of papers on his desk as if recalling those days of decision. 'I also got lots of calls from actors' agents suggesting their clients. It really is a plum job, you see, even with all the demands on both private and public life. One of these calls was from Sylvester McCoy's agent who suggested that I went to see him at the National Theatre in London where he was appearing in *The Pied Piper*. It was 6 January 1987, I remember. I was very impressed with Sylvester's performance and decided to meet him. He later came into my office and we sat chatting for about two hours.'

Right: 'Colin Baker had a wicked sense of humour and I was happy to be in his company,' says John of the sixth Doctor.

Again, John talks of this meeting with the enthusiasm of a showman who has spotted a new star. 'There is this wonderful, natural, eccentric quality about Sylvester. There is a sort of disjointed way that he speaks – the gestures are never quite in the right place at the right moment. I found myself riveted and quite happy to go on listening to him.'

After the interview, John studied a number of cassettes of shows in which Sylvester McCoy had appeared. 'The most fascinating one was a half-hour interview for Channel 4 in which he talked about himself and *The Pied Piper*. And it was the same thing I had seen in the office – the words and the gestures just gripped me! Well, I would have been quite happy to have booked him then and there – but my head of department asked me to spread my net a little wider and do a few screen tests with other actors.'

Beyond question there was enormous interest in the selection of the new Doctor, and a number of very well-known actors were being mentioned as possibles. What John was thinking of doing, however, was picking a comparative unknown for one of the most sought-after roles in British television. 'Anyhow, I did the tests with Sylvester and some other actors and – with no disrespect to the others, Sylvester was the Doctor I was looking for. I had always envisaged a Troughtonesque quality and here it was. Mind you, I don't think Sylvester and Pat Troughton are madly similar, but there are little characteristics which are the same. I also wanted somebody who was much smaller than Colin Baker.'

It was satisfying for John to find somebody who fitted the rough identikit picture of the seventh Doctor – who had already been built into the scripts for the 1987 season some of which were virtually complete by this time. Now there was just the matter of some adjustments to the text and coaching the actor into his very special part – as well as the little matter of preparing him for the amazing change in his life that being the Doctor would bring.

'Sylvester had a tremendous baptism of fire,' John goes on. 'We clinched the deal on a Friday, launched him to the press on a Monday, and on Wednesday he and I were on a plane to America for more press receptions and a convention! And even though I talked to him *ad nauseam* about what the reaction was going to be – the loss of his anonymity, becoming an institution, and so on – he was still taken aback. He was going from one radio station to another, one TV show to another, all day long. And that was only the start of it, in both America and Britain. But he coped wonderfully well. *Such* is the interest in the Doctor!'

After all the hullabaloo, however, Sylvester McCoy then had to *become* the Doctor on screen.

'The first story he filmed was, in fact, the first of the season, "Time and The Rani" by Pip and Jane Baker. Here he had the assistance of an established companion, Bonnie Langford, who had already done six episodes with his predecessor, and the vastly experienced and accomplished television actress Kate O'Mara as his adversary, The Rani.

Below: 'Sylvester McCoy has a Troughtonesque quality and is a very physical performer,' says John of the seventh regeneration of the famous Time Lord, here with Bonnie Langford and Kate O'Mara making 'Time and the Rani' (1987).

'Bonnie helped bridge the change-over of Doctors very well. She established a very good relationship with Sylvester, they got on extremely well. Actually, they had worked together before on the stage in *The Pirates of Penzance*. I know there are those who love Bonnie or hate her, but to my mind that is the mark of somebody who is making an impact. I think she has been very good for *Doctor Who*.

'I also think you can see Sylvester's confidence visibly building up during the four episodes of that first story,' John says with the benefit of hindsight. 'And by the time he was doing the second, "Paradise Towers" by Stephen Wyatt, he was settled.'

Selecting an actor and helping him to 'settle' into the part of the Doctor is, though, just one part of John Nathan-Turner's job as a producer. He has also been described as a 'promoter, salesman, publicist and ambassador', and talking to him about his work, each of these elements gradually becomes apparent.

Of crucial importance obviously is the creation of the Doctor's adventures, which also start to take shape in Room 303 at Union House. '*Doctor Who* is planned season by season,' John explains, 'and at the moment that means fourteen 25-minute episodes which will be transmitted one a week in the autumn. The first thing the Script Editor, Andrew Cartmel, and I do is sit down and plan the "shape" of a season and how this is going to be achieved. By "shape" I mean the kind of stories we will have in the season. In a typical one now we have four stories, and of these we may well decide to have a "traditional" story to start with, then a "bizarre" one second, with a "kooky" or really mad one third, and another "traditional" one to end on. This done, Andrew and I will consider possible writers for the stories we have in mind,' he says.

John will also call in the assistant whose shoes he once filled, Production Associate Ann Faggetter, to discuss how the season he envisages can be achieved with the resources that are available. If the budget is not sufficient, then he may well decide to try to obtain extra funding by looking for a co-production deal and prepare a document for BBC Enterprises to try to attract outside investment.

Once John and Andrew have decided on who will write the new season's stories, the business of script writing begins in earnest. 'Andrew is very good at his job,' John goes on, 'and he is keen to encourage new talent, which is most important because *Doctor Who* is very demanding and any writer can dry up on Who-ish ideas after four or five stories.

'The actual writing process is quite protracted and can take anything between three to six months depending on the writer and the way he produces. We don't give the writers a commission straight away. They go away and produce a two- or three-page outline which describes roughly what the story is and approximately where the "cliffhangers" (episode endings) fall. Andrew, the writer and I then get together and kick the idea around and if we feel that in the end we are going to come up with something that will work, we commission him or her' – and John puts a clear emphasis on the distaff side – 'to write episode one. And if that works out we will commission the remaining three parts.'

John stresses that there can be a number of rewrites called for during the creation of a script, and even completed scripts are not guaranteed to reach the screen. Indeed, usually more scripts than are required are commissioned, to avoid being suddenly left short of material. The history of *Doctor Who* is, in fact, full of instances of stories that had to be dropped or cancelled for reasons of cost, time or similar problems.

'While all this is going on I am busy setting up my team,' John takes up the story again, indicating the wall chart to his right. 'First, the directors. Knowing what kinds of stories we are having will affect my decisions. If, for example, the first story is going to be a "traditional" one then I might get in somebody totally new to the series in the anticipation that he can bring a totally new impetus to the series. I would never risk somebody on *Doctor Who* that I did not have the greatest faith in, though. For the second story, if it's an "oddball", then I would most likely get in somebody whose work I knew well. It is all a case of pairing the right kind of talent to the right story.'

John also has to liaise with various other BBC departments to book his designers, costume makers and other personnel for the production. Then he needs to draw up a production schedule for rehearsals, studio and location time, and filming.

The director of any particular story will join *Doctor Who* about seven weeks before actual production begins, to plan the work which lies ahead with his team which consists of a production manager, an assistant floor manager and a production assistant.

'Another round of meetings then begins,' John continues. 'The director will have script meetings with Andrew and me and this may well result in rewrites. We will also cast the various actors and actresses for the other roles. Planning meetings likewise take place with the set designer, costume designer, make-up artist, technical manager, visual effects designer and several other television servicing departments.'

Rehearsing a *Doctor Who* story takes place about ten days before the actual studio recording. The current four-part adventures normally involve one week's outside location work and five days of studio recording. This inside work is usually split into two sessions of two and three days, with at least a ten-day rehearsal gap.

'Once everything gets under way we soon get into an overlap situation,' says John. 'For example, we can still be working on the script for the last story of the season while filming of the first is taking place. There is a time, in fact, usually about June, when I need to be in about three places at once. Then it's murder!'

Despite the pressure, John keeps a very close watch on what will actually be seen on the screen. 'When the actual production begins I personally go to everything,' he explains. 'I know some producers don't – but I don't like surprises. Even before shooting starts I go to a script read-through of the whole story – and I also watch the entire shoot whether it is on location or in the studio.'

Once the complete story has been filmed and recorded on videotape, it is edited. This is called the post-production work, and again John is heavily involved. The edited tape will be reviewed by the director, composer and radiophonics expert who will decide where the music and special sound effects should be placed.

The composer will then write the score, record the music, and at the 'cypher-dub' – which is the final stage in making the programme – the music and sound effects are dubbed on to the edited tape.

Lastly comes John's moment of truth when the result of months of planning and gruelling hard work – the completed programme – is viewed by the BBC drama executives. Having recited in a matter of minutes what amounts to a year's work, John relaxes – as he is briefly able to do only when the season's stories are complete – and mentions almost as an aside how the cycle has already begun all over again even before *Doctor Who* is appearing on the nation's TV screens!

During his decade with the programme, John has religiously involved the various actors playing the Doctor in this creative process. He says:

'Take Sylvester. He and I meet quite often – usually on trains, where we can talk. I have always been keen to capitalise on anything the Doctors can give. Sylvester, for example, is a very physical performer so I want to include his physical attributes in the show.

'I remember when we were making the first story, "Time and The Rani", filming in a quarry at Frome. One evening after the shoot, we were all relaxing in a bar. One or two people were singing and a member of the cast was juggling – when suddenly Sylvester got hold of some spoons and started playing them. So we put that in the script.

'There are constant discussions going on between the actors and the production team and I am usually receptive to suggestions. I have always said there is no substitute for a good idea – whether it comes from the tea lady or the star!'

Once a season of *Doctor Who* is complete, the business of publicity and promotion gears up once again – though such has become the media interest in the series that stories about it are usually generated all year round whether or not it is being transmitted.

Again, this is something that demands a part of John's time. 'Because *Doctor Who* is a serial we need to promote and publicise it regularly,' he says. 'I think publicity is tremendously important, and I am surprised that there are some people in television who don't pay enough attention to it. We regularly issue information from this office to all the press so they can provide details about the show for people to read in their morning papers. Do you know, before I was a producer I used to think that somehow the *Daily Mail* or the *Sun* had watched every television programme before they wrote about it!' he admits with an almost sheepish grin.

To cater for the requirements of the media, John and a BBC publicity officer will meet and decide what to put in the weekly press release. On top of that, he will liaise with the Picture Office to release suitable photographs from the serial which tie up with the release. 'I am also very keen on co-operating with other programmes like, say, *Breakfast Time*, who ask if they can come and film us at work or get an interview to mark something special like an anniversary. I know some producers consider that to say yes is asking for trouble because of the extra people it will bring on to the set – but I encourage it, even when I have to feed a visiting unit of five out of my own budget!'

John also arranges press showings at the beginning of each season to show the national newspaper journalists the first two episodes of the opening story.

'When the occasion arises I like to have a screening which is a bit of an event. For example, I thought that Malcolm Kohll's "oddball" story "Delta and the Bannermen" from last season (November 1987) was so strong and so funny and so different that it should have a separate preview. What clinched the idea for me was something that happened earlier in the year.

'I had been approached by a company who wanted approval to produce some art cards with holograms of *Doctor Who* characters on them. They also invited me to their studios to have a look at the things they could do with holograms, just in case I thought they might be of use in the show. Well, this *is* something we are toying with using – but as soon as I saw they had a video theatre I thought what a marvellous place it would be to launch a special *Doctor Who* story.

'So we set up the showing for "Delta and the Bannermen" and instead of giving the press the usual brochure – glamorous though it always is – we decided to be even more stylish and have the information printed on the back of the hologram cards. That, plus the fact the people dispensing the coffee and drinks to the press were dressed like Bannermen, made it just that bit more memorable. I saw it as part and parcel of my job, but at the same time I was producing an *event*.'

Another of John's unseen jobs is providing the 'recaps' which appear before every episode of *Doctor Who*. 'Because the show is a serial, I have the option of having a "recap" at the beginning of each subsequent episode giving details of where the Doctor is and what has happened previously,' he explains. 'Andrew writes these "recaps" and I go to the photographic library to select the stills to be used to illustrate them. *Doctor Who* is also on CEEFAX, and we have to supply cassettes and scripts that are exactly as broadcast so that deaf viewers get precisely what is shown on the screen.'

The business of licensing manufacturers to produce *Doctor Who*-related items, while not primarily John's preserve, is still a factor that comes into his job, as all the dozens of souvenirs in his office bear witness. 'I suppose it is because I have been associated with the programme for so long that merchandising requests come my way,' he

Opposite: A typical piece of *Doctor Who* promotional material – a 'biography' of the Doctor sent to his admirers!

WHO IS DOCTOR WHO?

Just about the most popular character of British television, that's 'Who'.

For 24 years now, the mysterious Time Lord, who bears this name has been shuttling through time and space, sorting out galactic problems and vanquishing monsters, to the immense delight of a weekly multi-million audience.

The Doctor is a national institution; an outstanding character of modern fiction whose charismatic quality has triggered off one of the biggest merchandising packages associated with a British tv programme; as well as a score of active fan clubs throughout the world.

Sixty countries share the British enthusiasm for the Doctor Who series.

The Doctor is a Time Lord, the possessor of two hearts, a body temperature of 60 degrees fahrenheit and over 900 years old. Bored with Gallifrey, his own super-advanced planet, and fellow Time Lords, he roams through space and time in a personalised ship - the Tardis (Time And Relative Dimensions In Space).

In practice his space-ship is temperamental and unreliable. The chameleon circuit having jammed on a visit to London in the sixties left the Tardis exterior as a police box!

Nor is the Doctor himself infallible. Part of his appeal is his problem-solving capacity when things go wrong, making do with bits and pieces of electronic gadgetry that just happen to be around.

The Doctor has the ability to regenerate into a new body; to date there have been 7 Doctors, each very different, played by William Hartnell, Patrick Troughton, Jon Pertwee, Tom Baker, Peter Davison, Colin Baker and currently Sylvester McCoy.

Doctor Who is not a children's programme - it appeals to all age groups and to people from all walks of life.
It is a fantasy programme of good against evil - a departure into fun and adventure ....

Five Doctors Who are left to right: William Hartnell, Patrick Troughton, Jon Pertwee, Tom Baker, Peter Davison

says. 'Many of the people associated with *Doctor Who* have moved on, and when new people come into something like merchandising they have to start from square one. They may have no idea what a Zygon or a Tractator is, so requests to produce items like that come to my office for approval and referral to whoever is the copyright holder. In fact, we've become very much a focal point for that kind of manufacturing!'

Although *Doctor Who* cannot be seen to be endorsing any product on the screen, the Production Office has been approached from time to time by manufacturers with offers of help. John recalls with wry amusement that when there was talk about changing the TARDIS, the makers of Superloo sent him masses of brochures and a suggestion that they might be allowed to make a new time machine for the show!

Another aspect of promoting the series entails John and the members of the cast of *Doctor Who* attending fan conventions in Britain and America. They are invited to a considerable number each year and accept as many as is possible, filming and other commitments permitting. To date, all the Doctors bar William Hartnell, and virtually every companion, have appeared once or more at these gatherings – which can often run to thousands of people!

John believes much of the credit for *Doctor Who* taking off in America is due to the dedicated work of his actors visiting the country to promote the show – in particular Peter Davison and his co-stars. 'They really got us started there – Peter even went before he had played the Doctor,' recalls John. 'People may imagine that it is really glamorous to go to these conventions. But often all you see during the course of a weekend is an airport lounge and the hotel where the event is being staged. You have to get up, perform; sleep, get up and perform; then go home. Initially, the *Who* people did it for nothing because I had a hunch it was important and they agreed. Now, of course, they all get paid, but I think we all owe them for their dedication.'

John has never ceased to be surprised at the range and complexity of questions concerning *Doctor Who* that are directed to him and the actors at conventions. Some have called for the showman in him in the answering, but all have made him well practised in dealing with even the most unexpected enquiry. 'I guess one of the most frequent concerns apparent contradictions in the stories. To these I always reply, "Ah, but you are assuming that *everyone* in *Doctor Who* always speaks the truth. I'm not saying the Doctor is a liar, but he may have had a very good reason for saying something at the time."'

Right from the day he inherited the Producer's seat, John has been very aware of fandom and the varying degrees of interest large numbers of people of all ages take in the show. He has always listened to comments and suggestions and taken a keen interest in the thousands of letters which pour into Union House from all over the world – some addressed with nothing more than 'Doctor Who, England'.

Though attitudes towards him and his work among fans have swung sharply from one end of the scale to the other during his eleven years, he has developed a very objective attitude towards this aspect of his working life. 'As with any fan group, the *Doctor Who* people are a mixture of the ordinary and the weird,' he says, picking his words without any sign of rancour.

'There are some superb people, too, especially in America where there is a tremendous feeling of warmth towards the programme. I don't feel the same predominance of warmth in the UK. Certainly there is a small faction of people here who hate my work – and they are quite entitled to their opinions. But there do seem to be one or two who are trying to become stars in the fan world by being deliberately sensational in what they write.

'Some of the criticism I have seen levelled has been quite ridiculous – and I've been in and out of fashion so many times during my years in this chair that it is absurd. It is the difference between constructive and destructive criticism that concerns me. I don't mind about personal criticism, as long as it doesn't go so far that I have to take legal action, but what I *do* care about are actors who rely on reviews being attacked in a derogatory and destructive way, because it is their livelihoods that are at stake.'

John is also very aware of the almost obsessive quest on the part of some fans to find out what is going to happen in the programme in the future – a measure, of course, of the extraordinary interest the show generates. There is, he says, a well-developed system of 'moles' persistently seeking out information about *Doctor Who*.

'I used to find the constant attempts by certain of the fans to find out what was going to happen intensely irritating,' he admits. 'In a vast organisation like the BBC with information going all over the Corporation by computer, it is comparatively easy for the "moles" who are *Doctor Who* fans to tap into this information and then spread it outside.

'At one time I used to put phoney information on my chart. On one famous occasion, I put up a title, "The Doctor's Wife" by Robert Holmes, and then tried to keep a list of everyone who came into the office. Of course, that proved impractical – but the very day after we gave up, what should I read in one of the fanzines than a report we were doing a story called "The Doctor's Wife"!'

John smiles at the memory and then goes on: 'The thing is, I don't mind people having the information about what we are doing if they can resist the temptation to tell as many people as possible about it. I used to want to stop information getting out because I believed it would spoil the viewers' interest if they knew what was going to happen – especially the fan groups. If you know what is going to happen, why watch? Now I don't bother, for I think they are probably spoiling it for themselves.

'I suspect there are an awful lot of fans who would love my job – and therefore whoever *does* have it is bound to come in for criticism,' he adds with what most listeners would probably agree is considerable understatement!

But this said, what *is* the future for *Doctor Who*? Obviously, in writing a book such as this a year before its publication, programme plans for the twenty-fifth anniversary year were still very much in their infancy. What John was in no doubt about, however, was that the season would again consist of four stories in 14 episodes, these being screened from September to December and including the magical date of 23 November when the whole *Doctor Who* odyssey began.

The season will appropriately start with a return of the Doctor's most famous enemies, the Daleks, in a four-part story, 'Remembrance of the Daleks' by Ben Aaronovitch, with guest stars Simon Williams and George Sewell. This will be followed by 'The Greatest Show in the Galaxy', written by Stephen Wyatt and co-starring Peggy Mount and Jessica Martin.

Scriptwriter Kevin Clarke is the man who has been entrusted with the story to mark the 25th anniversary, and his three-part adventure, provisionally entitled 'Nemesis', will embrace the show's history in what John calls 'a "silver theme" celebration'. This story, or alternately Graeme Curry's 'The Happiness Patrol' (also in three parts) will wind-up the season.

All the adventures re-emphasise John's deep-rooted commitment to the present Doctor being part of a continuing and expanding story. A story he believes still has far to go.

'Do you know,' he said with a certain air of exasperation, 'for months I've been hearing rumours that Doctor Who is going to finish at the end of the twenty-fifth anniversary season. Well, I don't know anything about *that* – no one has told *me* to wrap it up!

'I really believe we have seen the worst times in the history of *Doctor Who*. The hiatus caused by the cancellation period is now behind us and we achieved very satisfactory ratings in excess of five million people during the 1987 season – and that doesn't include all those people who video the show to watch later. We are also going great guns in America – there are 208 Public Broadcasting Service outlets there and we are seen on 200 of them. If we can just make eight more then we shall start getting US ratings and they could be enormous!'

A full-length movie is to be made by Coast-to-Coast Productions, on which John is acting as creative consultant. This will feature the Doctor in a specially written 90-minute adventure which will hopefully reach the cinemas in time for the anniversary.

'I am very keen that Sylvester should appear as the Doctor, because it is misleading to have one person on the television and someone quite different in the cinema,' John says, with a passing reference to the only two earlier movies in the 'sixties which starred Peter Cushing in the central role. 'But the problem is we shoot our episodes all through the summer, and the film-makers want to shoot in April to June for a November release.'

John was unable to comment on the then current rumours that Tom Conti and Tim Curry were just two of the leading British

Above: Caroline Munro, who will play the Doctor's companion in the *Doctor Who* movie.

actors who had been suggested for playing the Doctor.

What has been confirmed is that the Time Lord's screen companion will be Caroline Munro, the statuesque brunette actress who shot to fame in the Navy Rum advertising campaign, and later starred in several Hammer horror movies and the James Bond picture, *The Spy Who Loved Me*. Recently, she was seen as a hostess on the popular ITV quiz show, *3-2-1*.

Caroline, who is a fan of *Doctor Who* and a lover of science fiction in general, has a considerable cult following in Britain and the USA, which one newspaper has described as 'Munromania', with a nod in the direction of the most famous of all American movie queens.

The *Doctor Who* movie has been budgeted at £7.7 million, allowing for a host of special effects.

'Obviously with that kind of money, the film will be really spectacular,' John Nathan-Turner commented, 'but we also have some surprises up our sleeves to mark the Doctor's quarter of a century.'

John has also announced that at the end of the twenty-fifth anniversary season he will be relinquishing the Producer's chair himself. He leaves with many happy memories of what has been more than a decade of his own life. He has certainly left his own mark on the programme as indelibly as Verity Lambert and all his predecessors in the job.

Like the TARDIS awaiting each new Doctor, Room 303 at Union House overlooking Shepherd's Bush Green awaits a new occupant to sit at the heart of the remarkable world of *Doctor Who* and guide the famous time traveller on his next series of adventures. . . .

THE SEVEN FACES OF DOCTOR WHO

SYLVESTER McCOY AND HIS PREDECESSORS

It seemed almost like a journey back in time in the TARDIS. For nearly thirty years ago I spent a holiday in the self-same Welsh location in which the seventh Doctor had dramatically appeared in his time machine. To be more precise, on Barry Island, the south Glamorgan holiday resort where the newest Time Lord's third story, 'Delta and the Bannermen', was filmed on location in the summer of 1987: the first *Doctor Who* story since 1975 to be made entirely outside the BBC studios.

Just as in July 1959 I had visited the pleasure island that faces what is left of Barry docks, once among the largest of their kind in the world, so here was the latest regeneration of the Doctor re-enacting in the grounds of the majestic holiday camp a dramatic encounter with the sinister warlord Gavrok and his evil Bannermen in hot pursuit of Delta and her precious charge. The year was the same – except that in 1959 when I had been there, *Doctor Who* had, of course, been no more than a twinkle in Sydney Newman's eye!

The remarkable coincidence, however, gave me a particular interest in 'Delta and the Bannermen', and seemed an ideal starting point for a discussion with the energetic and impishly humorous actor who has become the Doctor's seventh persona, 43-year-old Scottish-born Sylvester McCoy.

Working in the holiday camp, which was packed with holidaymakers at the time, proved no hardship for Sylvester, whose 'wonderful and exotic career' – as he calls it – has taken him as far afield as the ice-bound Arctic Circle! Indeed, the almost-tropical Welsh weather in July when shooting took place made his transition into the Doctor's role all the more pleasant.

At first sight, Barry Island seems an unlikely place for the Doctor to turn up – but not only did it prove an ideal background for the story, it even had some interesting Who-ish elements about it!

What, for instance, could sound more like an alien enemy than Argoed, Fonmon or Sarn (they are actually nearby communities on the mainland), while the very names of Cold Knap Point and Dunraven Castle, a few miles along the coast, could be localities straight from an exciting Earthbound *Doctor Who* story. The town of Barry itself, which in the late nineteenth century expanded from a population of under 100 to almost 13,000 through the development of the docks for exporting Welsh coal, has seen commerce dwindle and has become a brash and booming centre for holidaymakers like some far-distant world in the galaxy where technology has taken over from an old way of life (rather like the Leisure Hive which the fifth Doctor visited on Argolis, perhaps?). Indeed, in a scrapyard near Porthkerry Country Park lie rusting the hulks of dozens of old steam locomotives, relics of a time long by-passed by air and even space travel.

Sylvester McCoy enjoyed the location from the moment he arrived in the last week of June, and helped by one of the most glittering casts of famous actors to be recruited for the series, produced a story that has all the hallmarks of being regarded as a classic in years to come.

Opposite: Sylvester on location filming 'Delta and the Bannermen'.

'They were wonderful weeks,' Sylvester recalls in his gentle Scots accent. 'It was a fun story to do and all the people in it were a great laugh. Nobody was trying to act the star – which some of them had every right to do. I was still a bit of a new boy as the Doctor, but they were very welcoming and good fun to be with.'

Although he was well aware that he had just taken on one of the most famous roles in television, Sylvester was delighted about one early public reaction to him. 'It was one of the first days on location and very hot,' he says. 'So hot, in fact, that between takes I took my coat off. To get a bit of a breather, I wandered off down the street just wearing the jumper with the question marks on it and the tweedy trousers. And do you know, no one noticed me! I was very pleased about that – because I had achieved one of the things I wanted as the Doctor: a costume that I could walk about in without creating a fuss! Although there was one man who came up to me . . .' Sylvester pauses, and not for the only time during our discussions, falls into an accent. This time it is the unmistakable Welsh lilt. 'The chap says to me, "Oh, I like your pullover man, that's very nice. Did your mother knit it for you?" I was so surprised I said, "Oh yes!" – to which he replied, "I wish I could get that pattern!"'

However, if the seventh Doctor was able to enjoy a little anonymity for a while, he very quickly found out that playing a Time Lord can also have its dangers. 'We were filming this sequence on a rooftop with explosive charges going off all around me,' he says. 'One of them went off a little too early and this banged my head a bit, but we were able to keep on. Mind you, with the tight schedules we have, we *had* to – and I suppose that I learned right there and then that the one thing one would like more of on *Doctor Who* is time!'

He would certainly have loved more time with the comedian Ken Dodd, who played the part of The Tollmaster. 'Ken is one of my heroes and he was lovely to work with. Yet he was only with us for one night – we did his whole sequence in a single night's shooting. The remarkable thing about Ken is that he is such an ordinary bloke until he has to do his performance. But once he begins, he is a real professional. The funny thing was he was a bit concerned about appearing in *Doctor Who*, because he hadn't done a lot of that type of acting before!'

In fact, Ken Dodd actually visited the BBC studios in London before appearing in 'Delta and the Bannermen' to watch filming of the new Doctor's second story, 'Paradise Towers', which starred another famous name, Richard Briers, who was similarly making his debut in the series. Ken's part, though, was not filmed on Barry Island, but about twenty miles away at the Llandow Trading Estate near Cowbridge. Here a huge hangar belonging to British Tissues became The Tollmaster's Gate for a night – until he met a nasty end at the hands of Gavrok.

It wasn't only Sylvester McCoy who was impressed by Ken Dodd's professionalism. Producer John Nathan-Turner has an equally strong admiration for the Liverpool-born comedian. 'Being a stand-up comic, Ken is

Top: The Doctor with the 'wild-eyed space nutter', Ken Dodd.

Bottom: Don Henderson as the villainous Gavrok.

used to travelling around with all his props, like his dinner suit and his tickling stick, in the boot of his car,' John says. 'Well, our script called for him to appear blowing a razza and our property buyer hunted high and low to find him a selection of these musical instruments to choose from. And what happens – he turns up with his own!'

Ken Dodd himself was just as thrilled to have been asked to appear in the series. 'It was a great honour,' he said after filming. 'In fact I was tickled, for *Doctor Who* is one of the great British traditions, like test-matches and pantomimes!'

As ever, 'Doddy' provided newspaper reporters with his own highly individualistic description of The Tollmaster. 'He's a sort of wild-eyed space nutter in a lilac suit with lots of spangles who guards a galactic toll gate. I suppose he's a cross between David Bowie and Nigel Lawson because he wears fantastic clothes and takes people's money off them!'

A very different character was played by Don Henderson, the well-known character actor who has specialised in villainous roles and most recently starred in the series *Bullman*. Don played the black-hearted Gavrok.

'The amazing thing about Don is that although he plays all these villains, he's the gentlest man you could wish to meet!' says Sylvester. 'And he does it *so* well – if only people knew what a nice bloke he really is!'

Hugh Lloyd, another character actor who played the inoffensive Welsh bee-keeper, Goronwy, also delighted Sylvester McCoy. 'It was lovely to appear with him because he's

Below: The American comedian Stubby Kaye, who played a bumbling agent, and Morgan Deare.

worked with all the greats. I was a fan of his when he was with Tony Hancock and later Terry Scott. As a kid I always identified with his downtrodden little men continuously at the mercy of all those pompous people.'

Last, but not least, there was Stubby Kaye, the American comedy singing star, who played the bungling secret agent, Weismuller. Sylvester says of him:

'The thing about Stubby is that because he's made so many musicals, he's always breaking into song. There was one particular incident I remember, which also happens to be on film. In fact, at the end of the shoot, the technical boys made up a compilation of out-takes – the mistakes we make which you *don't* get to see – and among them was this wonderful scene with Stubby. He was just about to start acting when he heard the sound of an aeroplane in the distance. And immediately he began to sing [Sylvester mimics the actor as he retells the story]:

"There's a plane coming,
You can hear it,
You can hear it,
There's a plane coming over the hill!"

He was always doing things like that – just bursting into song at any moment!'

This general feeling among both the cast and crew of having fun and enjoying each other's company continued throughout the whole of the shoot on Barry Island – Sylvester remembers – while all around them hundreds of holidaymakers were also enjoying themselves in the camp. Obviously, certain sections had to be cordoned off for filming, but the relationship between the film-makers and pleasure seekers remained very good. 'I think some of the people were a bit puzzled by the old bus which turned into a spaceship,' the seventh Doctor recalls, 'but everyone knew exactly what the TARDIS was. Of course, there were people who wanted autographs and also wanted to take photographs, but it was as happy a location as any I've ever been on.'

Before Sylvester left Barry Island there was one challenge that he could not resist – though it had nothing to do with *Doctor Who*. 'Across the road from where we were filming was this fairground, and in it was a huge swingboat which kept catching my eye,' he says. 'It was one of those things that goes right up and over. Well, the idea of going in it scared me silly, but I kept telling myself I would *have* to have a go. Then, on the last day after we'd finished work, I plucked up courage and went for a ride. I was never so frightened in my life! Hanging upside down, the money dropping out of my pockets, I just prayed to get back safely on to the ground again. But once I'd done it I was so glad,' he grins ruefully.

In fact, that story somehow sums up Sylvester's character, his quirky sense of humour and absolute determination to give of his best as an actor. Certainly, these are two of the characteristics that made John Nathan-Turner select him to be the latest Doctor, the background to which he describes with a mixture of modesty and good humour.

Sylvester was born in Scotland, on the banks of the River Clyde, the son of Irish Catholics, and his parents' earliest intentions for him were to join the priesthood – a fact which incidentally links him to his predecessor, Tom Baker, who also trained for a time to be a priest. After four years, however, he quit, and at the age of 16, inspired by a chance remark of his grandmother's that he was 'predestined' for the stage, Sylvester packed his bags and left for London. Following an unhappy period working for an insurance company (which went bust), he joined the staff of the famous Roundhouse Theatre and after several months as a jack-of-all-trades behind the scenes, at last made it on to the stage with the *Ken Campbell Road Show*, where one of his contemporaries was another actor destined for stardom, Bob Hoskins.

This was the beginning of Sylvester's varied career which has seen him playing everything from Shakespeare to light comedy. He began to develop his special talent at mixing comedy with drama and even pathos – which he hopes will become a hallmark of his Doctor – by playing two of the world's most famous film comedians, Buster Keaton and Stan Laurel.

'I had always wanted to play Buster Keaton because he had such an interesting life,' Sylvester recalls. 'You see, apart from his fame on the screen, Buster had this drink problem and at one stage was confined in an alcoholic ward. I got together with writer Peter Fieldson and he devised this show for me called *Buster's Last Stand* about the comic's life in the ward in which he relived his past through alcoholic fantasies. I was on stage for two and a half hours and I didn't say a word! It was rather like a silent movie – a very bizarre mixture, in fact, though wonderfully exciting to do. Sadly, it didn't quite work.'

Gone with Hardy was Sylvester's interpretation of the period of Stan Laurel's life when he lived for about eight years with an Australian actress before he became famous. Again, the use of flashbacks was employed to tell the story of the couple's life, and although the play was taken across the Atlantic to Canada, it did not achieve the success that Sylvester had hoped for.

Not that all his stage work has featured only comic figures. At Stratford East he played Bram Stoker's immortal vampire count, Dracula; and later at the Lyric Theatre was cast as the lunatic, Renfield, in another production of the play. He was once more associated with the tale in 1979 when he played the mad servant, Walters, in the Universal film starring Frank Langella and Lord Olivier.

Again by way of contrast, he broke into television, soon making a mark for himself in a number of children's programmes, including *Tiswas*, *Jigsaw*, *Vision On* and *Eureka*, the latter two both produced by Clive Doig, who was to play a significant role in helping him get the part of the Doctor. 'The thing about children's programmes is that they are very imaginative and they stretch you,' he says. '*Doctor Who* also stretches an actor because of the type of character it is. Actually, though, I enjoy *every* part I play.'

By a curious coincidence, Sylvester also appeared at the Haymarket Theatre in 1985 with soon-to-be-famous Timothy Dalton in *The Taming of the Shrew* (in which he played Tranio) and *Antony and Cleopatra* (as Pompey). 'When I heard that Roger Moore was quitting as James Bond I remember saying to Tim, "You should go for that. You'd make a great James Bond!" Then six months after he became Bond, I got *Doctor Who*! It was quite a bizarre change of fortune for both of us – to go from being hard-working professional actors to landing two of the most famous roles around! The only difference between us is that his bank manager is luckier than mine – he gets more money!'

How, though, did Sylvester McCoy become the seventh Doctor?

'Actually, it was a role I had wanted for some time,' he says. 'I remember that three years earlier when Colin Baker got the part, I heard about it a bit too late, but I still thought to myself, "I wish I'd known about that – I'd quite like to have tried for it." So though I wasn't actually pursuing it all the time, it was a role that I fancied doing. Then when I heard on the news that Colin was leaving I phoned my agent and told him that there was a job going at the BBC,' he continues, only just able to repress a smile. 'By a coincidence, so was the Director Generalship – but I didn't get that, so they gave me *Doctor Who* as a consolation!

'Actually, what happened was that my agent phoned John Nathan-Turner, and immediately he had put the phone down, Clive Doig also came on the line and told

John he should take a look at me. Apparently John said, "Wait a minute, are you and his agent in cahoots?" As it was, John was obviously interested enough to come and see me at the National Theatre where I was playing *The Pied Piper*. This had been specially written for me by Adrian Mitchell based on the poem by Robert Browning. I had played quite a big part in creating the role, and what with working with groups of 50 kids at each performance, I guess it was a pretty good audition piece for the Doctor,' he says.

Sylvester then spent a couple of hours talking to John Nathan-Turner in his office. 'Usually, an interview lasts for half an hour even when it's going well – but this went on for two and a half, and I kept thinking to myself, "Help, I'm going to run out of charm soon!" Anyhow, we got on very well and after that I saw his boss, Jonathan Powell – for about five minutes, I think.'

Sylvester is quick to admit that the BBC obviously had certain reservations about him. 'I think they weren't quite sure whether I would be strong enough to stand up to the many villains I would have to meet in my career as the Doctor. So I did a couple of tests with Janet Fielding, who had been Peter Davison's companion. They were specially written – one was a "good-bye scene" (a sad one, that is) and the other a confrontation with an evil enemy. And I *still* got the job!'

Once the coveted role had been given to Sylvester he was then faced with the formidable task of bringing his own interpretation to a character who was, after all, already an institution. 'The thing is, I'm not really a fan of science fiction and I hadn't read many books of this kind, but I already had some ideas about how I would play the Doctor when I was talking to John,' he says, 'although they weren't really clear. However, once I got to the studios and got the costume on and had a script in my hand, it all seemed to come together. I am very much an instinctive kind of actor.

'I was also involved in the process of picking the Doctor's outfit. The panama hat is actually exactly the same as the one I wore to the interview. In fact,' he smiles mischievously once again, 'the reason John gave me the part was because he liked the hat. I said to him, "Well, if you want the hat I go with it!" I wanted a baggy jacket with pockets for all sorts of paraphernalia, and the jumper is based on a 1930s golfing sweater. We did consider the idea of the Doctor wearing glasses – as I normally do – but it was decided my eyes could be seen better without them. The umbrella with the red question mark for a handle was all my own idea.

'I have always felt the Doctor is somehow a late Victorian or Edwardian, plus there is a bit of the professor about him. Yet he is still the sort of person who could walk down the street today and wouldn't be considered too eccentric – until you get close up, that is. Anyhow, that is what I am after in my interpretation,' he says.

Although Sylvester is very emphatic about making the point that he is not the Doctor, but an actor playing the part, he has a very

The present and seventh Doctor, Sylvester McCoy, with the first of his companions, Mel, played by the vivacious Bonnie Langford.

Liz Shaw (Caroline John)

Jo Grant (Katy Manning)

Sarah Jane Smith

THE *Doctor's* FAVOURITE FEMALE COMPANIONS

Romana II (Lalla Ward)

Nyssa (Sarah Sutton)

Tegan (Janet Fielding)

(Elisabeth Sladen)

Leela (Louise Jameson)

Romana I (Mary Tamm)

Peri (Nicola Bryant)

Ace (Sophie Aldred)

definite idea about what *sort* of person the Time Lord is.

'He's someone who loves the Earth, and therefore humanity. But he is also a very wise man who sees the follies of man – and also those in himself. Those are his strengths. But he also has his weaknesses which are equally interesting. Take his passion for minutiae, and innocently wandering into obviously dangerous situations that perhaps he should see: maybe does, maybe doesn't. He's also a rebel and doesn't really like authority, which is something I like in him. Because, you know, authority has to prove its worth – just because it *is* authority, it shouldn't be accepted. It should be questioned – and the Doctor does and it gets him into trouble. He's also a bit of an anarchist as well! There is even a bit of Doctor Johnson in him – you know, one of those people you admire who stand up and say what they think.

'In fact, he is a mixture of all sorts of things, but at his most basic he loves the Earth. He is a man who should not use violence, I believe, but his wits and his intelligence to get him out of any tight corner.'

Sylvester is determined that during his tenure as the Doctor he will bring a little of each of his predecessors to the role because, 'I believe there is a logical sense in doing that.' He has, in fact, been a fan of the programme since he was in his twenties, though the demands of his career have made it difficult to keep up with the adventures of all of his predecessors.

'I actually started watching *Doctor Who* when Patrick Troughton was the Doctor,' he says. 'I don't know why I didn't start watching earlier – I think it was because I didn't have a telly! Then I got one, and became hooked on the series thanks to Patrick Troughton.'

Nevertheless, his comments on all the six Doctors before him are both perceptive and revealing.

'I have seen William Hartnell's performances on video, and I like his crabbiness and bad-temperedness. When I first approached the role, I thought I would try and get what I knew of him in it – so every now and then I try and get a bit crabby.

'I was particularly sad not to have had the chance to meet Patrick Troughton because I had always wanted to work with him. What made it even sadder was that I was making one of my first visits to America as the new Doctor and I was in Washington when he was already there talking to fans in Georgia. That was where he died. As I said, he was the first Doctor I watched and in a sense it is rather like your first love. He was the one who first attracted me to the series and, with no disrespect to the other Doctors, he was my favourite. It was Troughton's sense of comedy that I enjoyed, but he could also suddenly turn very serious and save the day. I liked that about him, and that's something else I want to bring back.'

Sylvester makes the point that each generation has had its favourite Doctor, and hopes that in time viewers will also enjoy him. Someone he also loves is the third Doctor, Jon Pertwee. 'I was a great fan of his before he became the Doctor. I have been lucky enough to meet him and appear with him at fan conventions. He is a lovely performer in front of an audience and that is something I enjoy doing, too.'

Sylvester pauses for a moment to give an imitation of Jon Pertwee's unmistakable burbling voice which made him a favourite with radio listeners long before he joined *Doctor Who*.

'He took a very different direction to that of Patrick Troughton and I think that was a very wise thing to do,' Sylvester continues. 'I had loved Jon as a comic performer, so when he first appeared as the Doctor and played it very straight I thought, "Hey, wait a minute, this is not the comic performer I know." But it was still very good – especially that whole dandy thing he built up.'

And Tom Baker? 'I watched him with great interest, too, and in a sense he brought both the seriousness and the comedy together. He had a long run at the role and really beefed it up. He certainly played a major part in helping the series break into the international market.'

Sylvester has also met the fifth Doctor, Peter Davison. 'We bumped into each other in the BBC canteen when he was filming some new stories for *All Creatures Great and Small*. He is a lovely man and I can understand why he was so well liked by everybody. I didn't see that many of his stories, because at that time I was very busy in the theatre and that makes keeping up with serials a bit difficult. I didn't have a video, either!'

And of his immediate predecessor, Colin Baker, Sylvester says, 'Again I didn't see his series very much because of my commitments. But everyone tells me what a nice man he is, and what a shame it was that he and the BBC had that falling out.'

Without that 'falling out' – as he puts it – Sylvester might well not have become the seventh Doctor. But the suddenness of Colin Baker's departure did create some problems for him. 'I inherited one script meant specifically for him,' Sylvester explains. 'That was "Time and The Rani", and some of the lines sounded just like Colin Baker saying them. It was a very bizarre situation – it was almost as if he was saying them through me! The others were written for "an unknown Doctor" as the writers didn't know precisely for whom they were writing.'

Another major problem was the regeneration of the Doctor from Baker into McCoy, as Colin Baker had declined to take part in this crucial scene. 'I had to dress up in Colin's costume with a silly wig and I looked like Harpo Marx,' Sylvester recalls with a grin. 'I had to lie down on my face and then turn over. For just an instant I did look surprisingly like Colin, and then the picture went all funny and it returned to normal, I was me – much to my horror when I looked in the mirror!'

One factor that was of enormous help to Sylvester coming so dramatically into the series was, he says, working with an old friend, Bonnie Langford, playing the Doctor's companion, Melanie. Plus Kate O'Mara, for whom he has the greatest admiration, as the first star guest.

'Bonnie and I had appeared together in the Gilbert and Sullivan musical *Pirates of*

Opposite: The Doctor's lively companion, Mel, played by Bonnie Langford.

Penzance at Drury Lane,' he recalls. 'We became friends and, in fact, ended up getting married every day and twice on Saturdays! She says, under threat, that she enjoys working with me – perhaps because I'm one of the few actors who are only just taller than she is!

'Anyhow, I was pleased she was there because it meant I had a friend. She was a great help. Kate O'Mara was also wonderful. She could have been like some stars are – a pain in the neck – but she turned out to be really professional, good fun, and we got on very well. My first studio session was with her and it lasted for almost twelve hours – we were both on our knees at the end, but great mates!

'In fact, right from the beginning there was a good feeling both in front of the cameras and behind them. No one made me feel I was the new boy and had to prove my worth. The Director of that first story was Andrew Morgan, who had done my screen test for the series. And because I sensed right from that initial meeting that he was the sort of guy who would give me a chance, it was wonderful to work with him on the first story. It felt almost like coming home, and I said to myself, "Hey, I belong here." It was very funny – I didn't worry. I felt relaxed. I just had to learn my lines and not bump into the monsters!'

In his second story, 'Paradise Towers', Sylvester was lined up with another top television star, Richard Briers. 'He was also someone who leapt at the chance of appearing in *Doctor Who*,' Sylvester recalls. 'We just got on from the word go.'

Richard Briers, playing a villain for the first time on TV, similarly enjoyed his encounter

Above: Sylvester with Richard Briers, the Chief Caretaker, in 'Paradise Towers'.

with the Doctor. 'It was a fascinating experience, if a bit of a macabre one,' he said afterwards. 'Certainly, it was a change from my usual roles, playing a kind of fascist dictator complete with Hitler moustache who feeds people to his monster!'

Only a couple of clouds have appeared on Sylvester McCoy's horizon to dampen to any degree his enthusiasm for the role of the Doctor. The first was the publicity which greeted the announcement that he was to be the seventh Doctor with headlines such as 'Sylvester Who?'. The other has been the attitude of certain fans. 'As you know, I've done a lot of things in my career other than stuffing ferrets down my trousers,' he says with a rueful grin. 'In fact, I've had a wonderful and exotic career, but the press just hadn't done their homework.

'Mind you, I was thinking only the other night that perhaps it is not such a bad thing when the press consider you, rightly or wrongly, an unknown, because if you arrive and make a success of a part then everyone sits up. If they don't know what I've done before *Doctor Who*, they'll judge me from that part onwards – which is no bad thing because it is such a good one. And it should help me with work afterwards – because there *does* seem to be life after *Doctor Who*, as the other Doctors have shown.'

And the fans? 'I was actually going to America even before I had played the Doctor, and they were absolutely wonderful. At first I thought they were rather strange, with all that dressing up, and I was uncertain about them. But the more I have come into contact with them, the more I have grown to love them as a body of people. I really look forward to sitting on a stage and talking to them because they are genuinely enthusiastic – they love the programme and they are very giving.

'It has been a bit different in Britain, though, because some of the fans were attacking me even before I'd been seen on television – and I just don't understand that,' Sylvester says. 'I actually told one person that he shouldn't call himself a fan but a critic. said, "You're knocking the programme so much you are going to put a nail in its coffin. *You'll* kill it!"

'What I say to the critics is this: things change. You became fans for different reasons – now it is not your programme, so please leave it alone and don't hang around and try to destroy it. There are people who see different things in it and they *like* what they see. There is a new public for *Doctor Who* coming along all the time and they are what will help it continue to be successful.'

These are strongly held views by a dedicated actor determined to see that the twenty-fifth anniversary year of the show is not its last. 'Though do you know there are already rumours going around that it will be!' he says.

Away from *Doctor Who*, Sylvester lives contentedly in Hampstead with his wife (a nurse), and two sons, Joe (11) and Sam (9). Are they fans? 'The boys watch now, but at the time when they might have started watching, when they were about seven or eight, the show was off the air for eighteen months,' Sylvester says. 'They do enjoy

25 GLORIOUS YEARS

Doctor Who, though, and they don't have any preconceived ideas based on my predecessors. Of course, they've seen me on TV a lot over the years so they are almost blasé. "Oh," they say, "that's just what my dad does – he's on the telly!"'

Sylvester grins for a moment and then recalls a record he recently made for charity. 'Now if that should ever get played on *Top of the Pops* and I appeared, then they would look at me in a new light. That *would* impress them!'

And how does the latest Doctor see his future? 'I'm looking forward to the anniversary season very much. I've had a chance to discuss all the stories with John and the Script Editor, Andrew Cartmel, and I think we shall be emphasising the *mystery* of the character of the Doctor more.

'I have been asked if there is ever likely to be any love interest for the Doctor. Certainly, I would like to see a bit more emotion in the relationship between him and his companion. But they say the Doctor is above anything *sexual*. Mind you, there was a sequence in "Delta and the Bannermen" where the Doctor was talking to the young man Billy who was about to do a species cross – he was going to marry an alien. The Doctor said, "I can't condone it, but love has never been known for its rationality." My delivery of that line was that somewhere – in the deep, dark, distant past of the Doctor – he *knew* that pain.'

Sylvester says that he now really feels settled in the role. But how long will he play the Doctor?

'I've been asked to do it for three years, but who knows? After all, they can get rid of me at any time they want to! You'll laugh, but as soon as I read that Michael Grade was going to Channel 4, I thought, "My God, is he going to take *Doctor Who* with him?"

'Joking apart, if at the end of three years they ask me to do more, then I'll consider my situation at that point. I'm enjoying it now, and if I continue to enjoy it, then there is a very good chance that I would agree to go on. But that's all pure conjecture. It's fantastic that the series has lasted for 25 years and I want to ensure that it goes on for a good many more years yet. There are still so many more places and possibilities to be explored . . .'

Spoken, surely, like a *true* Time Lord!

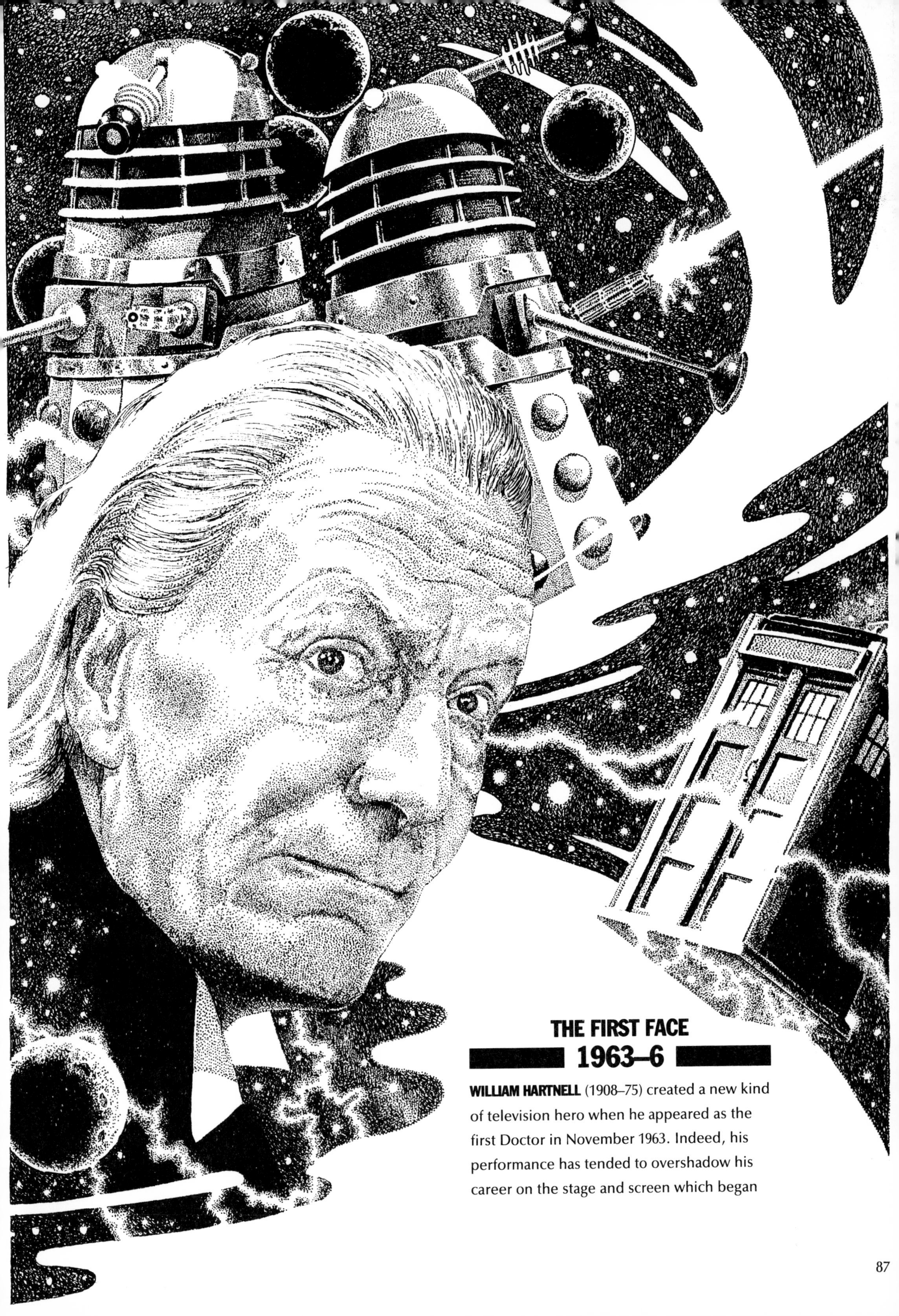

THE FIRST FACE

1963–6

WILLIAM HARTNELL (1908–75) created a new kind of television hero when he appeared as the first Doctor in November 1963. Indeed, his performance has tended to overshadow his career on the stage and screen which began

Above: 'The Doctor represents a cross between The Wizard of Oz and Father Christmas' – William Hartnell with Peter Purves in 'The Massacre' (1966).

as a boy actor with Sir Frank Benson in 1924 and took him through dozens of plays and over 60 films. It was his performance as the old Rugby League talent scout in the Richard Harris movie *This Sporting Life* in 1963 which led to him being selected to play the Doctor, a role he enacted for three years until ill-health brought about his retirement. He was married to the former actress and playwright Heather McIntyre, and they had one daughter. William Hartnell delivered this verdict in 1971 on the role he created:

'I was fortunate in being given almost *carte blanche* with the part. This gave me a tremendous opportunity to improve and build upon the original outline of the Doctor as a senile old man unable to control his space machine.

'I think the Doctor represents a cross between the Wizard of Oz and Father Christmas, though I was always adding fragments to it and trying to expand it. Though he is often snappy and a bit arrogant, I would like to have had the chance to bring more humour into the part.

'I loved every moment of being this eccentric old man, and the children calling me "Mr Who" and even "Uncle Who". To begin with, when I said it would run for at least five years, I was universally scoffed at by the press and other producers. But I believed in the show because it was magical.

'*Doctor Who* is certainly a test for any actor, because children are renowned scene stealers – so are monsters – and we had both! Look at the Daleks, who appeared in the second story and were an immediate success.

'*Doctor Who* gave me a certain neurosis – and I know it was not easy for my wife to cope with. I used to get a bit agitated about things and that sometimes made me a little irritable with people.

'Occasionally I had to put my foot down with a new director and tell him, "I know how to play the Doctor and I don't want you to intrude on it or alter it."

'In a way, I had to become hypnotised by the part. Whenever I looked at a new script it seemed unbelievable and so I had to allow myself to be hypnotised by it so that I could make the story believable to the young viewers. To me, kids are the greatest audience – and the greatest critics – in the world.

'I haven't done much television since leaving the series, but I don't regret that because I'm over 60 and it's time to start taking things a bit easier.

'Although I believe a bit of the magic of *Doctor Who* will always cling to me, I do regret that it is no longer a programme for children. That's why I hardly ever watch it.'

THE SECOND FACE 1966–9

PATRICK TROUGHTON (1920–87) was responsible for a unique moment of television history when his whimsical, heavily-jowled and elastic-featured persona took the place of the irascible William Hartnell as the second Doctor on 5 November 1966. No major TV hero had ever before been replaced by a new actor, and the success of the 'cosmic hobo', as Troughton became known, helped to create the element of regeneration which has since explained the introduction of each new Doctor to the series. Trained as an actor in London, Patrick won a scholarship to the Leighton Rollin's Studio in New York and following distinguished service in World War II he became one of the busiest character actors in England. He appeared in numerous television series before being somewhat reluctantly talked into playing the Doctor by the Producer, Innes Lloyd. Though Patrick was also reluctant to publicise himself while playing the Doctor, he had in later years begun to appear at *Doctor Who* conventions on both sides of the Atlantic, and it was while attending one at Columbus in Georgia that he collapsed and died. He had been married three times, and left a widow, Sheila, four sons, two daughters, a stepson and a stepdaughter. Talking about his role as the second Doctor, he said in 1984:

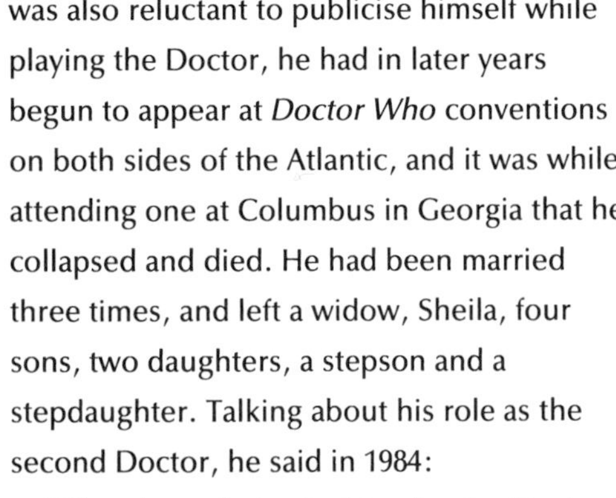

'When I was first asked to play the Doctor I had a feeling that perhaps it had been done to death and that it wouldn't last. So when I did agree, the character had to be completely different to Billy's Doctor.

'My daughter was about twelve and my sons maybe ten and eight, so obviously I had them in mind when I was playing the role – and I really tailored it to that. Perhaps if I'd had a grown-up family, it might have been a different character that emerged; but with my children being young, one had that in mind – I didn't want to make the character too frightening for the children.

'I was left pretty much to devise the character of the Doctor myself, though they did all want this Chaplinesque element to him. I mellowed him a bit as we went along, but he was always off-beat. I even tried to make him a bit naughty at times, because if you are going to be totally moral all the time it becomes boring. But, of course, when there were villains about the Doctor *had* to be on the side of right!

'*Doctor Who* was just one of many character parts I have played, but it was certainly more fun than most of the others!'

Below: 'There was this Chaplinesque element to the Doctor and I even tried to make him a bit naughty at times!' – Patrick Troughton in 1967.

THE THIRD FACE
1970–4

JON PERTWEE (1919–), who came from a theatrical background and had worked as a circus performer, vaudevillian, cabaret entertainer and radio star, was the first actor actually to put himself up for role of the Doctor when Patrick Troughton decided to

Above: 'I have always been an adventurous soul and I wanted the Doctor to be a man of action.' – Jon Pertwee being attacked by a Pterodactyl in the 'Invasion of the Dinosaurs' (1974).

leave – and to his surprise found himself already second on the list being drawn up! Like his two predecessors, Jon totally changed the Doctor's image to that of a dandy who was also a man of action. He came to the part after a varied acting career which had got off to an inauspicious start when he was thrown out of RADA, but later led to public acclaim when he starred in BBC Radio's *The Navy Lark* (he had been at sea himself during World War II serving on HMS *Hood*) in which he remained for 18 years. Jon was the first Doctor to appear in colour, as well as being confined to the Earth for most of his adventures. He has a German-born wife, Ingeborg, and they have two grown-up sons. Jon talked about his interpretation of the Doctor in 1985:

'Because I had played a lot of comedy roles before I joined *Doctor Who*, I found it difficult to keep that element down and play the part straight. After all, the series bears little relation to reality, so if you play it straight at least people will accept it. I think you have to be completely truthful within fantasy.

'Mind you, I have always been an adventurous soul, fascinated by danger and speed, and I wanted the Doctor to be a man of action. I introduced the use of the martial art Aikido, and whenever possible I was keen to include my love for motorcycles, speedboats, fast cars and gadgetry in general. Two cars were built to my specifications – "Bessie", the mock-Edwardian veteran, which was in complete contrast to my "Whomobile" – probably the most revolutionary vehicle ever made for the series. It looked just like a flying saucer!

'I always loathed the Daleks because I thought they were boring, and I wanted my monsters to be down-to-earth. I believe there's nothing more alarming than coming home to find a Yeti in your bathroom. OK, you might expect that in the Himalayas, but not in the average suburb!

'I suppose on reflection my Doctor was a kind of science fiction James Bond with a touch of the Renaissance Man. I was also a protective Doctor – my cloak was a bit symbolic of the mother hen!'

THE FOURTH FACE

1974–81

TOM BAKER (1934–   ), who became the fourth Doctor after being spotted by producer Barry Letts playing a magician in the film *The Golden Voyage of Sinbad* (1974), brought a unique charisma to the series and also helped to establish it as an international success

Below: 'The Doctor is very much a heroic stereotype, and because he is an alien there must always be a sense of magic about him.' Tom Baker in 'Masque of Mandragora' (1976).

during his record seven-year tenure. Like the seventh Doctor, Sylvester McCoy, Tom grew up in a Catholic family (in Liverpool) and for some years trained to be a monk, but instead settled for the wandering, Bohemian life of an actor, and when he joined *Doctor Who* he introduced much of his own love of flamboyant behaviour and off-beat comedy into the role. With his famous floppy hat and trailing scarf he also achieved an instant rapport with children, and his affection and regard for them – which is reciprocated – has been described in many stories. Twice married (once to his companion in the series, Lalla Ward), Tom has two grown-up sons. He talked in 1985 about playing the Doctor.

'I knew early on that the Doctor was very much a heroic stereotype, and though the patterns of his behaviour were well established, the challenge was to make his character as interesting and diverting as possible.

'The costume was very important in this, and what I wore had just the right amount of extravagance. Actually, it was totally impractical from an acting point of view because I was forever tripping over the scarf!

'I always took great care playing the Doctor, and I honestly believe that after a time I knew what he could and could not do better than any writer or director. You see, I never wanted any of the children who watched to be disappointed in him – and this meant I had to carry the concept of him being an almost-perfect man into my private life, which was very exhausting at times!

'Because the Doctor is an alien I also felt there should be a sense of magic about him. But he had to have a naïve innocence that countered his enormous wealth of knowledge – which I believed made him more vulnerable and therefore more interesting to the audience.

'I could never understand the complaints we got about the Doctor being violent. I hate violence myself, and the Doctor used to outwit his enemies rather than blow them up. Sometimes we even laughed our villains to destruction!

'Another thing that puzzled me were the fans who lived and breathed the programme. It was more real than real life to some of them, and though I was always very pleased at the compliments they paid me, I still had to insist that I was just an actor who had been lucky enough to play the role. And it *was* a thrill to play the Doctor.

'I've been asked if *Doctor Who* is my albatross? I suppose it probably is – but I just hope it doesn't turn out to be my nemesis!'

THE FIFTH FACE
1982–5

PETER DAVISON (1951–   ) was the first actor to play the role of the Doctor who had been a fan of the series as a youngster, and he again brought a new dimension to the show by appearing as a much younger, almost boyish figure. Having decided on a career in acting because he wasn't sure what else to do, Peter gained a sound training at the Central School of Speech and Drama before breaking into TV in a science fiction series not unlike *Doctor Who* called *The Tomorrow People*, made in 1975 by ITV. It was while playing Tristan Farnon in the very successful BBC series *All Creatures Great and Small* that Peter met John Nathan-Turner, then the production unit

Below: 'Although the Doctor is from Gallifrey he is very much an honorary Englishman, and there's nothing more English than cricket!' Peter Davison in 'Terminus' (1983).

manager, who in 1982 offered him the chance of following Tom Baker. Peter is married to the actress Sandra Dickinson. He discussed his role as the Doctor in 1987.

'The idea was to make the Doctor younger and a bit more physical in his approach to problems, but I have to admit I was worried because I had never imagined he could be anyone as young as me! I had watched the series since it had begun and I suppose I had this preconceived idea he was an older man.

'Once I had realised the part was just too good to refuse, I decided to fall back on what I knew of the first two Doctors in building up my interpretation. Tom Baker's very dominant image was still too much in everyone's mind, so I went for a mixture of Hartnell's brusqueness and Troughton's vulnerability.

'I suppose Troughton's influence was the stronger because he was the one I had watched most as a kid, and I really admired his lighter touch. What I added myself to the part was a kind of innocence and impetuosity – plus the cricketing costume which I liked because I'm rather fond of the game. I also felt that although the Doctor is from Gallifrey he is very much an honorary Englishman, and there's nothing more English than cricket!

'I always vowed that I would not appear in the series longer than three years – a view that was underlined to me by Patrick Troughton when we met at the BBC one day. He also featured in one of my favourite memories of the show.

'A while after I had left, I returned to do a series for the BBC called *L Driver*. This was being made in a studio at the same time that my successor, Colin Baker, was filming "The Two Doctors" with Pat Troughton. Well, when they were just about to shoot a scene together I crept up behind Colin and tapped him on the shoulder. He turned round and, you can imagine, got the shock of his former lives!'

THE SIXTH FACE
1985–6

COLIN BAKER (1943–) had the unique distinction of appearing in *Doctor Who* as a Gallifreyan guard named Maxil in the January 1983 story 'Arc of Infinity', before landing the role of the Doctor himself. In this story he shot Peter Davison's Doctor, though not, as he later explained, 'to get the Doctor's role!'. Colin was born in London and actually trained for five years to be a solicitor before going into acting. Work in repertory followed, and then stardom as the unscrupulous Paul Merroney in the popular BBC TV series *The Brothers*. Colin immediately accepted John Nathan-Turner's offer in the autumn of 1984 to play the sixth regeneration of the Doctor,

Opposite: Famous horror-film star, Peter Cushing, has twice played the Doctor in cinema movies. In 1966 he appeared with Bernard Cribbins and Jill Curzon in *Daleks – Invasion Earth 2150 A.D.*

Above: 'The Doctor is unpredictable – so I gave him a more extrovert personality and a sarcastic turn of phrase.' Colin Baker talking in 1987.

but two years later in December 1986 left the series following a much-publicised dispute, without filming a regeneration link with his successor, Sylvester McCoy. Colin, who is married to actress Marion Wyatt, has a daughter, Lucy, but tragically lost a baby son, Jack, in a cot death. He talked in 1987 about his ill-fated period as the Doctor.

'As soon as John Nathan-Turner offered me the Doctor's role I got hold of about twenty or thirty old tapes of the series and watched all my predecessors in the hope of finding out just *who* the Doctor is. I learned that he is actually what the actor makes him.

'That's why when I started filming he was mostly Colin Baker with a little bit of each of my predecessors: irritability, wit, action, extravagance and some recklessness. I did also try to make it obvious that he is an alien, and though he may look like any other human being he doesn't necessarily have the same values. For example, although my Doctor believed in justice and truth he was not as sentimental as an Earth man.

'The "bad taste" outfit was John's idea to match the Doctor's more extrovert personality and sarcastic turn of phrase. It all went to make him what I most wanted him to be, unpredictable, and therefore better able to hold the audience's attention because they can't be quite sure what he'll do next.

'Despite what happened, I can honestly say that working on *Doctor Who* was one of the happiest professional experiences of my life. We had a good team and lots of fun together. I was convinced that I was a good Doctor – certainly on an equal footing with my predecessors – and I would have liked to have carried on playing the role for a good few more years. Especially because I believe the Doctor has become one of our greatest heroes.'

WHO ARE THESE
DOCTORS!

25 GLORIOUS YEARS

Although seven actors are widely recognised for having played the Doctor's various incarnations during the past quarter of a century, several other performers have also portrayed the Time Lord on television, in films and even on the stage. Their names are undoubtedly worthy of record in this anniversary year, as their performances range from the Hartnell era to the present day.

The earliest man to don the first Doctor's mantle – as well as his black frock coat, checked trousers, long white wig and Astrakhan hat – was Brian Proudfoot, who doubled for him in a short sequence of location footage for 'The Reign of Terror' (August–September 1964). This was where the Doctor is seen walking along a path towards the camera in long-shot, and marked the earliest use of actual location work in *Doctor Who*.

The next actor to double for the Doctor was a versatile character actor, Edmund Warwick. Warwick's first role in *Doctor Who* was as the inventor Darrius in the 1964 Terry Nation story, 'The Keys of Marinus', and when William Hartnell was unavailable for recording episode four of 'The Dalek Invasion of Earth', Edmund's close resemblance to Hartnell was remembered and he was brought in for the one episode to double for the Doctor as required. This substitution proved so successful that in Terry Nation's 'The Chase' in 1965, when a robot double of the Doctor was created by the Daleks to destroy the real Doctor, Warwick was once again engaged to play the robot double.

The next occasion that a double was required was during Brian Hayles's 'The Celestial Toymaker' (April 1966). William Hartnell's health had been steadily failing him and as time went on he was increasingly unable to stand up to the vigorous demands of a hectic recording schedule. Therefore, when the opportunity arose during 'The Celestial Toymaker' to make the Doctor invisible, Hartnell could take a much needed rest, only having to pre-record his spoken part. This technique was used quite a lot when the regular cast took holidays and the like. They would pre-record their lines which were later played in at the appropriate times during the episode.

During the playing of the Trilogic game in the 'Celestial Toymaker', only the Doctor's hands were seen and these actually belonged to actor Albert Ward, who later doubled for the Doctor again in the studio recordings of episode three of 'The Smugglers' in 1966, Hartnell's penultimate story. Another actor also stood in for Hartnell during the location filming for this episode. This was David Blake Kelly (who was actually playing Jacob Kewper in the story) and he took the Doctor's mantle for the tricky scenes involving embarking and disembarking from a boat.

For Hartnell's regeneration story, Kit Pedler and Gerry Davis's 'The Tenth Planet' (October 1966), another actor, Gordon Craig, doubled for the Doctor in several scenes during episode one. Unfortunately, due to Hartnell's ill health, these were rather more frequent with the result that sharp-eyed viewers could spot the differences where the Doctor has his

Opposite: Stunt man Terry Walsh, who has been associated with *Doctor Who* since the days of William Hartnell and has doubled for the actors playing the Doctor on numerous occasions. He is pictured here working with Tom Baker on 'The Android Invasion' in 1975.

hat and scarf almost covering his face.

With the debut of Patrick Troughton as a much younger (mid forties) and sprightlier Doctor, there was less need to call on the services of a stand-in. However, Chris Jeffries did double for Troughton in 'The Wheel in Space' (April–May 1968) and 'The Dominators' (August–September 1968) when the need arose, and Tom Laird doubled in 'The Space Pirates'.

When Jon Pertwee became the third doctor in 1970, an early feature of his adventures were stories crammed with dangerous and explosive scenes; a factor which he encouraged, because he happened to love stunt work. Indeed, Jon was keen to take part in as many of these scenes as possible, particularly those in which high-powered vehicles were involved, because of his own skill and daring behind the driving wheel. Only the firmness of several directors and the special talents of a remarkable stunt man called Terry Walsh prevented Jon from endangering his life above and beyond the call of duty.

Terry Walsh had, in fact, already been associated with the programme since the days of William Hartnell – having appeared in the penultimate story, 'The Smugglers' by Brian Hayles, where he came to two sticky ends in a sword fight, playing the deaths of both a pirate and a revenue man in a fight sequence! But Terry lived again to become one of the most regularly employed 'unseen' stars of *Doctor Who* throughout both Jon Pertwee's and Tom Baker's eras.

Terry was an ideal substitute for Jon

Pertwee, in fact, looking remarkably like him physically, and only an inch shorter in height. He was not only proficient with most weapons but could drive any motor vehicle from a motorbike to a tank. Talking about his work in 1973, Terry said:

'*Doctor Who* is a great programme for me because it's so wide-ranging and you never know what's coming next. I've been involved in sword fights, gun fights and motor chases. I've been knocked down and blown up. I've been run down by a car and banged over an 80-foot bank. I've had stair falls, cliff falls, car falls, falls from ladders, falls on boxes and falls into water.

'Sometimes I've even had arguments with Jon Pertwee about stunts. If it's not dangerous and it looks fun – like falling over backwards from a whack – he likes to do it himself. "All right," I say, "but make it look difficult or I'm out of a job!" That soon became a joke. I'd be about to do a 60-foot fall or something hairy and Jon would shout out, "Make it look difficult!"'

The fourth Doctor, Tom Baker, was as keen as his predecessor to do his own stunts, but again where things were just too dangerous and there was a risk that the show might be without its star for weeks or even months if he got injured, Terry took over – complete with coat, flowing scarf and hat, and a very voluminous wig!

Terry's skill was seen at its best during a lengthy fight sequence in 'The Sontaran Experiment' by Bob Baker and Dave Martin (February–March 1975) and in a spectacular high jump in Robert Holmes's 'The Talons of Weng-Chiang' (February–April 1977).

In the Tom Baker story 'The Leisure Hive' by David Fisher (August–September 1980), not one but *three* stand-ins had to be recruited for episode one when the Doctor apparently fell apart in the Tachyon Generator. His various anatomies were played by Derek Chafer, David Rolfe and Roy Seeley, all *Doctor Who* regulars.

Tom's successor, the youngest of the Doctors, Peter Davison, had little call for a stand-in during his fifth incarnation, but the sure-footed Gareth Milne saw him through some tricky moments in 'Warriors of the Deep' (January, 1984) and 'The Caves of Androzani', (March–April 1984).

Perhaps the most remarkable of all the stand-ins for the Doctor was created by the veteran stage and radio actor Richard Hurndall, who played the part of the first Doctor in the twentieth anniversary special, 'The Five Doctors', screened in November 1983. Not only did Hurndall look almost identical to Hartnell's first Doctor, but he had the most extraordinary effect on actress Carole Ann Ford who had appeared as the first time traveller's grand-daughter. 'Richard gave a marvellous performance,' she said afterwards. 'It was wonderful, but also rather spooky. He didn't deliberately try to be Bill, but somehow he just looked and sounded like him. It was a wonderful piece of casting.'

Tragically, Richard Hurndall died only a few months after giving this performance, in April 1984.

Since the Peter Davison era, neither of his successors, Colin Baker and Sylvester McCoy,

Opposite: Richard Hurndall, who looked uncannily like the first Doctor when he played William Hartnell's role in the anniversary special, 'The Five Doctors' in 1983.

has required a double – special effects being able to transport them safely through most hazards.

The stories of *Doctor Who* have not, of course, been solely confined to television, and in 1965 and 1966 the Doctor appeared in two movies, played by the 'gentleman of horror', Peter Cushing. The films, *Doctor Who and the Daleks* (1965) and *Daleks – Invasion Earth 2150 AD* (1966), were both produced and written by Milton Subotsky, with Gordon Flemying as the Director. Peter Cushing's Doctor was presented as an eccentric inventor living in London who had created the TARDIS, a machine capable of travelling in time. His companions in the first picture were Roy Castle and Jennie Linden (as Ian and Barbara); and in the second, Bernard Cribbins and Jill Curzon (as Tom and Louise). A young actress, Roberta Tovey, played his grand-daughter, Susan, in both.

Peter Cushing, who was a veteran of numerous horror and fantasy films made by Hammer Pictures, was deliberately chosen for the Doctor's role in preference to William Hartnell because Milton Subotsky felt a star name was essential to sell the picture outside the areas of Britain and Australia where the series was then being shown.

'It was a curious experience taking over Bill

Above and opposite: In 1965 Peter Cushing played the leading role in the first of the cinema movies, *Doctor Who and the Daleks*, with the youngest-ever companion, Susan, played by Roberta Tovey.

Hartnell's role while he was playing it on television,' Peter Cushing has recalled. 'Especially as I knew Bill and I know he would love to have played the Doctor on film. Although I did not consider myself a fan of the programme, I did watch it when I agreed to take the part. I decided my Doctor had to be a bit less eccentric and crabby, and a bit more lively and amusing.'

The big box-office success of the first film encouraged Milton Subotsky to produce the second, which featured the Daleks even more prominently. 'I am afraid my memory of that picture is not too clear because I was quite ill during much of the shooting and they had to work around me a good deal,' Peter recalls of a time that seems with hindsight almost a replay of William Hartnell's closing months with the television series. 'But I did enjoy playing the role because it was a change from all the horror pictures, and made me popular with children, which I was very pleased about. I still believe that Doctor Who as a heroic figure is one of the best parts any actor could play.'

Although Milton Subotsky had the rights to produce a third *Doctor Who* movie, the lack of success of the second picture has so far

Above: Trevor Martin, who had appeared in the TV series, took the part of the Doctor in Terrance Dicks's stage play, *Doctor Who and the Daleks: Seven Keys to Doomsday*, which was put on at the Adelphi Theatre in London in 1974.

deterred him from doing so – although Tom Baker did bring him a project in 1975 called *Doctor Who Meets Scratchman*, which was based on a completely new script that he had devised with his co-star in the TV series, Ian Marter. Tom wanted to star in the movie with Peter Cushing's fellow horror star, Vincent Price, as the villain of the title.

Talking about the film, Tom Baker explained, 'The script was about scarecrows becoming animated when a fertiliser on Earth goes horribly wrong. The scarecrows were able to create other scarecrows, and they all went on the rampage raiding stores and using their sticks as weapons. The Cybermen were involved, too, and there were wonderful scenes of them coming out of the sea.

'The whole plot hinged on the fact that somewhere out in space was this creature called Scratchman, which is an old-fashioned name for the Devil. The ending was going to be amazing – we were going to turn the whole studio into a giant pinball table. The Doctor and his companions were stuck on this table and Scratchman was firing these balls at us. The balls disappeared down holes which were sort of gateways into other hells.

'It was a very violent film, but very funny too. The BBC Production Office saw it and hated it – but I thought it was marvellous,' Tom added of the film that, unhappily, did not materialise.

A *Doctor Who* story that did reach the public and presented yet another Doctor was a London stage play, *Doctor Who and the Daleks: Seven Keys to Doomsday*, which opened at the Adelphi Theatre in The Strand on 16 December 1974. Written by Terrance Dicks, one of the most prolific script writers to work on the series and for a time its Script Editor, the play starred Trevor Martin as the Doctor and Wendy Padbury, who had played companion Zoe Herriot during the second Doctor's time, as Jenny. The story told of yet another struggle between the Doctor and the Daleks on the mysterious planet Karn.

Terrance Dicks recalls the play – and its fate – very vividly. 'There was a lot of enthusiasm for the production,' he says, 'and the staging was very impressive, with huge sets, some new monsters called Clawrantulars, and this great Doomsday Machine for the finale. It was a very splendid production.

'At the time we were between Doctors. Jon Pertwee had finished his era, and though we wanted him to appear in the play he had other commitments. Tom Baker, of course, hadn't yet been seen in the role. So we decided to cast Trevor and opened the play with a scene showing him regenerating from Jon. It worked very well, I thought, and certainly the whole play got some marvellous reviews,' Terrance says.

Trevor Martin combined a little of all his predecessors in the title role. A long grey wig like Hartnell's was completed with baggy trousers such as Troughton had worn and a dashing coat and necktie that could well have been taken straight from Jon Pertwee's wardrobe. Trevor's style of acting was inevitably influenced to a degree by the three earlier stars, but still managed to be both individual and entertaining.

Trevor was actually not a complete

newcomer to the world of *Doctor Who*, although the part was unlike anything he had done previously. After training at the Guildhall School of Music, he had worked with the BBC Radio Drama Repertory Company for three years, later joining the Royal Shakespeare Company and after that the National Theatre Company. In 1969 he appeared in *Doctor Who* in the final Patrick Troughton story, 'The War Games', where, appropriately as events transpired, he was cast as a Time Lord!

'Actually, I had been a fan of the programme for some years before that,' Trevor said during a press conference for the opening of the play. 'My four children had been avid watchers since the days of William Hartnell and they got me to watch it whenever I was at home. I think they believed I would really become famous when I played the Doctor!'

Sadly – as Terrance Dicks has also explained – this was not to be. 'I think the economics were against us – and also the IRA! The Adelphi was a great barn of a place and the show cost a tremendous amount to set up. Although we got very good attendances for the afternoon matinees, I don't think adults were keen to come in the evening to a children's show. Plus the fact that the IRA were running a bombing campaign in London that Christmas, which certainly didn't help us. I remember there were several bomb scares and we actually heard some explosions during the course of the four-week run!

'Still, it was a great experience for all of us who were involved, and it was marvellous for me to have my name up in lights in the West End, if only for a few weeks!' added Terrance. In fact, all was not lost for him, because he later incorporated some of the material from the play into the Tom Baker serial 'The Brain of Morbius', which was screened in January 1976.

Recently, an attempt to mount a new play featuring the first American Doctor was instigated in Chicago, the heart of *Doctor Who* fandom in the USA. Entitled *The Inheritors of Time*, the play was written by John Ostrander, who hoped to produce it himself at the Pickwick Theatre in Park Ridge, Illinois.

Heralded among American fans as 'promising to be the hottest theatrical production in Chicago', the lavish play featured the Doctor after his twelfth regeneration, the fate of the Time Lords, and the destiny of the human race. To date, the play has had only a read-through given by Patrick Troughton at the 1983 Chicago Convention.

In Britain, two young film-makers belonging to the Doctor Who Appreciation Society have been working for five years to produce an epic-length movie about the Doctor in which he once again pits his wits against the Daleks. In their film, however, the Doctor has a new companion, Amber, and encounters a new race of frog-like aliens called the Korvens. Designer and model-maker Julian Vince has created precise replicas of the Daleks as well as the ingenious Korvens, and his partner in the enterprise, Paul Tams, who is in his early twenties, wants

Below: Trevor Martin (far right) as one of the three judges at the trial of the Doctor in 'The War Games' (1969).

to be the youngest ever Doctor! Both hope for a much higher degree of sophistication than two earlier DWAS attempts at movie-making, the two-hour *Oceans in the Sky* and their own previous effort, *The Image Makers*.

Talking about the project in *Movie Maker* magazine, Paul said, 'We want to make a thoroughly professional movie – but as amateurs and on an amateur budget. We see no reason why, in terms of quality, this film should be any different as far as production values are concerned from the two *Doctor Who* films made by Milton Subotsky.'

And Julian Vince added, 'In a way, we see this as the third of a trilogy. Subotsky had the option to make a third one, and we're making what he might have done if he'd taken up the option.'

In fact, as has already been mentioned, the major project by Coast-to-Coast Productions, *Doctor Who: The Movie*, seems likely to reach the public before either of these two ideas. Yet there is no denying that all of them stand as further evidence of the incredible interest in the enigmatic figure of the Doctor – *whoever* may be playing him.

THE DOCTOR WE PRESUME?

THE TIME LORD AS SEEN BY HIS FAVOURITE FEMALE COMPANIONS OVER 25 YEARS

BARBARA WRIGHT

Schoolteacher

Played by Jacqueline Hill, 1963–4

The Doctor's first companion (aside from his grand-daughter Susan), and to date the oldest of his female co-travellers. Jacqueline Hill was a former fashion model with stage experience and appearances on both American and British television, who made her debut in the first story, 'An Unearthly Child', as the mature and intelligent Coal Hill Secondary School history teacher who became unwittingly involved with the wayward time traveller. Speaking of her days with the first Doctor, she said at a recent *Doctor Who* convention:

'Bill Hartnell deserves much of the credit for *Doctor Who*. He was very firmly at the helm right from the start and created this sense of unity among everyone working on the programme. It was a great show for inventive new talents. Bill also made everyone from the director right through to the production assistant stretch themselves. Things were never easy because the studios at Lime Grove were very cramped and we were always working to a very tight schedule. You can't believe how different it was to the Television Centre which is used today!

'Mind you, Bill could get very annoyed if things weren't being done in what he thought was the right way. He cared a great deal about the programme and he was always very proud about all the letters he got from children. Some of them he would show to us to emphasise a point he was making.

'I enjoyed my part because Barbara had to stand up to the Doctor's know-it-all attitude. I suppose I was one of the few companions who actually stood up to him and didn't dissolve into screams.

'My favourite stories were those with the Daleks because they were such fascinating things. It was impossible not to want to try them out for yourself and we all did! I think it was easy to suspend belief when acting with them, and that's what gave them such an impact.

'I was very fond of Bill Hartnell and I think the only disagreement we ever had was over the fact the series was in black and white. I thought that lent the right air of mystery to the stories. Bill was keen that it should have been in colour – and in that way he was ahead of his time, I suppose. But then, he was never in any doubt that *Doctor Who* would last.'

Opposite: 'I enjoyed my part because Barbara had to stand up to the Doctor's know-it-all attitude.' Jacqueline Hill.

DOROTHEA 'DODO' CHAPLET

Schoolgirl

Played by Jackie Lane, 1966

An irrepressible Cockney teenager whom the first Doctor met on Wimbledon Common when she stumbled into the TARDIS and immediately reminded him of his grand-daughter, Susan. Born in Manchester, Jackie Lane first worked in the theatre and then broke into television, often playing children because of her height (only five feet tall) and very youthful looks. As Dodo, though, she was one of the first girls on TV to wear a mini-skirt and is regarded as the first of what has become a long line of 'trendy' female companions. Commenting on her relationship with the first Doctor, she said recently:

'The regular cast of Bill, Peter Purves and I got on extremely well together. We had a marvellous working relationship which is what helped us get over any problems that faced us.

'I found Bill a very generous man, but also a very lonely one. Often he would take Peter and me out to dinner after we had finished rehearsing or filming. Because of our continuous schedule in those days, we had to work from Monday to Friday every week and Bill had to stay in a small hotel all week and only return home at the weekend.

'That is what he found so lonely – but being a true professional he just got on with the job. His wife Heather was marvellous about it, too.

'I know there have been lots of stories about Bill being difficult to work with, but I did not find him any more argumentative or irritable than any other actor I have come across. In fact, he was actually rather shy. But he did not suffer fools gladly and took a very dim view of practical jokes being played on the set – unlike some of his contemporaries.

'He would argue with the directors about points of continuity which he considered important. Especially about the operation of the TARDIS – after all he *was* the Doctor, and it *was* his ship and he *ought* to know how to operate it!

'I think his most endearing quality was his ability to ad-lib. He would forget his lines sometimes but this wouldn't stop him, and unless what he said changed the plot of the story the director would leave it in. I thought that made things more believable, unlike today when everything has to be so precise. You know, people don't go through life without fumbling and slurring and occasionally not saying what they mean.

'My favourite story was "The Celestial Toymaker", which was actually the hardest to make because of the tiny studio we worked in. I remember "The Savages", too, because the cast had to destroy the control room in the TARDIS at the end of the story. There could only be one take, so everything had to be just right. The Director, Christopher Barry, told us to pick up something and smash away. We absolutely loved doing it, and I remember Bill saying at the end, "There was something very satisfying in destroying that!"

'I sometimes wonder whether there wasn't more to that remark than any of us thought at the time.'

Opposite: 'Bill would argue with directors about points of continuity – after all he *was* the Doctor!' Jackie Lane.

Above: 'Patrick and Frazer Hines were absolutely marvellous – even if they did have fun at my expense!' Deborah Watling.

VICTORIA WATERFIELD

Victorian scientist's daughter
Played by Deborah Watling, 1967–8

The second Doctor's demure and pretty companion, who underwent an almost overwhelming culture shock when she was propelled from the peaceful environment of Victorian England into the time traveller's many worlds of terrifying monsters and constant danger. The daughter of actor Jack Watling (who himself twice appeared in *Doctor Who*), she followed in the family tradition of going into acting, and made an immediate impact playing Alice in a BBC TV version of *Alice in Wonderland*. Her face on the front cover of the *Radio Times* led to her being offered the role of Victoria. She speaks of her days with Patrick Troughton with amused affection.

'I was a bit nervous about joining an established show like *Doctor Who*, but Patrick and Frazer Hines were absolutely marvellous – even if they did have fun at my expense quite a bit of the time! Although I was cast as a Victorian girl, I was very much left to decide my own interpretation of the role. I had to do a lot of screaming to begin with, which earned me the nickname of "Leatherlungs". Actually, I loved working with all those monsters, especially the Yeti, which were rather cuddly, and the Daleks, which I thought were really funny things!

'I became sort of the Doctor's adopted daughter, but some of the things he got me into I'm sure no father would *ever* let happen to his child. I mean, he had such a sense of humour you never knew what he was going to do next. We were once filming on my birthday in the depth of winter – which Pat and Frazer both knew about. Well, they gave me the bumps, which wasn't so bad – but then they threw me straight into a load of foam and sand that was being used in the story! I was frozen!

'Sometimes I was able to get my own back with a little help from Frazer. I remember when we were filming "The Enemy of the World" and Pat had to play both the Doctor and the dictator Salamander. He had to be serious in the Salamander scenes and we couldn't resist sending him up. Even when he did manage to get the lines out, usually one or other of us would make a mess of what we had to say and Pat would have to start all over again!

'Although we all got on so well together, we rarely met when we were not working. Pat was a very private person, and didn't like the limelight. He had lots of close friends, though, and I suppose the best description of him would be an actor's actor. I felt I had lost someone close when I heard about his tragic death.'

Above: 'I think Patrick was the best Doctor Who they've had.' Wendy Padbury.

ZOE HERRIOT

Computer scientist

Played by Wendy Padbury, 1968–9

A young lady of super-intelligence whom the second Doctor encountered working on a space station, Zoe could match wits with the time traveller but was occasionally baffled by the most everyday of experiences. Wendy Padbury, with her elfin-like looks, made a speciality of playing girls younger than herself on both TV and in films, and after 49 episodes with Patrick Troughton had a break of four years before appearing in the London stage play *Doctor Who and the Seven Keys to Doomsday* in which Trevor Martin played the Doctor. She spoke recently of her days with the series.

'It was the best break I'd ever had joining *Doctor Who*. I was twenty and I had only done *Crossroads* and a few other bits and pieces on television. What made it even better was that Patrick Troughton had been my favourite actor since I was a child, and he and Frazer Hines made me very welcome though they played a lot of pranks. They used to call me "Padders".

'There are lots of funny stories from our time together. Like the time we were rehearsing in a church hall and I'd fallen asleep during the lunch break. I was wearing one of those wrap-around kilts that tie with a buckle. While I was asleep, Frazer had undone the buckle and then he and Patrick shouted, "Rehearsals, Wendy!" I sprang up, the kilt fell down, and I ran screaming into the corridor only to bump straight into the vicar! Pat always insisted that I mumbled, "Good afternoon, Vicar" and curtseyed. I don't remember!

'We made a good team because we all had very specific parts to play. When Patrick complained one day that he had all the lines to say and all we had to do was to ask him "How?", Frazer came up with a marvellous reply. "You're being paid to say all the lines," he said. "Wendy is being paid to get the dads in from the kitchen and I'm paid to keep the girls from doing their knitting!" A very good answer, I thought.

'I encountered a lot of monsters, but the creatures I disliked most were the Ice Warriors – they were horrible. They had scaly green make-up, were very tall and had awful hissing voices. They were cold and slimy-looking and sent shivers down my spine – even though I knew the actors underneath! I don't like reptiles at the best of times.

'I still think Patrick was the best Doctor Who they've had. When he and Frazer and I all left at the same time I really thought it had to be the end of *Doctor Who*. But how wrong can you be!'

LIZ SHAW

Scientist

Played by Caroline John, 1970

A scientist who combined brains and beauty, Liz Shaw was the third Doctor's first companion who initially resented being coerced into working with the Earth-exiled Time Lord and ultimately left because she could not get on with him. Caroline John came to the series from a background of theatrical companies ranging from local rep to the National Theatre Company, having deliberately broken away from them to join *Doctor Who*. She found both the series and Jon Pertwee's Doctor a fascinating challenge.

'I had been used to theatrical work so *Doctor Who* offered a good change. It was also a super opportunity to be in at the time when the programme was changing and being taken more seriously. Jon Pertwee was also starting to create a completely different kind of Doctor, a more scientific one.

'The curious thing was that though I played a scientist, I'm not a science fiction person. In fact, I'm very gullible. I actually used to believe most of the programmes myself. Before I joined *Doctor Who* I didn't realise that there were these poor men sweating away inside the Daleks. I just thought they must be remote controlled!

'The series was very hard work, not only for me but also for Jon. But he is a tremendous inspiration to everyone he works with, and he knows just how to relieve tension and get the best out of actors. The fact that he is so passionate about scientific gadgets was a great help, too. I loved that old car of his called "Bessie" – and I even got to drive it, though at the time I hadn't passed my driving test!

'During 1970, *Doctor Who* was being made more technical and aimed more at grown-ups. In fact it was a tremendous training ground for a virtual beginner to TV like me. Nevertheless, I was determined to quit at the end of a year so that I didn't get stuck with the character.

'We had our laughs on the show, of course. I remember filming a sequence on location in Madame Tussauds for the first story, "Spearhead from Space". In the story some of the waxworks were supposed to come to life and I was standing waiting for my cue when I happened to glance at what I thought was one of the waxworks – and it blinked! Well, I nearly died of fright. I hadn't realised it was another actor also waiting for his cue!'

Opposite: 'Jon Pertwee was a tremendous inspiration – he knows just how to relieve tension and get the best out of actors.' Caroline John.

JO GRANT

Espionage agent
Played by Katy Manning, 1971–3

Jo was the petite, mini-skirted and scatter-brained blonde who swept into the third Doctor's life fresh from her training as an espionage agent. Katy Manning, the daughter of a famous Fleet Street journalist, came to the series after just two jobs in TV, including the highly acclaimed ITV series *Man at the Top*, and found playing Jo very much an extension of her own personality, the extrovert fun-lover.

'I had watched *Doctor Who* since I was a child. William Hartnell was the Doctor then, and I used to watch him battling the monsters, absolutely terrified out of my wits from behind the sofa. I loved the monsters, in fact, so when I joined the show acting with them just meant recalling that feeling. And the monsters are what doing *Doctor Who* is all about, aren't they?

'I had actually met Jon Pertwee in the foyer of the Television Centre some months before I joined the show. But I still felt very nervous when I came to start filming. In fact, I learnt everybody's lines as well as my own so that I wouldn't make any mistakes.

'What I hadn't realised, of course, was that they don't shoot the scenes in the order you see them on television, so I couldn't follow the story at all!

'Things weren't made any easier because both Jon and Nicholas Courtney, who played the Brigadier, can be a bit overwhelming when you first meet them, and I'm afraid I giggled an awful lot. I have always been a giggler, even when I was at school. They treated me a bit like a kid sister to start with.

'I'm also short-sighted, so after I'd walked into things a few times, Jon started leading me about to save me hurting myself! I also adored Roger Delgado who played The Master, and despite his appearance on TV he was one of the most genuine and funny men I have ever met.

'In fact, making *Doctor Who* became a fun thing. Practical jokes were being played all the time. There was one occasion when people's cigarettes kept blowing up and I got the blame. But Jon was the villain of the piece! And whenever anyone giggled during rehearsal the director would always scream at

Opposite: 'Making *Doctor Who* was a fun thing – I think Jon was a superb Doctor.' Katy Manning.

me – though Roger was often the culprit.

'We all became a close team very quickly: we used to go out together after work and even go to each other's parties. Jon was always the star of these parties because he tells such incredible stories – most of which *are* just stories!

'One of the things about the series I really enjoyed was the stunts. Jon and I did quite a number of the stunts ourselves because we were both keen on a bit of excitement. Some were just too dangerous and they wouldn't let either of us do them. I remember that my stand-in was actually a man wearing a blonde wig, who was several inches taller than me!

'Jo was a lovely character to play because audiences identified with her. She cared for the Doctor, and he cared for her, too. I think Jon was a superb Doctor; he looked absolutely right in the part.

'I was sorry to leave the series, but as Jon and most of the others were going at that time, it seemed the right moment. I'm sure I shall be in my bath-chair before *Doctor Who* actually ends!'

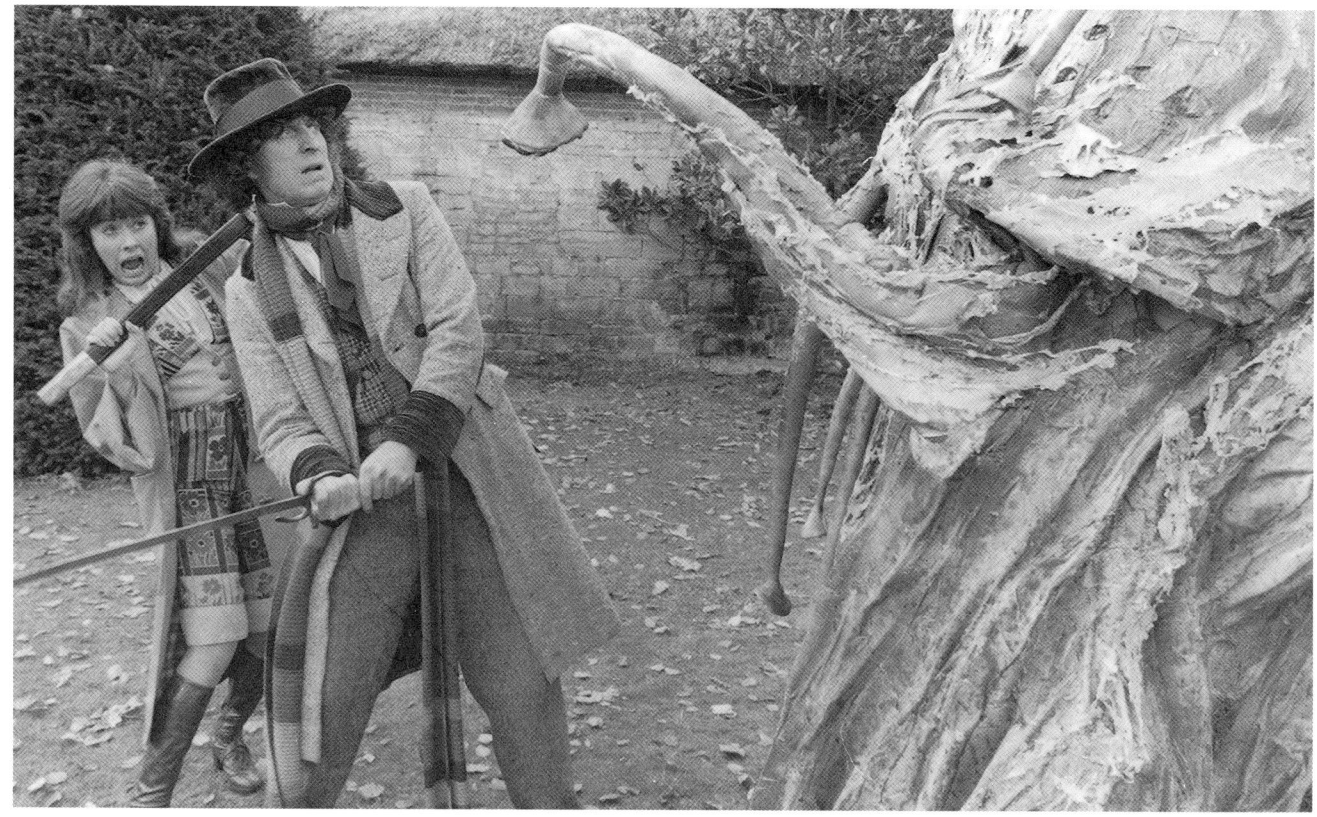

Above: 'Whatever you try to make of the character of one of the Doctor's assistants, there is no getting away from the fact that no-one can eclipse the Doctor!' Elisabeth Sladen.

SARAH JANE SMITH

Journalist

Played by Elisabeth Sladen, 1973–6

Sarah Jane, a new style heroine and firm believer in women's lib, developed a better relationship with the Doctor after he had regenerated into his fourth identity. Independent by nature and with an insatiable thirst for facts, she was played by Elisabeth Sladen, who had previously worked in local rep and done a little TV work since leaving her native Liverpool (a birthplace she shares with Tom Baker). Her entry into the world of *Doctor Who* came as a complete surprise.

'I had no idea that Katy Manning was leaving, so when I was asked to go for an audition for *Doctor Who* I assumed it must be for a small role of some kind. I hadn't been a regular watcher of the series, but I thought it might be a rewarding experience and so I was very pleased when the producer, Barry Letts, offered me a part.

'I was lucky in that Barry gave me tremendous freedom in developing Sarah Jane Smith, so that it was possible to make her different from the Doctor's other girls. She changed, of course, as anyone would going from one extraordinary environment to another in the company of someone like the Doctor!

'My style of acting is rather different to Jon Pertwee's – he likes to work every move out, while I'm all instinct – but I think we made a good partnership. Tom Baker was a first-rate actor, too – warm and charming, if a bit eccentric. It was a marvellous time for me, because everyone seemed to get on so well, and though we spent a lot of our time going from one quarry to another in the most freezing weather conditions, we always managed to laugh.

'Although Sarah Jane always wanted to be in control, she was afraid of creepies – like me! – which was where the Doctor came in to offer protection. Whatever you try to make of the character of one of the Doctor's assistants there is no getting away from the fact that she is a foil, a plot device. *No-one* can eclipse the Doctor!

'I encountered most of the famous monsters – Daleks, Cybermen, Ice Warriors – but I think I liked the robot in Tom Baker's first story the best. It was a beautiful piece of craftsmanship, but a nightmare for the poor actor inside. He nearly fainted more than once because of the difficulty of breathing and often fell over with the most tremendous crashes!

'Working with the robot K9 was unpredictable, too, and it was a real surprise when I was asked to come back and do the spin-off show, "K9 and Company". Because Tom wasn't in it, it was rather like being a female Doctor, in control, if you like – and I think it worked rather well.

'Originally I had not planned to stay with the series longer than a year, but I enjoyed working with Tom so much that I stayed for three. Although it's years since I was in *Doctor Who* I still get loads of fan mail. Occasionally, I go to the conventions, and the interest the fans take in the series and the actors is incredible. It can be a bit claustrophobic, but any actor will tell you that it's wonderful to receive appreciation for your work. I loved my years with *Doctor Who*.'

LEELA

Sevateem warrior

Played by Louise Jameson, 1977–8

Leela was again a complete contrast to her predecessor at the Doctor's side – a tough and beautiful warrior from a tribe of savage hunters whom the Time Lord tried not altogether successfully to turn into a civilised lady. Louise Jameson, a member of the Royal Shakespeare Company and an experienced dramatic actress was put up for the part by her agent and found that it brought a whole new dimension of experience into her life.

'*Doctor Who* was an opportunity to learn the television business quickly. In fact, it taught me all about TV technique and for that I'll always be grateful. The show itself is such fantasy, although a bit frustrating for anyone playing a companion because there are only so many ways you can say "What is it, Doctor?"

'Leela was quite a dramatic change in the

Above: 'Tom Baker is a very forceful personality and there is no doubt he was mainly responsible for the enormous appeal of the show.' Louise Jameson.

type of companion, and I'm not sure that Tom Baker wanted her in the series to begin with. There was a lot of discussion going on then about violence, and Mrs Mary Whitehouse even used to ring me up after certain episodes.

'Tom Baker himself is a very forceful personality and there is no doubt he was mainly responsible for the enormous appeal of the show. He's a genuine eccentric, and could be very domineering when we were working. If he didn't like a script he would often hurl it across the rehearsal room!

'On one occasion when we were making "The Robots of Death" I nearly killed a cameraman, throwing something. I had to throw this knife into someone's back – but I miscalculated and it missed this chap by about half an inch! You see, I was wearing red contact lenses to turn my blue eyes to brown and they were difficult to see through because I am naturally short-sighted. When we did the second take everyone in the studio was moved behind me with the exception of this one poor quaking cameraman! The following season I was able to get rid of the red lenses and revert to blue, which was quite a relief for everyone I think!

'I had to fight hard to develop my character. Too many scripts just called for me to scream and run away and hide. I had to convince the producer and the director that Leela would actually stand and fight in the situation. Sometimes the sex-symbol thing was a bit annoying, but I always tried to make the audience believe that Leela was bright as well as tough.

'Because of all the special effects used in *Doctor Who*, you have to use a lot of discipline and put up with all kinds of working conditions. Anyone who imagines making the series is glamorous should try a few hours on a *Doctor Who* location on a typical winter's day!

'I was a little disappointed not to have been asked back for the anniversary show "The Five Doctors", but I think that was because Tom refused to appear and they could only use the material from "Shada" with Lalla Ward. I believe that's why neither Mary Tamm, my successor, nor myself was involved.

'I have said since that the only thing that would make me return was if they made *me* the Doctor!'

Opposite: 'Both Tom and I would have liked to have developed the love/hate relationship between the Doctor and Romana.' Mary Tamm.

ROMANA

Time Lady

Played by Mary Tamm, 1978–9

Lady Romana was the first companion not chosen by the Doctor – albeit accidentally – but introduced to him by the White Guardian in order to help him in his search for the Key to Time. And as played by Mary Tamm, an experienced stage and TV actress who, by a curious twist of fate, had been at RADA at the same time as Louise Jameson, Romana proved to be quite a match for the fourth Doctor. Mary herself found life working with Tom Baker no less challenging.

'From the outset I decided to appear in just one series, and being the type of show it is, one year with *Doctor Who* seemed a very long time! But it educated me in the making of a TV series and showed me that the most important thing is to set up a good working relationship with the Doctor. Tom Baker made me feel welcome right away and helped me a lot.

'When I first started work, though, it was a big shock. It was a six-day-a-week job and absolutely exhausting. I lost a stone in weight within the first month!

'Tom is a fascinating man and very refreshing to work with, if occasionally a bit difficult. He was certainly unlike anyone I had worked with before and suited the part of the Doctor right down to the ground. He made everyone feel that it was very much "his show".

'Actually, I am not a bit like Romana, and I usually prefer parts that enable me to play someone completely different from myself. I think it was for my appearance and manner of speech that I was picked to play Romana – as someone who really looked as if they could stand up to the Doctor and be his equal in intelligence.

'Both Tom and I would have liked to have developed the love/hate relationship between the Doctor and Romana, but I think everyone else was a bit frightened of that because it would have been such a radical departure from the established formula of the series.

'One love of mine I did have plenty of opportunity of exploring was my love of dressing up and wearing glamorous clothes. Romana was a very glamorous person and the costume designers were always very good at letting me have my say over costumes.

'I have not lost touch with the show since I left, and in 1983 I attended this extraordinary event in Chicago to celebrate the show's twentieth anniversary. All the actors who have played the Doctor were there – with the exception of William Hartnell, of course – along with many of the other actors and actresses past and present. We were all flown out and put up in this enormous hotel for a two-day convention.

'The show is hugely popular in America and 10,000 fans turned up for the convention, some of them queuing for hours to get our autographs. We were treated like royalty, and everywhere we went we had up to six bodyguards looking after us. On one occasion I went to the loo escorted by two huge guys with walkie-talkies!

'The things a *Doctor Who* girl has to endure!'

NYSSA

Consul's daughter

Played by Sarah Sutton, 1981–3

Nyssa was the beautiful daughter of Consul Tremas of Traken whose body was taken over by The Master; she joined forces with the fourth Doctor in the hope of reclaiming her beloved father. She remained with the Doctor after his regeneration into his more youthful fifth persona. Nyssa was played by the versatile Sarah Sutton, who had made her acting debut on the London stage at the age of nine and entered the world of television when only just in her teens.

'It was my agent who got me an audition for *Doctor Who* and even when I was offered a part in "The Keeper of Traken" I had no idea it was going to last beyond that one story. Playing an alien gave me plenty of scope with the part and I was able to develop it once I became a member of the team.

'Because Nyssa was supposed to be intelligent and had a technical mind I had a lot of fun saying some of those unpronounceable words, and I liked it when they gave me the facility of extra-sensory perception in "Time-Flight". What, of course, the viewers don't see is the actors getting tongue-tied over the scientific lines, or else breaking into fits of laughter when trying to be terrified by an actor in a monster's costume who can scarcely see and keeps bumping into things!

'*Doctor Who* is like any long-running series in that the cast tend to look to the star to set the general tone. I didn't really get to know Tom Baker, who seemed to me a very intense

Opposite: 'Peter Davison was very aware of the importance of preserving the Doctor's image.' Sarah Sutton.

and elusive man. But I do remember that when he was in a good mood, rehearsals and filming could be a lot of fun.

'Peter Davison was very different, much more open and relaxed. In fact, we shared a similar sense of humour and got on very well together. Peter was able to transmit this air of relaxation to everyone on the set, from actors right through the production team – but he had a serious approach to the job. He was very aware of the importance of preserving the Doctor's image.

'I also got on very well with Janet Fielding and we developed a real rapport as the series went on. I loved all the costume changes, too, from my "fairy" dress at the beginning to the more adult look that came later.

'One of my favourite stories was "Black Orchid", because it was so different from all the others. I especially enjoyed dancing the Charleston because I have always been keen on dancing. But it wasn't all fun, because we filmed in freezing weather and I was wearing the skimpiest outfit!

'I still smile when I remember how the Production Office kept getting letters of complaint about Nyssa being too covered up. So that's why when I left the series in "Terminus" I decided to drop my skirt as a parting gesture to all those fans who had written in.

'Mind you, it caused such a stir at the time, and as I'm still being asked about it when I am interviewed, I'm not sure it was a wise thing to have done!'

TEGAN JOVANKA

Air hostess

Played by Janet Fielding, 1981–3

Airline hostess Tegan was another very different type of companion for the fifth Doctor – the time traveller's first Australian assistant, in fact – and their quite different attitudes sometimes put a severe strain on their relationship. Brisbane-born Janet Fielding obtained a BA honours degree at the University of Queensland before coming to England and achieving her major breakthrough into television in *Doctor Who*.

'I watched *Doctor Who* as a kid in Australia – my whole family was brought up on it, in fact. But I have to admit that I told a lie to get my role in the series when I came over to this country.

'It was my first television part and there were 100 people up for it. I really needed it, because I didn't have much money, the fringe theatre I was playing in wasn't paying anything, and working in a wine bar wasn't what I'd planned when I left Australia.

'The Producer, John Nathan-Turner, looked me up and down and asked how tall I was. Quick as a flash, I replied in my best Australian accent, "I'm five feet two, the minimum height for an airline hostess in Australia. I thought about being one once, so I checked it out." Then I took a breath. You see, I knew they were looking for an Australian air hostess in the series, and of course I was lying through my teeth – Australian air hostesses have to be much taller. I don't think he believed me, but I got the job!

'John had conceived the part of Tegan as a bit like Lucy in Peanuts, a bossy but vulnerable sort of person. In some ways the Doctor can be an irritating character, and though he is also very lovable, all that whimsicality can be a bit much. I had to put those kind of sentiments into words.

'Peter Davison was a lovely person to work with, so full of fun, very considerate and hard-working. His Doctor was more vulnerable, more fallible than Tom Baker's flamboyant character. Peter made us into a team – and even when we've got together since for conventions, the same kind of feelings emerge all over again between us.

'We did have the odd argument, of course, but a bit of healthy disagreement is an important ingredient in making any show successful, I believe. Someone once described me as a "tank" actress, which means I have a tendency to come on strong, but there's not a lot of me so I've got to make my presence felt somehow!

'While I was with the series the image was moved a little more into the adult world. In particular, the costumes changed from up to the neck and down to the knees into shorts with low-cut tops, corsets and bodices. And I don't mind telling you they were not the easiest things to run in, or if you had to climb heights. I popped out more than once!

'It seemed a good point to leave the series in a story like "Resurrection of the Daleks" because Peter had decided to go, and everyone knows the Daleks *are Doctor Who*.'

Top picture: 'In some ways the Doctor can be an irritating character, and though he is also very lovable, all that whimsicality can be a bit much!' Janet Fielding.

Bottom picture: 'Colin Baker has a great sense of fun, and worked really hard at the role when he became the sixth Doctor.' Nicola Bryant.

PERPUGILLIAM 'PERI' BROWN

Botany student

Played by Nicola Bryant, 1983–6

Peri, as the fifth Doctor's last companion was more familiarly called, shared his company only briefly before he regenerated into the formidable shape of Colin Baker's Time Lord. She also brought the accents of a new continent, America, into the Doctor's adventures and, indeed, acting newcomer Nicola Bryant holds both British and American passports.

'I suppose it was a terrific gamble for John Nathan-Turner to pick a drama student like me fresh out of drama school (the Webber Douglas Academy) for such an important role. Particularly as I had competition from both American and Canadian actresses who had flown over specially to audition. But I was a real fan of the series and had been ever since I could remember.

'My sister and I used to watch it every Saturday evening and we wouldn't leave until it was finished. My mother would sometimes get cross that we wouldn't come for tea, but at the end we were both petrified to leave the sofa in case there might be Daleks behind it!

'I remember that as soon as I read the part of Peri I was in no doubt that I could play it. I just knew the girl so well – she was *me*! People have asked me if I did any research into the other companions before I started rehearsing, and I have to say no. Peri was not like anyone who had appeared with the Doctor before. She was quite new, and that was how I approached her.

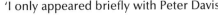

'I only appeared briefly with Peter Davison, but his relaxed style and humour were a tremendous help. Colin Baker had a great sense of fun, too, and he worked really hard at the role when he became the sixth Doctor. As he was already an experienced actor before he joined *Doctor Who*, it never occurred to me that he might like any advice from a newcomer like me. In fact, when we became good friends he asked me why I had never said anything about the way a scene could be played. He thought I had been snubbing him, when in fact *I* thought it would have been very big-headed for an actress of a few months to make suggestions to an actor of many years!

'Colin was a great practical joker, and he really set me up when we were making "The Two Doctors" with Patrick Troughton, who was another prankster. It was a scene where Colin had to splash some water on my face to revive me. It was the last we were going to shoot that day, so it was important to get it right.

'Well, we played it and then Colin asked to do it again. This time, though, he threw the whole jug over me, and though I was absolutely drenched I did my best to say my lines. It was only when they all burst out laughing that I realised I had been set up. The first take had been perfect!

'While we were filming that same story in Spain, this huge American tourist suddenly walked by. "Hey," he said, "are you making a movie? You must be from Hollywood." Immediately, Colin shouted back, "No, we're better than that – we're British!"'

Above: 'Melanie certainly enjoyed teasing the Doctor, but he obviously cared a great deal about her and didn't want anything nasty to happen.' Bonnie Langford.

MELANIE BUSH

Computer programmer

Played by Bonnie Langford, 1986–7

The bright and energetic Mel, played by flame-haired song and dance star Bonnie Langford, joined the sixth Doctor during the course of his 'trial' on Gallifrey, and was around to lend a hand after his sudden and dramatic regeneration as Sylvester McCoy. Twenty-three-year-old Bonnie came to the series with a wealth of acting experience, having made her TV debut on *Opportunity Knocks* at the age of six and becoming still more widely known playing the obnoxious Violet Elizabeth Bott in the LWT series *Just William*.

'I can hardly claim to have been a fan of the series before I joined *Doctor Who* because I was usually working at the time it was on TV. That's one of the problems of being a child actress. In fact, when I was very little I was too scared to watch it, though when I realised it was all pretend I did see some of Tom Baker's stories.

'I was certainly aware of *Doctor Who* as I grew up and I heard from other people in the profession that it was a fun show to do. So when I got a phone call from John Nathan-Turner and an invitation to play this character called Mel I was more than happy to accept. I was appearing in *Peter Pan* on the stage at the time, and Colin Baker and I got some amazing publicity, including being photographed flying through the air!

'Actually Colin and I were already friends, having previously appeared together as well as sharing the same agent. He is a lovely man to work with and we had a lot of giggles – though it's not easy to laugh when you're blue with cold on some wet and windy location!

'I enjoyed the development of the slightly antagonistic relationship between Melanie and the Doctor, because it was easy to nag him about his health – although this was always a bit tongue in cheek. Melanie certainly enjoyed teasing the Doctor, but all the time she knew he was in charge and there was only so far she could go. For his part, the Doctor obviously cared a great deal about her and didn't want anything nasty to happen.

'I wasn't aware of having to make any great changes in Melanie when Sylvester took over as the Doctor. It was certainly nice to be working with someone else whom I had already appeared with, and though he is a very different kind of actor to Colin, we soon had a rapport.

'Obviously there were differences in the way we worked, but I was never conscious of thinking, "That's not the way Colin would have done it." When we first met, I treated the new Doctor like some kind of nut – but then, imagine how anyone would feel at such a dramatic change in a person!

'*Doctor Who* was a change for me, and a really fun thing to do.'

ACE

Waitress

Played by Sophie Aldred, 1987–

The seventh Doctor's latest companion is the first of a new breed of girls, a cherub-faced teenager whose innocent expression masks a tough and resolute character, and one who is well aware of the ways of the world despite being only 16! In fact, Sophie Aldred, who plays Ace, is 25 and has worked mainly in the demanding world of fringe theatre as well as being a presenter on the BBC children's programme *Corners*. While filming her introductory story, 'Dragonfire', Sophie talked about her role.

'I can't quite believe this is happening to me – it's an absolute dream come true. I used to watch *Doctor Who* when I was a kid and Jon Pertwee played the Doctor. In fact, I was the typical scared child peeping at it from behind the sofa, and my Mum banned me from watching it because I had nightmares about the Cybermen!

'When I became an actress I always hoped I'd get a chance to appear in the series. I actually went along to audition for the part of someone who could ride a motorcycle, because I've got one of my own. But John Nathan-Turner decided I'd make a better Ace.

'She is a character from present-day Earth – from Perivale – who to begin with is working as a waitress in a milk-shake bar on a trading colony called Iceworld. She hates the job. She's much more interested in chemistry and explosives. Joining up with the Doctor provides her great escape.

'Ace is not a bit like Melanie. She is tough

Left: 'Ace is tough and very street-suss in her attitudes, and her relationship with the new Doctor is going to be bumpy.' Sophie Aldred.

and very street-suss in her attitudes. She wears very trendy clothes: a satin jacket covered in badges, cycling shorts and Doc Martin boots. She also has a great sense of humour and a very colourful line in slang words!

'Working on the series with Sylvester is such fun – and it probably helps that we were both born under the same star sign and actually share the same birthday. I'm really looking forward to our time travels together – though I'm not sure I want to bump into the Cybermen!'

Commenting on Ace, John Nathan-Turner added:

'She will be more self-reliant and independent than the Doctor's other assistants – very indicative of today's young women, in fact. Her relationship with him is going to be bumpy.

'For example, she keeps on calling him Professor. And because of her interest in explosives she'll be rather like Leela, who would always get out her knife to challenge somebody as the answer to all problems. Ace, though, will tend to get out a home-made can of nitroglycerine!

'I took a great deal of interest in the casting of this character, because we weren't sure whether Bonnie would stay on to do another season. When she decided not to, Ace made an ideal replacement. What I was most anxious to avoid – having started the 1987 season with a new Doctor – was to have to start the anniversary season with a new companion. For such an important moment in the show's history, it is vital that the line-up is firmly established.'

STORIES OF INTER-GALACTIC GUEST STARS

On the morning of Thursday, 6 August 1987, the Head of Drama at the BBC, Jonathan Powell, stood up before a crowded room of journalists who had gathered at the Television Centre to see and hear details of the Corporation's plans for drama productions to be screened during the coming winter months. The smartly-dressed, bespectacled figure paused for silence to fall and then began to speak.

'If I told you,' he said, 'that the next programme for the winter season stars Brenda Bruce, Elizabeth Spriggs, Judy Cornwall, Clive Merrison, Richard Briers, Hugh Lloyd, Stubby Kaye, Ken Dodd, Don Henderson and Edward Peel you would probably think it was one of Shaun Sutton's Theatre Night Specials. But you would be wrong – it's *Doctor Who*!'

Those people present at the press launch remember a gasp going around the room. For this was the very series that not so long ago had seemingly been in danger of ending its long run. Now it was evidently being relaunched with a host of top-name stars.

In fact, *Doctor Who* has attracted leading actors and actresses ever since its inception in 1963 – some of whom were already stars and others who were destined to achieve fame in the future. This element of the series' success has tended to be rather overlooked in the overall picture, a state of affairs which deserves remedying at this important moment in its history – for as the current Producer, John Nathan-Turner, has also said: '*Doctor Who* has become the show that *everyone* wants to be in. No matter how big a star you are, each and every one has children, or grandchildren or even young relatives who watch the programme. And nothing seems to impress these kids more than for someone to appear with the Doctor.'

And to this, John adds: 'I have been misquoted as saying that I think *Doctor Who* is the Morecambe and Wise situation comedy show. I didn't say that at all – I said it has become the Morecambe and Wise Show of the BBC in that everybody who is anybody wants to be in it. Which is a wonderful position for a producer to be in – for it means you have a spectacular array of talent available to you!'

Turning back the pages of *Doctor Who*'s history it is easy to discover by talking to those familiar names who have appeared in the series just how this desire to be in it developed, and how much they have all enjoyed being part of the Doctor's adventures. What follows is a comprehensive account of the stars who have guested on *Doctor Who* during the past twenty-five years.

The WILLIAM HARTNELL Era

The first well-known actor to appear in *Doctor Who* in December 1963 was one of the best known 'baddies' of his time, yet his part was quite overshadowed by the debut of the evil machines destined to ensure the success of the embryonic programme – the Daleks, created by Terry Nation. The actor was **Alan Wheatley** who, in the years from 1955 to 1959,

Previous page: Bernard Bresslaw as the awesome alien leader, Captain Varga, in 'The Ice Warriors' (1967).

Left: Alan Wheatley (Temmosus) in 'The Daleks' (1963).

had become a household name playing the nasty Sheriff of Nottingham in ITC's production of *The Adventures of Robin Hood*, starring Richard Greene in the title role. Although by nature a quietly spoken and courteous man, he made something of a speciality of playing villains, though his stage work included Shakespeare and, curiously, one play called *The Doctor's Dilemma*! In all, Alan played the scheming Sheriff in 145 episodes, and is the first to admit that the role left him very typecast.

'After the Sheriff of Nottingham stint I was lucky indeed not to have to rely on my acting for my living,' he says. 'It so typed me I was unable to get the parts I wanted, and films simply closed down for me. Even when I travelled by air, customs officers used to look in my baggage and say, "Any arrows to declare, Sheriff?"'

It was the shrewd investment of his money and the participation in a partnership in a theatrical agency which ran the careers of people such as Sean Connery, Michael Crawford and Sheila Hancock that enabled Alan not to have to worry too much about acting.

'I did continue to work on radio and television, and it was very nice to be involved at the start of something that has become as successful as *Doctor Who*,' he says. 'Of course, at the time no one had any idea of what lay ahead, and my enduring memory of making "The Daleks" was what extraordinary, cumbersome things they were! I played Temmosus, the leader of the Dalek's enemies, and I came to a pretty swift end in the story – something that had not happened to me before in Robin Hood!'

Alan Wheatley remembers William Hartnell as being a very single-minded actor determined to make the series a success. 'Of course, once the children saw the Daleks the show never looked back. I went on to play other villains on television – including a very nasty and vain type who got electrocuted in *The Avengers* – but I never had any more to do with *Doctor Who*.'

A pair of popular actors, **Mark Eden** and **Derren Nesbitt**, appeared in the first of the Doctor's historical adventures, 'Marco Polo', which was screened from February to April 1964.

Mark Eden, who later became a regular on

Below: George Coulouris (Arbitan) in 'The Keys of Marinus'.

the hugely successful Granada series *Coronation Street*, played Marco Polo, and narrated the story of his journey to the Court of Kublai Khan into which the Doctor and his companions were inadvertently thrust. Derren Nesbitt, with his blond hair slicked back and sporting a beard, was Tegana, a Tartar war lord, who tried to sabotage the caravan and steal the Doctor's TARDIS. Nesbitt later appeared in *Special Branch* (1969–73), the Thames Television series about Scotland Yard's security department, made by Euston Films with whom, of course, Verity Lambert was associated.

The second story by Terry Nation for *Doctor Who* was 'The Keys of Marinus', shown April to May 1964, which featured **George Coulouris** as Arbitan, the keeper of the machine controlling an island of glass amidst a sea of acid on the planet Marinus. George Coulouris had become a star on Broadway and in Hollywood in the late 'thirties and 'forties, where he built up a formidable reputation playing villainous roles in films. Among his best performances were those in Orson Welles's celebrated *Citizen Kane* (1941), an adaptation of Ernest Hemingway's *For Whom the Bell Tolls* (1943), and *An Outcast of the Islands* (1951). Later he made a number of pictures in England including *Doctor in the House* (1954).

'*Doctor Who* was the first time I had appeared in a science fiction story,' George Coulouris recalled later. 'And though I was not in the story very long, getting myself murdered by the leader of the villains (the Voord), it did lead to me working in some interesting fantasy films including *The Skull* (1965), based on a story by Robert Bloch who wrote *Psycho*, and *Blood from the Mummy's Tomb*, made in 1971.'

Because of his long association with Hollywood, George Coulouris has sometimes been referred to as the first American actor to have appeared in *Doctor Who*. In fact – and to set the record straight once and for all – he was born in October 1903 in Manchester, England!

With comedy now regarded as one of the continuing elements in *Doctor Who* over the years, it is worth noting that the first comedian to have appeared in the series was **Peter Glaze**, who starred as one of the super-intelligent Sensorites in the story of that title screened from June to August 1964. Glaze, a short, bespectacled man and a television veteran, became a favourite with very young viewers in *Crackerjack*, an early-evening BBC children's series of comedy and entertainment which ran for many years in the 'sixties and 'seventies. 'The costumes were like something out of a cartoon film,' Peter recalls with a grin, 'and the feet made you feel as if you were walking around in flippers! Still, I enjoyed being the villain, though I suppose I was more of a schemer than an actual baddie.'

The last story of the first season, 'The Reign of Terror' (August–September 1964), Dennis Spooner's tale which transported the Doctor back to the French Revolution, contained a

Above: Derek Francis as Emperor Nero in 'The Romans' (1965).

small part as a Parisian physician for a young actor in his early twenties named **Ronald Pickup**. He has since become a leading stage and television performer, receiving public and critical acclaim for his portrayal of Randolph Churchill, the father of Sir Winston Churchill, in the seven-part Thames Television production of *Jennie, Lady Randolph Churchill*, made in 1975.

The first major actor from abroad to star in *Doctor Who* was actually the versatile Australian, **Ray Barrett**, who played a dual role in the two-episode story, 'The Rescue', which was shown in the first two weeks of 1965. '*Doctor Who* was a good introduction to the demands of a British television serial,' Ray said some years later when he had become one of the most popular characters on British TV in the long-running serial *The Troubleshooters*. 'The schedule was tight and I had to fit into a team that had already been working together for some time – although Maureen O'Brien (Vicki) was introduced in the story and went on to become one of the Doctor's companions. I played a paralysed spaceman who was exposed by Doctor Who as a murderer.'

Barrett suffered a nasty fate over a cliff for his crimes in *Doctor Who*, and promptly went into the BBC's prestigious new serial about life in an oil company which was screened for a year as *Mogul*, and then in 1966 became *The Troubleshooters*. He played a young go-getter along with Robert Hardy, and helped to make the series compulsive viewing for five years.

Interestingly, the Script Editor of *The Troubleshooters* was Anthony Read, who in January 1978 became Script Editor of *Doctor Who* for a year during Tom Baker's era (later handing over the job to Douglas Adams of *Hitch-Hiker* fame), and also wrote one of the fourth Doctor's most dramatic adventures, 'The Horns of Nimon'.

'The Romans', another Dennis Spooner story which followed at the end of January 1965, featured one of the most familiar character actors on television at that time, **Derek Francis**, a portly and rather owl-like man who usually appeared in rather self-important roles. In 'The Romans' he was cast as one of the most pompous, and perhaps most evil, men of all time – the Emperor Nero. 'Every actor dreams of playing someone really outrageous who has left his mark on history – and Nero has to be just about the most outrageous figure of all,' Derek said in an interview a few years later. 'It was a clever story, too, because when Doctor Who frustrated my plans I used it as the excuse to burn Rome! Mind you, I don't think the children were at all frightened, because there was a lot of humour in the story.

'Bill Hartnell and I had worked together before,' he added, 'and we both enjoyed playing comedy, which made it all rather fun to do.'

25 GLORIOUS YEARS

Below: Julian Glover as Richard the Lionheart in 'The Crusade' (1965).

Certainly, 'The Romans' was arguably one of the most entertaining of all the first Doctor's historical stories, and the reactions of viewers to Derek Francis's performance were highly favourable. It is only to be wondered at that he was not called upon to appear again in the show before his untimely death in 1984.

The appearance of Shakespearean actor **Julian Glover** as King Richard the Lionheart in the historical drama of 'The Crusade' in March 1965 was to prove a milestone in the history of *Doctor Who*, for several reasons. Firstly, Glover's starring role in the series was heralded by national newspaper publicity – the first time that any actor other than the regular members of the cast had been so featured. Secondly, his appearance encouraged other actors who had previously been reluctant to take part in what was generally regarded as a 'kids' show' to accept roles. And thirdly, Glover enjoyed the experience enough to return to the series in Tom Baker's era in a completely different role, thus becoming the first actor to star with more than one Doctor.

By the early spring of 1965, when 'The Crusade' was made, Julian Glover was already an established star of the theatre and had received excellent reviews for two of his films, *Tom Jones* (1963) and *The Girl with Green Eyes* (1964).

'I was asked to appear in *Doctor Who* by the Director, Douglas Camfield, a most persuasive and talented man,' Julian recalls. 'I had actually done some SF on television a few years earlier in *Quatermass and the Pit*

(1958–9), which Rudolph Cartier directed brilliantly for the BBC. *Doctor Who* was quite different, of course, but it was a challenge to play King Richard, especially because of the extraordinary idea of him being rescued from a Saracen ambush by an old man travelling in a police box!

'Then in 1979 Graham Williams asked me to appear again in the series with Tom Baker. By this time my son, Jamie, who was ten, was also a *Doctor Who* fan, and so I really had no choice! Jamie was very amused when I ended up as a great scaly monster with one eye!'

Julian's role was actually a dual one: as Count Scarlioni, art thief, and as an alien called Scaroth. Also appearing with him were John Cleese and Eleanor Bron, who happily escaped his explosive fate. This was not, though, quite the end of the Glover family association with *Doctor Who*, for in March 1983 Julian's wife, the actress Isla Blair, played a noble lady opposite Frank Windsor's lord in a plot to stop the signing of the Magna Carta, which was thwarted in the fifth Doctor Peter Davison's adventure 'The King's Demons'!

Julian Glover's skill at playing in fantasy stories has since landed him a major part in the *Star Wars* sequel *The Empire Strikes Back* (1980), and in 1981 he played Kristatos in the James Bond movie *For Your Eyes Only*. Being cast as the villain in the movie brought this wry comment from him while he was filming: 'The ironic thing is that I was once up for the part of James Bond myself when Sean Connery dropped out. And I came pretty close to getting it.'

It is also a fact that Julian Glover once featured on a list of possibles to play *Doctor Who*!

There is another interesting link with *The Empire Strikes Back* in the form of a young performer who made his acting debut in the *Doctor Who* story which immediately followed Julian Glover's first appearance. The actor's name was **Jeremy Bulloch**, and he played Tor in Glyn Jones's four-part story 'The Space Museum' (April–May 1965). Jeremy reappeared later in the series as Hal, the archer who killed Linx, 'The Time Warrior' in the Jon Pertwee serial which ran from December 1973 to January 1974. Then, in 1980, Jeremy won himself an important part in *The Empire Strikes Back* as the impassive bounty hunter Boba Fett.

In fact, as shall be mentioned later, there was even a third *Doctor Who* veteran who appeared in the George Lucas space epic – David Prowse, playing the awesome Darth Vader.

'The Crusade' also provided a part for an actress whose name has since figured greatly in the story of *Doctor Who* – both on camera and off. In the role of Joanna, King Richard's sister whom the monarch tries to marry off to Saladin's brother, was a rising young star named **Jean Marsh**. She it was in 1970 who created the hugely successful London Weekend TV serial of early twentieth-century servant life, *Upstairs, Downstairs*, in co-operation with her close friend, Eileen Atkins. (Eileen, incidentally, had been Julian Glover's first wife.) For a time, too, Jean was the wife of the third Doctor, Jon Pertwee.

Jean came to *Doctor Who* after a career

which had begun as a child actress on the London stage, continued on Broadway and then into American television. 'I had my first taste of *Doctor Who*-type TV in 1959 when I worked in Hollywood on an episode of the *Twilight Zone* series called "The Lonely",' Jean recalls. 'I say *in* Hollywood, but actually the Director (Jack Smight) first took us on location to Death Valley, which was supposed to represent the location of the story, a remote asteroid.'

Jean was cast as a robot woman named Alicia with whom a stranded spaceman named Corry (Jack Warden) falls in love. His devotion is finally shattered when a supply ship arrives on the asteroid and the captain convinces Corry that the love of his life is no more than a mass of valves and wires. 'It was unbelievably hot filming that story,' Jean says. 'People kept collapsing in the heat, and when I lay on the ground to shoot the closing scene where the robot is destroyed, they put a thermometer on the ground and it read 140 degrees! After a couple of days we just had to go back to the studios!'

Though 'The Crusade' was supposedly set in an equally hot climate, Jean had to contend only with the heat of the studio lighting. However, she impressed Verity Lambert and the other members of the production team enough to be asked back to appear in the mammoth twelve-episode story of 'The Daleks' Master Plan' which ran from November 1965 to January 1966. In it she became the Doctor's shortest-lived companion, Sara Kingdom. 'I started out in the story as a hard-hearted security agent who even kills her own brother,' Jean says. 'But once Sara realised she was being duped into the service of the Daleks she went over to the Doctor's side and helped him defeat the plan – but at the cost of her own life. It was a challenging part, particularly having to change my character so dramatically during the course of the story!'

Though this was Jean's last appearance in *Doctor Who*, she was for two years married to Jon Pertwee. 'I think I was far too young for such a commitment,' she admits today. 'I must have been strange and exasperating for Jon, who was very mature, upper middle class and Rolls-Royce rich. I came from a real working-class Cockney background. I was always nervous and doing the wrong thing.

'We did have wonderful times when we were alone together, though, for he was so full of the joys of life. When things went wrong I left him – it was much more my fault than his. Still, I've always watched his career with interest,' she adds.

Terry Nation's Dalek story 'The Chase' (May–June 1965), which had the Doctor on the run from his deadly enemies, also showed the Time Lord bumping into some famous people from Earth's history including Abraham Lincoln, William Shakespeare, Roger Bacon and Queen Elizabeth, as well as such fictional characters as Frankenstein's monster and Count Dracula. There was also a brief appearance of the famous pop group The Beatles (a clip from a promotional film) and an up-and-coming actor, **Hywell Bennett**. The Welsh-born actor played the luckless Rynian caught up in the Dalek machinations, and after shooting his scenes for the series

Below: Jean Marsh (Sara Kingdom) looking rather like an Avengers girl in this publicity photograph for 'The Daleks' Master Plan' (1966).

went straight off to make the film which brought him to public attention and launched his film career, *The Family Way*.

The late **Peter Butterworth** holds the distinction of being the first Time Lord apart from the Doctor to have appeared in the series. Usually cast as a well-meaning bumbler, Peter had become a cinema favourite through his roles in the long-running *Carry On* series which began in 1958 and ran until two years before his death in 1979.

Peter played a devious monk, the title role of 'The Time Meddler' in Dennis Spooner's July 1965 story, in which he was attempting to interfere in the result of the Battle of Hastings in 1066 by giving King Harold an atomic bazooka! Although the meddling monk was outwitted by the Doctor, his comic impact on audiences was such that he returned for a reprise in 'The Daleks' Master Plan'.

'I had a string of television shows of my own at one time,' Peter said in an interview he gave in 1968, 'but I always preferred working as one of a group. The part of the monk in the *Doctor Who* series was right up my street because I liked everyone who was involved with the programme, and I'm sorry in a way that the BBC didn't develop the character more. Still, I suppose once you have been on the side of the Daleks there is no future for you!'

Another veteran British actor, the late **Max Adrian**, was cast as the comic Greek, Priam, in 'The Myth Makers' (October–November 1965). In fact, he and the Doctor never actually met on the set, as William Hartnell had expressed a wish not to have to act in scenes with an artist who was both Jewish and gay. A master of high camp, Max Adrian was, though, amused by the irony of having come into *Doctor Who* immediately after filming *Dr Terror's House of Horrors* for Amicus Films!

Andre Morell, who played the dignified Tavannes in John Lucarotti's February 1966 story of the St Bartholomew's Day Massacre which took place in Paris in 1572, was also becoming a regular in British horror pictures when he made this *Doctor Who* story. Earlier, in 1958, he had appeared in the lead role in the excellent BBC TV serial *Quatermass and the Pit* in which, as mentioned earlier, Julian Glover had also appeared.

Andre was actually a close friend of the star Peter Cushing (they had appeared together in *The Hound of the Baskervilles* in 1959), who at that time was filming the second of the two Milton Subotsky *Doctor Who* movies, *Daleks: Invasion Earth 2150 AD*. Ironically, but for this prior commitment to the BBC for the TV series, Morell himself would have appeared in the cinema version!

Michael Gough is the famous actor with the longest association with *Doctor Who* – which is perhaps most appropriate for a man who shares the same birthdate as that of the programme: 23 November! He was also for a time married to one of the Doctor's companions, Anneke Wills, who made her debut as Polly in the programme only a few weeks after his own in the memorable Brian Hayles story of an evil games-player dominating a fantasy world, 'The Celestial Toymaker' (April 1966). 'It was a curious

Below: Michael Gough in the title role of 'The Celestial Toymaker' (1966).

experience making that story,' Michael recalls, 'because for two of the four episodes William Hartnell was actually away on holiday and I only had his pre-recorded voice-overs to play the games against!

'Over the years I seem to have been cast quite often as brilliant scientists who meddle with things that they really ought to leave alone, so I suppose I have always had a more than passing interest in *Doctor Who*! I've actually played a number of doctors, and I remember when I appeared as Dr Livingstone in *The Search for the Nile* in 1971 I was always being greeted in my local pub with, "Dr Livingstone, I presume!"'

Michael has also been associated with three other popular fantasy series: *The Avengers*, in which he played the creator of the dreaded Cybernauts; *Out of the Unknown* (1965–6); and *Blake's 7*, in which he made a dramatic appearance as Hower in the story 'Volcano' (January 1980).

But his outstanding performance as the Toymaker was never forgotten in the *Doctor Who* Production Office, and in January 1982 he was cast as one of the Gallifreyan Time Lords, Councillor Hedin, in the Peter Davison story 'Arc of Infinity'. 'Of course, not only the Doctor had changed by then,' Michael says, 'but the series itself was much grander in scope and the sets dwarfed anything we had had on "The Celestial Toymaker". But the magic of the whole concept of *Doctor Who* was still there.'

In 'The Savages' (May–June 1966), the part of Chal was played by **Ewen Solon**, who in the late fifties had appeared opposite Rupert Davies in the much acclaimed BBC detective series *Maigret*, based on the novels by Georges Simenon. Ewen also made a return to the series in September 1975 when he played Vishinsky in the fourth Doctor's adventures on 'The Planet of Evil'.

'The War Machines', which was shown in July 1966, had portly **William Mervyn** guesting as the civil servant Sir Charles Summer. Later that year, William began his starring role as the Bishop in the BBC comedy series *All Gas and Gaiters*, which made stars of both him and Derek Nimmo during its four-year run.

A cameo appearance in this same story in episode four was made by the familiar BBC newsreader **Kenneth Kendall**, playing himself and announcing the appearance of the War Machines in the streets of London. 'I had to treat the part just like a real news bulletin,' Kenneth said later, 'and I was rather flattered when someone told me afterwards that they thought I'd been as convincing as Orson Welles in that radio broadcast of his about a Martian invasion, *War of the Worlds*, which actually made a lot of listeners believe that aliens had landed!'

Just as a famous actor had helped to usher the first Doctor into his role, so another well-known film star saw him out in 'The Tenth Planet' (October 1966), when William Hartnell took his leave of the series. The actor was **Robert Beatty**, the rugged Canadian-born actor who had made a number of successful movies about World War II and then starred in the Scotland Yard TV crime series *Dial 999* from 1957–8. He had also appeared with William Hartnell in two 1946 movies,

Above: Robert Beatty as General Cutler in 'The Tenth Planet' (1966).

Appointment with Crime and *Odd Man Out*.

'Bob' Beatty played General Cutler, the commander of a South Pole tracking station battling against an invasion of Cybermen. 'The thing I remember most was the heat of filming in the studios,' he says. 'The poor guys in those Cybermen suits nearly fried under the lights! Bill Hartnell also suffered in the heat, and if he looked exhausted and worn out at the end of the story it was because he *was*!'

Robert Beatty gained useful experience working on *Doctor Who* for when he was later cast in Stanley Kubrick's blockbuster film *2001: A Space Odyssey*, made in 1968.

The PATRICK TROUGHTON Era

A familiar figure on British television was an eye witness to the debut performance of Patrick Troughton as the second Doctor in the 'Power of the Daleks', which introduced him to audiences in November 1966. Playing the villainous Deputy Leader Bragen, on the planet Vulcan under threat from the Daleks, was the lean and incisive figure of **Bernard Archard**, whose first appearance caused many viewers to gasp 'The man from *Spycatcher*!'

Archard, a former repertory actor, had made his name in the BBC series in the 'fifties in which he played Lt-Col. Oreste Pinto, 'the hero with a heart of stone', an army officer who interrogated suspected spies. He continued to work in television after this, but also made a number of fantasy films including *Village of the Damned* (1960) and *The Horror of Frankenstein* (1970).

'I had worked with Patrick Troughton before, and I was not surprised that he managed to take over the role of Doctor Who so well from William Hartnell,' Bernard Archard says. 'He was a great character actor, and playing a sort of space clown was his idea of having fun. There were some worrying moments making that first story, but Patrick was a real professional. I think the Producer (Innes Lloyd) knew what he was doing in having the Daleks in the story because they pretty well assured it of success!'

Bernard is perhaps guilty of being somewhat modest about his own contribution to the 'Power of the Daleks' – and long-time fans of the series were delighted when he

Below: Hannah Gordon as the lovely Kirsty in 'The Highlanders' (1967).

returned in October 1975 in the Tom Baker story 'Pyramids of Mars', playing Professor Marcus Scarman, an Egyptologist who had been possessed by the spirit of an ancient god called Sutekh. 'It was quite a horrific story,' recalls Bernard, who was actually suggested for the part by *Doctor Who* script writer Robert Holmes, after he had seen the actor in the movie *The Horror of Frankenstein*. 'I had to wear this white powder all over my face and red rings around my eyes so that I looked half-dead. There was also a scene where I got shot in the back, and I had to wear an explosive harness to give the impression of being peppered by shotgun pellets. I don't mind admitting I was sweating a bit when the charges went off!'

The following story, 'The Highlanders', broadcast over the Christmas period from December 1966 to January 1967, featured beautiful **Hannah Gordon**, a long-time favourite of British television viewers, as a charming Scottish lass, Kirsty, in a story that was one of the last purely historical *Doctor Who* adventures. Set near the battlefield of Culloden in the year 1746, the role took Hannah back to her native land.

'There was a lot of trudging about over damp countryside I seem to remember,' says Hannah Gordon, 'but Pat Troughton was such a bundle of fun and practical jokes that he always kept you amused whatever the weather was like. I believe it was the story where he and Frazer Hines, who later became his companion, struck up their friendship. And I understand it was very much at Pat's insistence that Frazer was written into the

Right: Peter Barkworth (centre) as the scientist, Clent, in 'The Ice Warriors' (1967).

series rather than out of it as was originally planned. They actually filmed two endings – one leaving him behind in Scotland and the other going into the police box.

'I've seen *Doctor Who* a few times since my appearance, but I don't believe anyone has been quite as good as Pat Troughton. His death has been a sad loss to our profession,' she says.

Hannah later starred in several successful TV series including the very popular *Telford's Change* shown in 1979. In this, she played opposite the fine character actor **Peter Barkworth**, who also made his contribution to the *Doctor Who* legend when he appeared as a scientist named Clent battling the second Ice Age on Earth in Brian Hayles's story 'The Ice Warriors', screened in November–December 1967.

Two other familiar names to be found in the cast-list of 'The Ice Warriors' are **Peter Sallis**, now hugely popular in the series *Last of the Summer Wine*, who played the hapless Penley; and **Bernard Bresslaw**, a star of many of the *Carry On* films, who was the awesome leader of the aliens, Captain Varga. Bernard, who stands over 6 foot 7 inches tall, found the role both a rewarding and a rather surprising one.

'One morning, the Director, Derek Martinus, asked me to go along to this fibre boat-building company,' he remembers. 'When I asked why, he said, "To be fitted for your costume"! I thought the Ice Warrior I was playing was going to be something like a Viking in furs and a beard, so you can imagine my amazement when they plonked me into this suit which was a combination of a fibreglass shell with plastic limbs and latex rubber make-up! It was terribly restricting to wear and ever so hot, and often I couldn't see where I was going.'

Bernard made the part even more memorable by developing a hissing voice for Captain Varga. He also enjoyed working with Patrick Troughton, whom he found a complete contrast to William Hartnell with whom he had earlier appeared in *The Army Game*.

'The Moonbase', Kit Pedler's story which was aired in February–March 1967, firmly established the popularity of the Cybermen, still rated second in popularity only to the Daleks. Playing the commander of an embattled weather station on the Moon was another fine character actor, **Patrick Barr**, who had been a leading man in numerous successful films including *The Return of the Scarlet Pimpernel* (1938) and *Robin Hood* (1952) as well as several TV series.

'The Faceless Ones', screened from April to May 1967, introduced to the series two beautiful young actresses destined for stardom, **Pauline Collins**, who played the winsome, dimple-cheeked Samantha Briggs, and **Wanda Ventham** as the sexy Jean Rock. Both could have enjoyed long associations with the series – but only one has chosen to do so: Wanda Ventham.

'After appearing in *Doctor Who* I was asked if I would like to become one of the Doctor's companions, but I decided against it because I felt it would typecast me,' Pauline Collins says. 'Then, of course, I played Sarah in *Upstairs, Downstairs* and I'm still associated with *that* in many people's minds. I went over to America recently and it's going out all over again there. They regard it like history; like a classic.'

Wanda Ventham, however, has returned to the series not once but twice, and has worked alongside three Doctors, Patrick Troughton, Tom Baker and Sylvester McCoy. 'I actually started out studying scenic design at art school,' Wanda explains, 'but gradually I drifted into local rep and from there to TV. I cut my television teeth on series such as *Danger Man* (1959), *The Avengers* (1960), *The Saint* (1963), *The Prisoner* (1967) and *Doctor Who*. I don't think there was a film series going that I wasn't in for at least one episode! In fact, *Doctor Who* was just one more when I first appeared in it. But I loved working with Pat Troughton, and Tom Baker was such a character you never knew what he would do next!' she says. It was, of course, the BBC series *The Lotus Eaters*, in which she played opposite Ian Hendry, that turned her into a well-known face.

The Tom Baker story she appeared in was called 'Image of the Fendahl' (October–November, 1977) and she played Thea Ransome, an attractive medium who is unwittingly used by the Fendahl, an entity which feeds on life, to materialise on Earth. Exactly ten years on, Wanda returned once more to help launch the adventures of the seventh Doctor in 'Time and The Rani' by Pip and Jane Baker (September 1987). Gone, though, was the beauty, as heavy make-up turned her into the oppressed Faroon caught up in the evil scheming of Kate O'Mara's Time Lady, The Rani.

'It's satisfying to play something different after years of all those sexy glamour roles,' she says. 'I do love the chance to play character parts. It's also nice to be associated with something as long-running as *Doctor Who*, though I'm not going to say which of the three Doctors is my favourite!'

When the Daleks returned yet again in 'The Evil of the Daleks' (May–July 1967), they had enlisted the help of a Victorian scientist, Theodore Maxtible, to lay a trap for the Doctor. Playing Maxtible was **Marius Goring**, a versatile and experienced film actor who had

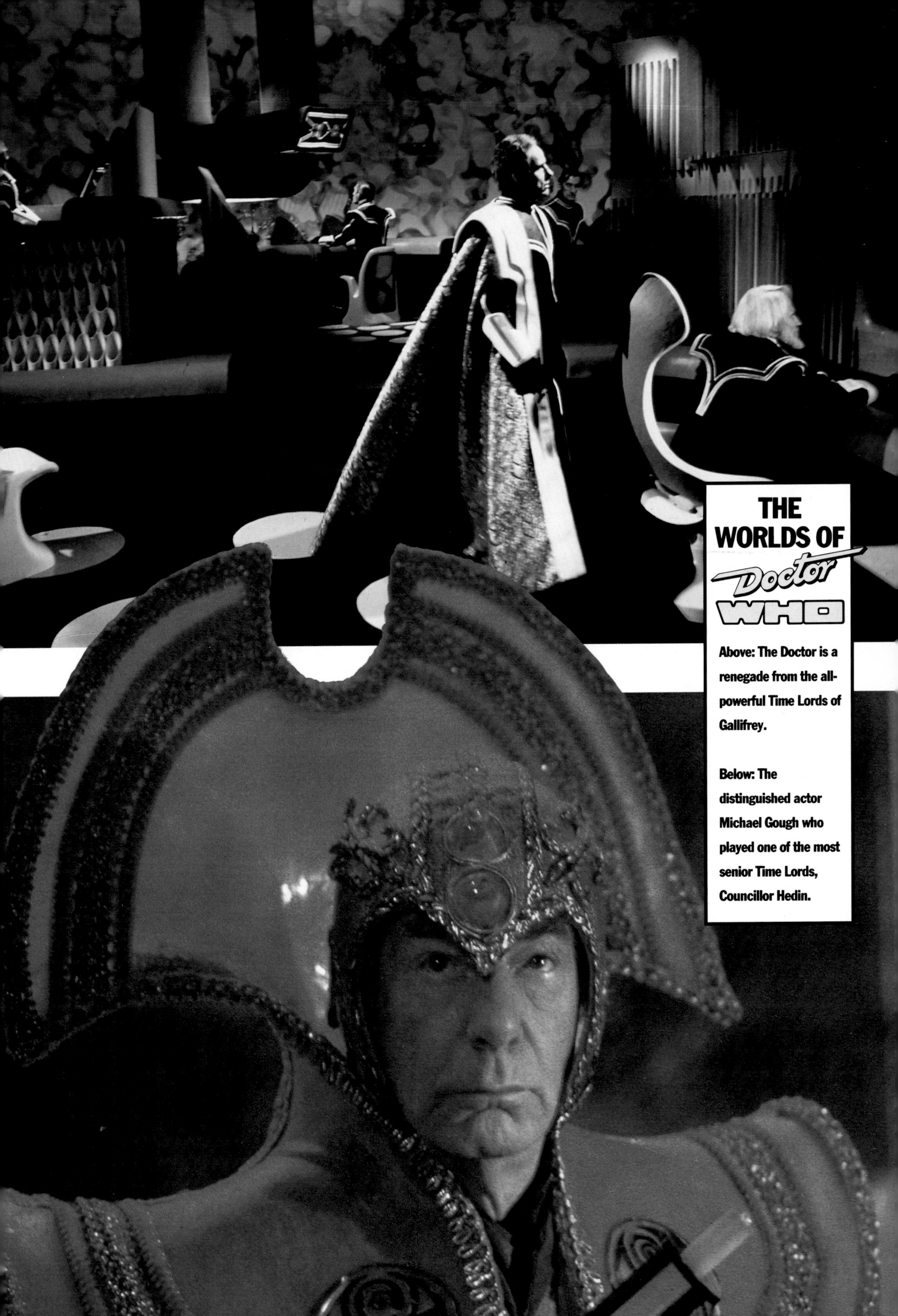

THE WORLDS OF Doctor WHO

Above: The Doctor is a renegade from the all-powerful Time Lords of Gallifrey.

Below: The distinguished actor Michael Gough who played one of the most senior Time Lords, Councillor Hedin.

Another renegade Time Lord is The Master – but his mission is to spread evil through space and time. In his first incarnation he was played by the late Roger Delgado, here confronting the third Doctor (Jon Pertwee).

Above left: Anthony Ainley, the current incarnation of The Master.

Above: K9 – the very popular robot, who starred in a one-off special programme, 'K9 and Company' with Elisabeth Sladen.

Left: The Brigadier – a long-time favourite in the series, played by Nicholas Courtney.

Each of the seven Doctors has faced many narrow escapes from death. (Above) the fourth Doctor, Tom Baker, in 'The Deadly Assassin', and (right) his successor Peter Davison in 'Four to Doomsday'.

Above: Marius Goring as the bearded Victorian scientist, Theodore Maxtible, in 'The Evil of the Daleks' (1967).

been making movies since before World War II and had starred in the BBC serial *The Scarlet Pimpernel* in 1954. Goring's performance, which culminated in him being turned into a Dalek-like creature, was memorable, and helped to make this one of the best of all the Dalek stories. A minor role in the story, that of Toby, was played by another character actor, the Welshman **Windsor Davies**, who was later destined for stardom as a bellowing sergeant-major (shades of the first Doctor here!) in the BBC comedy series *It Ain't Half Hot, Mum* (1973–81).

Professor Travers, a Yeti-seeking explorer, was a character who appeared in two of the second Doctor's adventures, played by **Jack Watling**. He turned up in 'The Abominable Snowman' (September–November 1967) and 'The Web of Fear' (February–March 1968). Jack was a youthful-looking film star who had been in many English movies since the late 'thirties, and who enjoyed the unique distinction in *Doctor Who* history of working with his pretty actress daughter, Deborah, the Doctor's companion, Victoria Waterfield.

'Pat Troughton and Frazer Hines were a real pair of practical jokers,' Jack recalls, 'and not only did they set up the guest actors, but even poor Debbie was not immune from some of their pranks. It was mostly harmless fun – though it could get pretty *risqué* at times – and you were always well advised to look carefully if you went through a set door or had to sit down somewhere when you were on location! But no one with a sense of humour could deny that it was fun making *Doctor Who* with those two!'

Another well-known TV actor who fondly remembers the prankish nature of Patrick Troughton is **Ronald Allen**, a long-time star of *Crossroads*, the soap opera serial about life in a Midlands motel which began in 1964. Allen appeared in 'The Dominators' (August–September 1968), playing Rago, one of the aliens of the title who took over the planet Dulkis with their robot servants, the Quarks. He made a return visit to the series in March and April 1970 when Jon Pertwee had become the Doctor, and played Ralph Cornish, in David Whitaker's clever story, 'The Ambassadors of Death'.

'The Krotons' by Robert Holmes, screened in December 1968–January 1969, saw the debut in the series of Welsh-born **Philip Madoc**, a master of the villainous role, playing Elek, the would-be leader of the Gonds. Interestingly, though, this was not Philip's first connection with *Doctor Who*, for two years earlier he had appeared in the second film based on the series, *Daleks – Invasion Earth 2150 AD*, which starred Peter Cushing. played this black marketeer called Ashton who was dealing in food with the Dalek's slaves,' he recalls. 'It was not an easy film to make because Peter Cushing was ill a lot of the time and the shooting schedules kept getting changed. Everything was a lot smoother on "The Krotons", which I was invited to appear in by the director, David Maloney.'

When David Maloney was again hired by the *Doctor Who* Production Office to make 'The War Games' (April–June 1969), he once more cast Philip, this time as the War Lord, a cruel alien organising the armies of human soldiers in their bloody battles.

In January 1976, Philip Madoc brought his total to three appearances for *Doctor Who* when he played the disreputable surgeon Solon, opposite Tom Baker's Doctor – a part which he still recalls as among his favourites. He was not so happy over a fourth and final appearance in 'The Power of Kroll' (December 1978–January 1979), when he played a refinery

Below: Philip Madoc first appeared in 'The Krotons' (1968), and is pictured here as the surgeon, Solon, in 'The Brain of Morbius' (1976).

Right: David Troughton, son of the second Doctor, appeared in his father's last story, 'The War Games' (1969).

technician called Fenner. He had expected to play the evil Thawn, controller of the refinery, a part which was given to Neil McCarthy.

The last appearance by Patrick Troughton as the Doctor in 'The War Games' also gave an acting break to his son, **David Troughton**, now acknowledged as a fine character actor in a similar mould as his late father. 'The part of Moore was offered to me by the Producer, Barry Letts, without even an audition,' David recalls. 'I don't know how much it had to do with the fact that it was my father's last appearance, or that I was a friend of Katy Manning, but it was a good way to launch my career on TV.

'Watching my father acting was fascinating, because he rarely discussed his work at home, and I owe a great deal to him. My family were very appreciative of all the tributes we received after his sudden death.'

David Troughton has made one further appearance in *Doctor Who* as King Peladon in Brian Hayles's story 'The Curse of Peladon', which featured the third Doctor, Jon Pertwee, and saw another return to the screen of the Ice Warriors.

The JON PERTWEE Era

It was perhaps a neat twist of fate that the first famous actor to be seen with Jon Pertwee should be another character player who, like the third Doctor, had built up his reputation on radio. **Hugh Burden**, who played Channing, the factory boss, secretly making deadly manikins called Autons in Robert Holmes's 'Spearhead from Space', had for years been referred to as 'one of the best-known voices in radio drama'.

Born in Ceylon (now Sri Lanka), he studied acting at RADA and with his distinctive voice and wide-ranging style, moved easily into the theatre and radio and later into television in the years just prior to the outbreak of World War II. Hugh appeared in several TV series, including *The Avengers*, *Public Eye* and *The Mind of J. G. Reeder* in which he starred as the engaging sleuth created by Edgar Wallace. In fact, he actually began work on this 16-part series shortly after his appearance in Jon Pertwee's debut show screened in January 1970.

'There were a lot of problems getting that story made,' Hugh recalled some years later. 'It was the first *Doctor Who* programme to be done in colour, and we had done a whole week's shooting at Television Centre when this dispute blew up with the lighting people. I remember it all came down to a case of going on location or scrapping the whole story. The Producer (Derrick Sherwin) decided to rejig the script and we literally learned our lines as we went along. Although this must have been very upsetting for Jon, who was just getting used to the part, he took it very well. As you know, he was picked for the part because of his versatility and because of his comic touch – and I sometimes wonder if he didn't make the part more serious, more straight if you like, because of the traumas making "Spearhead from Space"!'

Hugh, who died in May 1985 shortly after filming in the adaptation of Graham Greene's novel *Dr Fischer of Geneva*, gave a fine performance himself as Channing, and the debut story has since been praised for both its production and artistic qualities.

Another veteran star, the Scottish actor **Fulton Mackay**, appeared in the second of Pertwee's stories, 'Doctor Who and the Silurians', playing Dr Quinn, a scientist at a top-secret Derbyshire atomic research centre who became obsessed with the man-like reptiles of the title which lurked beneath the establishment. A grisly fate awaited Mackay at the end of the story – destruction by the Silurians – but four years later he scored a tremendous success as the prison officer in Ronnie Barker's comedy series about life in jail, *Porridge*. Mackay died in September 1987.

Above top: Hugh Burden as the factory boss, Channing, in 'Spearhead From Space' (1970).

Above bottom: Fulton Mackay (Dr Quinn) in 'Doctor Who and the Silurians' (1970).

Below: Paul Darrow, who played Captain Hawkins in 'Doctor Who and the Silurians'.

Geoffrey Palmer, another familiar face in BBC sit-coms, appeared alongside Fulton Mackay as Masters – and enjoyed the work on *Doctor Who* enough to return in the later Jon Pertwee adventure 'The Mutants' (April–May 1972), playing the sorely pressed Administrator on the planet Solos, later assassinated by the sadistic Marshal.

Apart from these two TV veterans, a young actor destined for fame in a later BBC series, *Blake's 7*, was cast in 'Doctor Who and the Silurians'. He was **Paul Darrow**, who in playing Captain Hawkins foreshadowed some of the characteristics that would make his Avon in *Blake's 7* such a central figure in the space drama. 'I happen to like playing the type of characters that I can develop on my own,' Paul says. 'The loner, if you like – for I can really go anywhere with him, can't I? That's why I tried to make Avon someone who was apparently unpleasant but doesn't believe he is.'

Paul made a second return to *Doctor Who* in 1985, his reputation as a star assured as a result of *Blake's 7*, which had become a cult series in the interim. This time he played opposite Colin Baker's Doctor in Glen McCoy's story 'Timelash'. Here he was Maylin Tekker, the conniving and untrustworthy Council President of Karfel, who lured the Doctor into his scheming and nearly ended Peri's life when he threw her to the savage Morlox. 'It was a part I just couldn't resist taking when the script was offered to me,' Paul said during filming. 'It offered me the chance to go really over the top!'

Paul Darrow, incidentally, is not the only

star from *Blake's 7* to have starred in *Doctor Who*: **Brian Croucher** (Travis) appeared as Borg in Tom Baker's 'Robots of Death' (January 1977); **Michael Keating** (Vila) played Goudry in the same Doctor's serial 'The Sun Makers' (November 1977); and **Jacqueline Pearce** (Servalan) played the Androgum cannibal, Chessene, in the Colin Baker story of 'The Two Doctors' (February–March 1985).

The cast list for 'The Claws of Axos', screened in March–April 1971, lists the name of 'Tim Piggott' playing Harker, one of the humans drawn into the latest of The Master's machinations. Tim is now better known as the international star **Tim Pigott-Smith**, who played the-man-you-love-to-hate, Ronald Merrick, in the award-winning Granada TV serial *The Jewel in the Crown* (1984). In this drama of India, Tim was an anti-Indian police officer with the kind of brooding malevolence that any villain in *Doctor Who* would have been proud of – and the performance won him the award of 'Actor of the Year'. It was just reward for years of hard work in the theatre and on television.

'I always seem to be cast as the outsider,' says Tim, 'the man with a strange twist in his character. My career got off to a good start with the Royal Shakespeare Company, including playing Doctor Watson in *Sherlock Holmes*, but when this work ran out I had to make another career in rep and on television. In fact, the television work built up to such a point that I became exclusively a TV actor for some years.'

During this period, Tim made a second return to *Doctor Who* in the Tom Baker era in

Opposite: Ingrid Pitt (Galleia) in 'The Time Monster' (1972).

'The Masque of Mandragora' (September 1976), playing one of the people caught up in a cult of devil worshippers in fifteenth-century Italy. It was a colourful role, and one where Tim could continue the development of his now-famous lip-curl and gift for dead-pan sarcasm.

Ingrid Pitt, the Polish-born film star, had already been dubbed 'The Queen of Horror' for her starring roles in pictures such as *The Vampire Lovers* and *Countess Dracula* (both 1970) when she was signed by Producer Barry Letts to appear as Queen Galleia in 'The Time Monster' by Robert Sloman (May–June 1972). As a young actress, Ingrid had fled from East Germany, where she was building a theatrical career, and gone to America where she broke into films.

'One of the first movies I made was in the *Doctor Who* tradition,' Ingrid says. 'It was a science fiction story called *The Omegans*, about these aliens trying to take over the world. But it was filmed in the Philippines on a pretty small budget with some really crummy monsters! Then in 1969 I got my big break when I was offered a part in *Where Eagles Dare* – and became famous as the actress who slapped Richard Burton's face; all for the sake of the film, of course!

'The next year I did *The Vampire Lovers*, which co-starred a couple of people who are also associated with *Doctor Who*. Peter Cushing, who played the Doctor on the screen, was one of them, and the other was Kate O'Mara, who has become quite a star of the series recently,' continues Ingrid. 'And after that I played another vampire in *The House that Dripped Blood*, which starred Jon Pertwee. He was a horror film actor who bought a flowing cloak and turned into a vampire! It was a bit like a trial run for *Doctor Who* in some ways, I suppose, and what was nice was that Jon asked for me to play the "vampish" Queen in "The Time Monster".'

Ingrid particularly admired the work of Roger Delgado playing The Master in 'The Time Monster', and was quick to confirm that his saturnine dark looks concealed a warm and generous personality. 'I played the Queen of Atlantis,' Ingrid recalls, 'and at first fell under The Master's charm. But in the end I had to betray him when I realised he wanted control of Atlantis for himself.'

Ingrid found working on *Doctor Who* great fun, and was happy to return in January 1984 when current producer John Nathan-Turner cast her as Solow in another 'underwater epic' called 'Warriors of the Deep', written by Johnny Byrne – this time set not in ancient history but in the year 2084 in a military sea base at the bottom of the ocean.

'The Time Monster' also gave valuable experience to two other performers whose fame still lay ahead of them: **Susan Penhaligon** and **Dave Prowse**.

The voluptuous Susan played Lakis, a member of the Queen of Atlantis's Court. Four years later, in 1976, she was to appear in the controversial London Weekend Television series *Bouquet of Barbed Wire*, in which she played opposite Frank Finlay as her father nursing an obsessive love for his married daughter.

Dave Prowse played the fabled Minotaur as

Opposite: 'Mrs Who', Lalla Ward, who played Romana, and for a time was the wife of the fourth Doctor, Tom Baker.

a prelude to the role which has since made him famous – the intergalactic villain Darth Vader in the *Star Wars* films created by George Lucas. Much of Dave's film and TV career has involved him being concealed behind a mask – and it was no different in 'The Time Monster', where he was masked under the head of a Minotaur to take on Jon Pertwee in mortal combat. 'I can play anything – and I have,' says Dave, a towering but very gentle man. 'Remember all the Frankenstein monsters in the Hammer films? They're all me – the fellow with the bolt through his neck. You name a monster or a creature – I've been it. If you want a hero to look good, let him fight me, kill me, and drop me over a balcony.'

As a former Olympic Weightlifting Champion and physical training consultant, Dave has become known as the 'Man in the Masks' in the film world, and there are few better performers when it comes to impersonating any alien creature – though he is a talented actor and has fancied himself as two of the great cinema heroes of our times, James Bond and Superman. As Darth Vader, though, he has found almost equal recognition and is much in demand at fan conventions on both sides of the Atlantic.

'Vader has become a cult figure just like Doctor Who,' he says, 'and just as the actors who have played the Doctor find that the fans know more about the character than they do, so *I* get told all sorts of things I never realised about my part! Do you know, children really believe in Darth Vader. They don't want him sent up or got at.

'I'm glad I usually play the villain in pictures,' he adds, 'because it's the villains in movies that people *always* remember.'

Dave Prowse was not the only *Doctor Who* actor to appear in the *Star Wars* films. Julian Glover and Jeremy Bulloch, who were mentioned earlier, were both able to use their experience from the series, as was **John Hollis**, who played Sondergaard in the Jon Pertwee adventure 'The Mutants' (April–May 1972); **Michael Sheard**, who is most remembered as Laurence Scarman in Tom Baker's 'Pyramids of Mars' (October–November 1975); and **Milton Johns**, who contributed to three stories between 1967 and 1978.

In 'Carnival of Monsters' by Robert Holmes, which was shown in January–February 1973, Jon Pertwee was reunited with an old friend from his radio days, **Tenniel Evans**. 'Jon was one of the stars of "The Navy Lark", which ran for over 18 years,' Tenniel Evans recalled in 1976. 'He was absolutely marvellous at inventing new personalities and new voices, and when I read that they were looking for a new Doctor Who I said he should apply. He thought I was crazy to even suggest it – but he got his agent to contact the BBC, and the rest you know.

'It was just like old times when I got the call to work with him on *Doctor Who*. He was obviously enjoying the part enormously, and said he would never have thought of going for it if I hadn't put the idea in his head. That started us off on all sorts of memories from "The Navy Lark" days, and in the end I think the Director, Barry Letts, got a bit tired of us and our stories. There were times when we

just broke up remembering something funny that had happened!', he recalled.

'Carnival of Monsters' was an important landmark in *Doctor Who*, for after three years of being confined to Earth, the Doctor was at last free to travel in space. Tenniel Evans played Major Daly, and the combination of the long-standing friendship of Pertwee and Evans plus the witty script made this a memorable story. Also in the cast was another comedian, **Leslie Dwyer**, later to become one of the cast of the long-running BBC holiday camp series *Hi-de-Hi*, which began in 1980.

In Jon Pertwee's final appearance as the Doctor, in 'Planet of the Spiders' (May–June 1974), the ruggedly handsome actor **Gareth Hunt** took time off from his work in *Upstairs, Downstairs* to play Arak, one of the colonists on the planet Metebelis 3 who were being enslaved by giant spiders. The cost of ridding the humans of their oppressors was, of course, the third Doctor's life. Hunt, though, went off to a co-starring role with Joanna Lumley and Patrick MacNee in *The New Avengers*, which ran for 26 episodes in 1976.

The TOM BAKER Era

In 1979, some years into his tenure as the fourth Doctor, Tom Baker was discussing the appearance of famous actors and actresses in *Doctor Who* with an Australian journalist, Peter Dean, during the course of which he made the following revealing suggestions. 'Can you imagine,' he said, fixing Dean with his infectious grin, 'Glenda Jackson as the imperious Queen of the Spiders on Metebelis 3, threatened with extinction by the terrifying Krynoids? Or American actress Elaine Stritch encased in silver armour as a Cyberwoman locked in an interstellar conflict with the gruesome Sontarans?

'Well, such treats could be in store for *Doctor Who* fans if the right scripts could be found for them, because the ladies are willing,' he went on. 'One hears such lovely feedback from people about the show. It's now so jolly and successful that it's a big thing with other actors – nearly everybody wants to be in it. It's six weeks of sheer fun to make!'

Of course, Tom himself played a major part in making *Doctor Who* such fun for actors during his fourth regeneration, which lasted from 1974 to 1981 – an observation that is borne out by everyone who appeared with him. One of the fourth Doctor's early co-stars was **Frederick Jaeger**, who appeared in 'Planet of Evil' in 1975, having first appeared with William Hartnell in 'The Savages' in 1966.

Frederick, whose blond, rather intimidating features make him a likely candidate for casting as a German, has a delightful sense of

Opposite: Frederick Jaeger (Professor Sorenson) in 'Planet of Evil' (1975).

humour and regards himself very much as a true-blue Englishman. Though born in Berlin, his Jewish parentage meant that he had to flee Germany to escape Hitler's purges – and yet, ironically, he found himself being cast in Nazi roles when he first broke into the acting profession in England. 'I needed a sense of humour appearing in that *Doctor Who* story,' he recalls. 'I played this professor [Sorenson] who was turned into a monster. I looked like an outer-space version of Dr Jekyll and Mr Hyde! Do you know, it took eight hours in the make-up chair to transform me into a mixture of Piltdown Man and Guy the gorilla!'

Frederick says that Tom Baker was not above bursting out laughing at the sight of him when they were on the set. 'Actually, though, that monster was nowhere near as worrying as the part I had in HTV's series about the Duke of Monmouth's rebellion in 1685. I was a German mercenary caught by King James and hanged in chains to be pecked by crows. Well, the studio couldn't find any trained crows so they got over the problem by making a mechanical crow worked by remote control. It seemed like a monstrous contraption and I was terrified its steel beak might get out of control and savage me! Fortunately, though, nothing went wrong and I was able to escape to fight again.'

In 'Planet of Evil', Frederick was also restored to human form, thanks to the Doctor's intervention. Two years later, in October 1977, he returned to the show as another professor, Marius, the inventor of a dog-like mobile computer called K9 in the story of 'The Invisible Enemy' by Bob Baker and Dave Martin. 'After the robot crow, K9 was easy to handle,' he recalls, 'and not half so dangerous – though the machine did have a habit of going in the wrong direction at times. No one had any idea whether the dog would catch on with the viewers, so the Director (Derrick Goodwin) filmed two endings to the story. In one, K9 stayed with me – in the other he went off with Tom Baker. Of course, he became one of the most famous props in the show, second only to the Daleks I believe!'

Another actor famed for his sinister appearance was the late **Tony Beckley**, who played Harrison Chase in Robert Banks Stewart's story 'The Seeds of Doom' (January–March 1976), about the discovery of alien life forms, the Krynoids, which took over an Antarctic base. Beckley was a wealthy and eccentric English botanist who stole one of the Krynoids and almost allowed it to turn all Earth plant life against humanity.

Interviewed in 1978, two years before his sudden and tragic death, Tony said: 'I seem to have got a real reputation for being "Mr Nasty" on the stage, in films and now in television. . . . Only a couple of years ago I nearly put paid to mankind in a *Doctor Who* story. However, that was a better experience than many of my television appearances because you usually have three weeks of rehearsals in a draughty drill hall in the suburbs, followed by a day of actually recording the play with an often strange and unfamiliar crew. With *Doctor Who*, Tom Baker really carried the show along and made everyone feel part of a team. It was one of my

Above: Russell Hunter as Commander Uvanov in 'The Robots of Death' (1977).

happiest TV experiences.'

Russell Hunter, the mournful figure of Lonely in the Thames TV secret service thriller series *Callan*, starring Edward Woodward, which ran from 1967 to 1973, made an impressive guest appearance in *Doctor Who* in January 1977. He was cast as Commander Uvanov, in charge of a vast mobile mining factory, under threat from a robot-obsessed scientist, in Chris Boucher's story 'Robots of Death'.

Robert Holmes's story 'The Ribos Operation' (September 1978) brought to the programme the bluff, often larger-than-life Scottish character actor **Iain Cuthbertson**, as Garron. Cuthbertson was by then a national favourite through his portrayal of Charlie Endell in the three-year-long Thames TV series about a London spiv, *Budgie*, starring Adam Faith. The producer of that show was none other than Verity Lambert. 'I am something of a rogue and a vagabond by nature,' says Iain Cuthbertson, 'having played in weekly rep in Scotland for years as well as never-to-be-forgotten one-night stands all over the Highlands. It meant I could take to parts like Charlie Endell, and Garron, who was an intergalactic con-man and always just an inch away from disaster at any time.' In 'The Ribos Operation', Iain Cuthbertson once again avoided an untimely end and was able to make good his escape in a spaceship laden with riches.

A trio of lovely ladies guested in *Doctor Who* at the opening of the seventeenth season in the autumn of 1979. **Suzanne Danielle**, now a highly regarded actress, appeared as Agella, a Movellan, one of a race of humanoids engaged in a deadly war with the Daleks on the planet of Skaro in Terry Nation's story 'Destiny of the Daleks' (September 1979).

In 'City of Death' by David Agnew (September–October 1979), **Catherine Schell** played Countess Scarlioni, the accomplice of Julian Glover's Count Scarlioni in a plot to steal the Mona Lisa painting. Catherine, playing a smouldering beauty ultimately killed by her ruthless husband, came to the show after two years of science fiction experience in Gerry Anderson's serial *Space 1999* (1975–6), about a space station travelling through the universe encountering alien civilisations.

Also appearing in 'City of Death' was the revue actress **Eleanor Bron**, who played an art critic in company with another of the country's leading comedy actors, **John Cleese**, famous for his *Fawlty Towers* series. 'I loved the opportunity to appear in *Doctor Who*,' she says. 'Any excuse for dressing up and being glamorous attracts me. The interesting thing about doing "City of Death" was that John Cleese and I didn't appear until the closing scenes, and we weren't mentioned at all in the cast list in the *Radio Times*, so most people were totally surprised when we turned up! However, when the story was re-shown a year later as part of a season of re-runs, there were stories about us in all the newspapers.'

In one of these reports, Producer John Nathan-Turner re-emphasised what Tom Baker had said earlier, when he told the *London Evening News* (20 August 1980): 'I don't think John Cleese took much persuading to do the show. *Doctor Who* is a bit like *The Muppets* – everybody likes the idea of popping up in it, if only to impress their children.'

Eleanor Bron actually made a much more significant appearance in the programme in 1985 when she returned in the Colin Baker story 'Revelation of the Daleks' by the show's Script Editor, Eric Saward. She played Kara, the head of the Food Corporation, who employed Davros to help her make food. 'It was a gruesome tale,' she remembers, 'because Davros was actually using dead bodies to make this food. Kara tried to get rid of him, but paid the price so many of the Dalek's enemies do by being killed very graphically!'

'The Creature from the Pit' by David Fisher, screened in October–November 1979, featured the lanky and eccentric character actor **Geoffrey Bayldon**, playing an Astrologer to the Court of the tyrant Lady Adrasta on the planet Chloris. Bayldon, a veteran of such films as *Dracula* (1958) and the James Bond movie *Casino Royale* (1967), was to enjoy his greatest fame when he switched to television in 1970 to star in the LWT series *Catweazle*. 'I played an old wizard from the eleventh century who accidentally transported himself to the twentieth century, so I had more than a little sympathy with Doctor Who when I was cast in "The Creature from the Pit",' Geoffrey says. 'I liked the part of the old astrologer, too, though I've never seen anything quite so bizarre as the monster which was supposed to be a huge translucent blob and was actually made out of a giant plastic bag with limbs stuck on it!'

Geoffrey Bayldon also has another association with *Doctor Who* in that he was later cast with the third doctor, Jon Pertwee, in the successful Southern Television series *Worzel Gummidge*, which was launched in 1978.

Adrienne Corri, a seductive redhead who

Above: Adrienne Corrie as the attractive Mena in 'The Leisure Hive' (1980).

had made her screen debut in *Devil Girl from Mars* (1954) and followed this with a number of horror movies in the 'sixties and 'seventies, gave a memorable performance in 'The Leisure Hive' by David Fisher (August–September 1980). She played Mena, the leader of the Argolins, keepers of the entertainment centre known as the Leisure Hive on the planet Argolis. Though her race was dying as a result of its warmongering activities, Mena was attempting to rejuvenate herself – a task which she ultimately achieved thanks to the Doctor. Co-starring with Adrienne was another veteran British film actor, **Laurence Payne**, who played Morix. It was the third time the couple had worked together, having previously appeared in the movies *The Tell-Tale Heart* (1961) and *Vampire Circus* (1972).

The story which immediately followed, 'Meglos' by John Flanagan and Andrew McCulloch (September–October 1980), offered long-time fans of the series not only a chance to see the Doctor's very first companion, **Jacqueline Hill**, return in a quite different role as Lexa, but also the delight of watching the versatile comedian **Bill Fraser** as General Grugger, the leader of a band of ruthless space mercenaries whom the Doctor only just managed to outwit. Fraser, of course, after a lifetime in the theatre, became a star as the spluttering Sergeant-Major Snudge opposite the diminutive private, Bootsie (played by Alfie Bass), in the TV series *The Army Game*, which later became *Bootsie and Snudge*.

Bill Fraser came to a nasty end in the

Above: Bill Fraser as General Grugger in 'Meglos' (1980).

explosive finale to 'Meglos', but gave such an impressive performance that producer John Nathan-Turner signed him for another appearance in the *Doctor Who* Christmas 1980 Special, 'K9 and Company', which starred Elisabeth Sladen. Though there was a special condition that Bill insisted upon if he was to appear – as he revealed in a light-hearted interview in August 1980. 'I play something horrible that comes from behind a tree,' he joked. 'I only took the part on condition that they would let me kick K9. I expect all the *Doctor Who* fans will hate me, but I have never been too keen on that tin dog!'

Bill also revealed that he had appeared with two of the other Doctors. In 1936, while running his own repertory company at Worthing in Sussex, he took on a would-be actor named Peter Cushing who was later to become a star of many horror films and the two *Doctor Who* movies. And in 1955 he co-starred in a movie called *Private's Progress* with William Hartnell.

Shortly before his death in September 1987, Bill Fraser said: 'Billy Hartnell was one of that whole gang of old troupers who gave such character to British films and TV during those important decades of development after the Second World War. He never really got the recognition he deserved, but I am sure he would be pleased that his creation of the character of Doctor Who is still remembered today and used as a yardstick. I would love to have appeared with Billy, and I could even imagine playing the Doctor myself!' he said with a mischievous grin and a roll of those expressive eyes.

Two more familiar British actors co-starred in *Doctor Who* before Tom Baker ended his record-breaking run in the role. In 'Warriors' Gate', Steve Gallagher's story of space pirates screened in January 1981, **Kenneth Cope**, the former *Coronation Street* regular and star of ATV's serial about a detective who is killed on a case and comes back as a ghost to help his partner, called *Randall and Hopkirk (Deceased)* (1972), was impressive as the conniving Packard. While in 'Logopolis' (February–March 1981), which introduced the new Doctor, Peter Davison, the handsome stage actor and film star **John Fraser** played the Monitor whose dramatic revelation that the Universe is being kept alive only by his people's calculations propels the fourth Doctor into a confrontation with The Master which he can successfully resolve only at the cost of his fourth 'life'.

The PETER DAVISON Era

Although the story 'Castrovalva' by Christopher Bidmead was the first of the fifth Doctor's stories to be screened, in January 1982, Peter Davison had actually first played the role while filming Terence Dudley's 'Four to Doomsday', which was shown the following month.

Cast as the leading villain, Monarch, the ruler of the Urbankans who are intent on pillaging Earth of its silicon, was **Stratford Johns**, familiar to all viewers as Charlie Barlow of the police series *Z-Cars*. It was an interesting piece of casting that had brought the veteran actor and the latest Time Lord together in this opening story, because, as Stratford Johns explained, his wife Nanette was a cousin of the very first Doctor, William Hartnell.

'I had watched *Doctor Who* on and off ever since its early days because of the family connection,' he explained. 'At the time I was in the series I was trying hard to break the typecasting because I was known everywhere as the fellow who had played Charlie Barlow.

'Just before this I had got a role in a story called "Games" in the *Blake's 7* science fiction series where I was a chess-playing master of the universe called Belkov. And then right after came this part as a power-mad frog in *Doctor Who*! It was great fun to do, a bit over the top. I thought even then that Peter Davison made a good Doctor – such a change from all the others. I was pleased he did so well.'

Interestingly, Stratford Johns's assistant in *Z-Cars* and its spin-offs *Softly, Softly* and *Barlow* – **Frank Windsor**, who played John Watt, also co-starred with Peter Davison in another Terence Dudley story, the historical drama 'The King's Demons' (March 1983). The versatile Windsor played the nobleman Sir Ranulf Fitzwilliam.

Above: Stratford Johns as the evil Monarch in 'Four to Doomsday' (1982).

The third Davison adventure, 'Kinda' by Christopher Bailey, featured two major stars in the story of the gentle people of the planet Deva Loka whose way of life was being threatened by an expeditionary force from Earth. The first of these was **Richard Todd**, the much-respected English film actor who had become famous as the leader of a very different force, a group of RAF bomber planes, in the classic World War II movie *The Dam Busters*, made in 1955.

Right: Richard Todd (Sanders) in 'Kinda' (1982).

Above: Beryl Reid as the gun-toting Captain Briggs in 'Earthshock' (1982).

Todd, who had earlier played two of the great heroes of literature, Robin Hood and Rob Roy, had actually been on one of the early lists of possible replacements for Patrick Troughton when the second Doctor decided to leave the series. 'I don't know that it is a part I would have accepted, even if it had been offered to me', the still-handsome leading man said while filming at the BBC Television Centre. 'You see, I had worked with Peter Bryant, who became *Doctor Who*'s Producer in the late 'sixties, when he was an actor. He had appeared in a BBC production of *Wuthering Heights* in which I had played Heathcliffe, and we became quite friendly.

'I did enjoy making "Kinda", which I thought had a most interesting and unusual script,' said Todd, who played Sanders.

Appearing alongside Richard Todd in this story was **Nerys Hughes**, the popular British comedy actress, who had come to public attention as one of *The Liver Birds*, and who more recently has enjoyed a quite different success in the drama series *District Nurse*. It was perhaps a taste of things to come that she appeared as Doctor Todd!

An even more famous English comedienne gave a compelling performance in the fifth Doctor's encounter with the Cybermen in Eric Saward's highly acclaimed story 'Earthshock' (March 1982). She was **Beryl Reid**, playing the gun-toting Captain Briggs.

Beryl threw herself into her part with all the infectious enthusiasm for which she is famous. 'I'm not known as Beryl the Peril for nothing,' she says with a grin. 'I enjoy doing lots of different things, that's what keeps you from going stale. Do you know, I went from doing an old-time music hall appearance into this futuristic *Doctor Who* story! It was great, and helped me in my continual fight to avoid being typecast.

'So you want to know how I got myself into that *Doctor Who* part? The same way I do with everything I play – by putting on the shoes! Once you've got the shoes right for a character, you get the walk right, and then

Above: Lynda Baron as the pirate Captain Wrack in 'Enlightenment' (1983).

the whole thing falls into place. I wouldn't like to have been in the shoes of the actors playing those Cybermen, though – but weren't they good!'

Another highly individual comedy actress, **Liza Goddard**, appeared in Steve Gallagher's grim story 'Terminus' about a spaceship carrying victims of a terrible disease (February–March 1983). The role was a far cry from her work in such light-hearted series as *Yes Honestly* and *Pig in the Middle*.

Barbara Clegg's story 'Enlightenment' (March 1983) brought a return to *Doctor Who* for the female star **Lynda Baron** – though the fact that it was a second appearance was probably unknown to most fans. For Lynda, who played the pirate Captain Wrack, had been heard but not seen in the William Hartnell western adventure 'The Gunfighters', which had attracted such appalling viewing figures in April–May 1966. Lynda had sung the ballad which made up the background music for much of the four-episode story. By the time Lynda returned to *Doctor Who* she was a star of the stage and TV – in particular, playing the apple of Ronnie Barker's eye, Nurse Gladys Emmanuel in the BBC series *Open All Hours* – and she made a swashbuckling figure in the story of a sailing ship race in space in which the Doctor became unwittingly involved.

'I did a lot of reading up on women pirates for this part,' she revealed after the transmission of the story. 'They were a terrifying lot – every bit as wild and wicked as the men, and some were even bare chested with it! Not me, though, but the costume I wore *was* based on old prints. Women buccaneers were extravagantly dressed and always wore the best hand-made boots, probably stolen!

'I know people now expect me to be jolly and rotund, but frankly I'm not as big as Nurse Gladys's navy-blue mac might lead you to think. In fact, I am not a bit like her or your average district nurse. Nor, come to that, your average pirate!'

Playing Lynda's second-in-command in the story was a young singer, Leee John (who does spell his name with three *e*s), leader of the group Imagination, who had just enjoyed two years of regular success in the charts.

Above: Peter Gilmore (left) as Brazen in 'Frontios' (1984).

There was a strong tang of the sea about **Peter Gilmore**, who guested as Brazen in Christopher Bidmead's story 'Frontios' (January 1984). He, of course, had become popular with viewers as James Onedin, the Victorian captain of a three-masted schooner, in the series *The Onedin Line*. 'I had been acting for twenty years without getting a name, so I won't be surprised when this bit of fame has gone,' Peter said in 1978. 'That's the reason I keep going back to the theatre. Publicity just embarrasses me. I've always managed without it.'

He was, though, rather taken aback by all the attention he received from the press when appearing in *Doctor Who*. 'It was just a job to me, but I soon realised that there is tremendous interest in *Doctor Who* and everyone who appears in it,' he reflects. 'And because the story was set on this fantastic planet, there were bits of it that rather reminded me of making *The Onedin Line*. People used to imagine we filmed the stories up the Orinoco or on the Spanish Main – while in fact, English rivers can look really exotic in the summer! *Doctor Who* has the same problem making a quarry or a studio set look like something out of this world.'

The most star-laden of all the Peter Davison adventures was undoubtedly the 'Resurrection of the Daleks', which pitted the fifth Doctor against his oldest foes. The Eric Saward story, screened in February 1984, again generated widespread publicity, not least because of the appearance of no fewer than five stars: Rula Lenska, Chloe Ashcroft, Rodney Bewes, Maurice Colbourne and Leslie Grantham. To be strictly accurate, though, fame still lay just around the corner for the last of these five. . . .

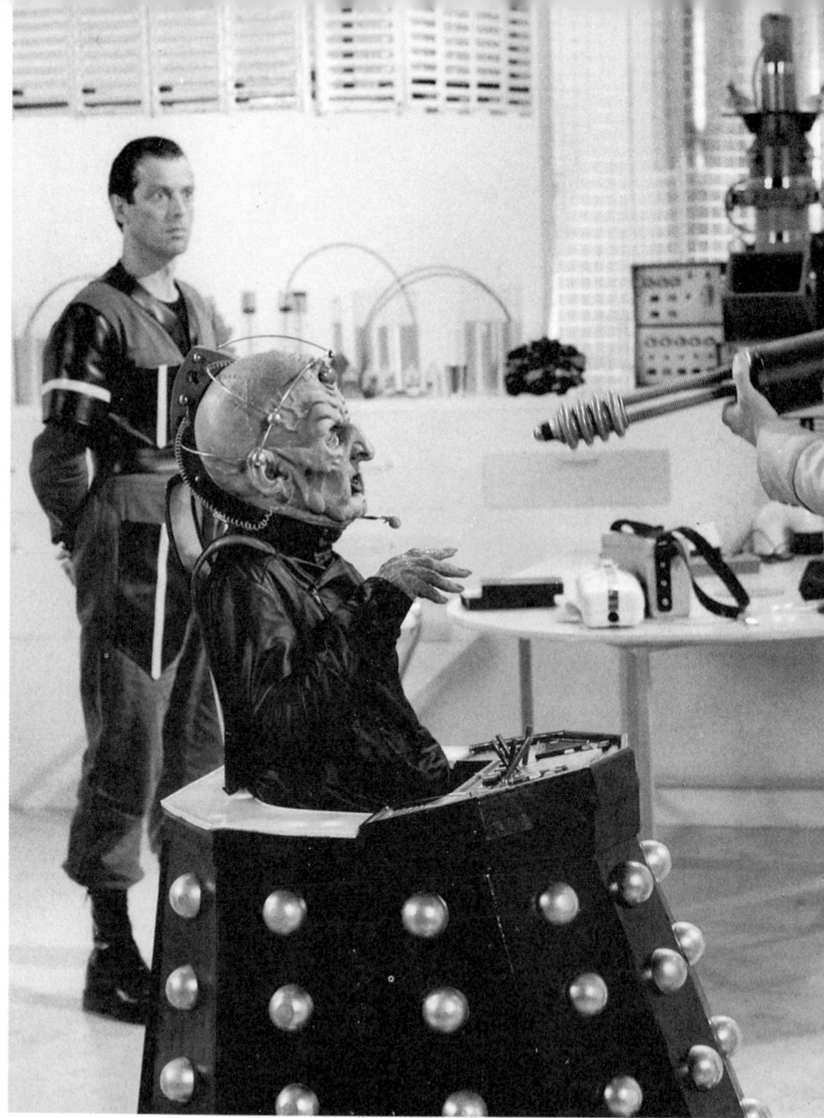

Above: *EastEnders* star, Leslie Grantham, who made a brief appearance as Kiston in 'Resurrection of the Daleks'.

The statuesque, red-headed actress **Rula Lenska** played a scientist called Styles; while **Chloe Ashcroft**, a favourite of the young children's TV programme *Play School*, was Laird. **Rodney Bewes**, the genial star of the long-running series *The Likely Lads*, proved not as amiable as he seemed, in the form of the double-dealing Stein; and **Maurice Colbourne**, the granite-faced leading character from the sailing series *Howards' Way*, played the mercenary, Commander Lytton.

Way down the cast list was Leslie Grantham, playing Kiston. Today, of course, he is often referred to as 'Britain's Number One Soap Villain' for his appearances in the BBC's hugely successful series *EastEnders*, playing the womanising publican, 'Dirty Den' Watts. Though 'Resurrection of the Daleks' has to date been Leslie's only appearance in *Doctor Who*, his connection with the programme is one of the most interesting in the annals of the show's history.

For, as is now generally known, Leslie was jailed in April 1967 for killing a taxi driver while serving in the Army in Osnabruck, West Germany. He served his term in prison and then set about making a career for himself in acting, which has been rewarded with the kind of fame he probably never dreamed possible. Along the way he has proved himself a very good actor – and the change in his fortunes is due in no small degree to another *Doctor Who* star, Louise Jameson, who played the fourth Doctor's assistant, Leela.

Speaking in 1985, Louise revealed that she had been a prison visitor in 1977 and had met Leslie Grantham during the course of his imprisonment. 'Leslie and I hit it off straight away when we met, and he wanted to know all about my work as an actress,' she said. 'He was so taken by my help and encouragement that he went to drama school after his release. I like to think that I helped him launch his acting career, and we have kept in touch.'

There is also another fascinating link between *Doctor Who* and *EastEnders* – one the longest running series on television and the other the most popular. For the woman who created *EastEnders*, the Producer, Julia Smith, was responsible as a young director at the BBC for filming two early *Doctor Who* stories, William Hartnell's 'The Smugglers' by Brian Hayles (September–October 1966) and Patrick Troughton's 'The Underwater Menace' by Geoffrey Orme (January–February 1967).

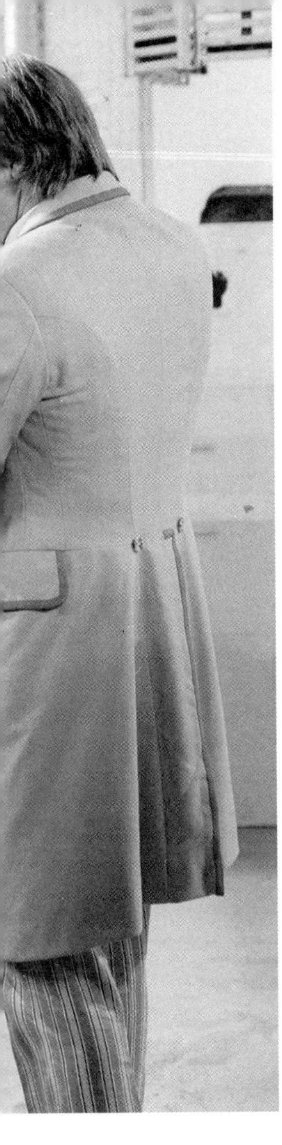

Right: Maurice Denham (Edgeworth) in 'The Twin Dilemma' (1984).

The COLIN BAKER Era

The appearance of the sixth Doctor, Colin Baker, in his first full-length adventure, 'The Twin Dilemma' by Anthony Steven, in March–April 1984, was not only a new landmark in the show's history, but also brought to the programme another actor, **Maurice Denham**, who had the unique distinction of having appeared with each and every one of the previous Doctors – though in quite different productions. Maurice, a veteran of stage, screen and radio, was most suitably cast as Professor Edgeworth, a Time Lord, and one of the Doctor's tutors when he was young on Gallifrey.

Here again, Maurice demonstrated his amazing versatility, which has made him constantly in demand since he came to public notice during World War II on the radio show *It's That Man Again (ITMA)*, playing two women, charwoman Lola Tickle and telephonist Ivy Clingvine. 'Mind you, I've never thought of myself as a funny man,' Maurice explains. 'They were just characters I worked on like any others. Fortunately, I was also given the chance to play everything from Shakespeare to modern drama and science fiction, and this has kept me busy.'

By the time Maurice came to appear in *Doctor Who* – an opportunity he was glad to accept, he says – he had appeared in innumerable stage productions, countless radio and television plays and serials, as well as over 100 films. 'It was while I was making "The Twin Dilemma" that someone pointed out that at one time or another I'd appeared with each of Colin Baker's predecessors: Billy Hartnell, lovely Pat Troughton, that great radio comic Jon Pertwee, and both Tom Baker and Peter Davison. It was a record I wasn't aware of, but when you've been in the business in this country for over fifty years like I have, nothing surprises you any more!' he quipped.

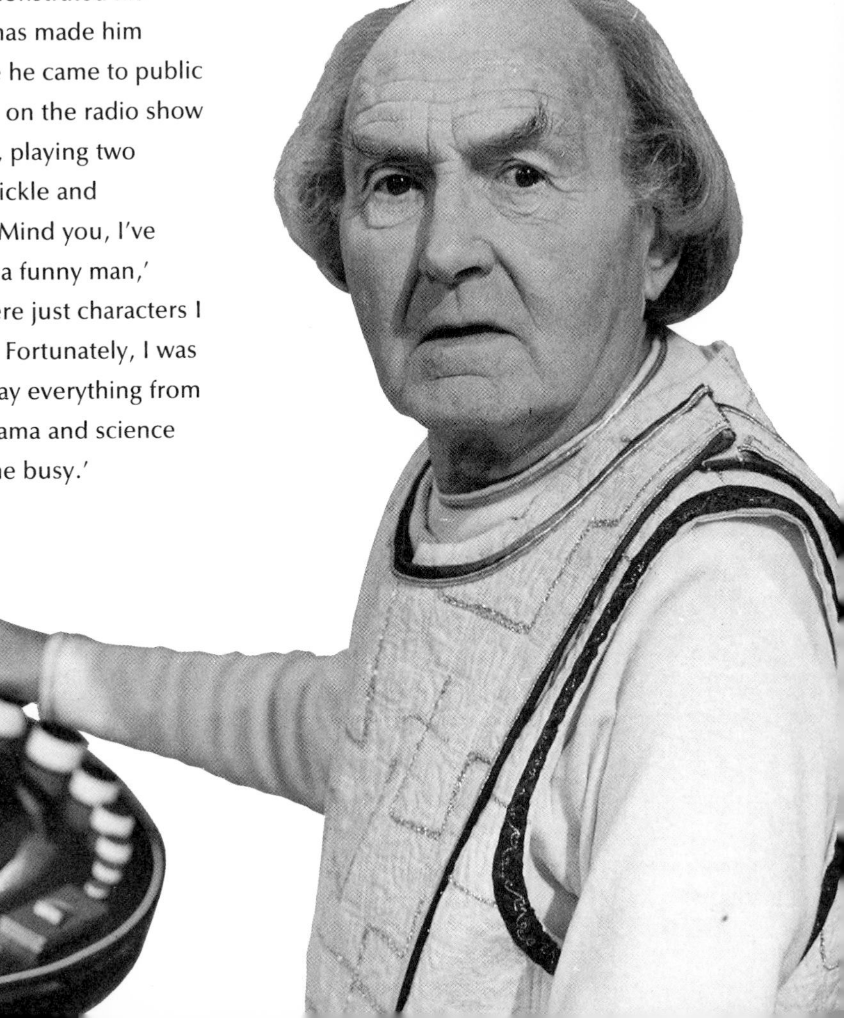

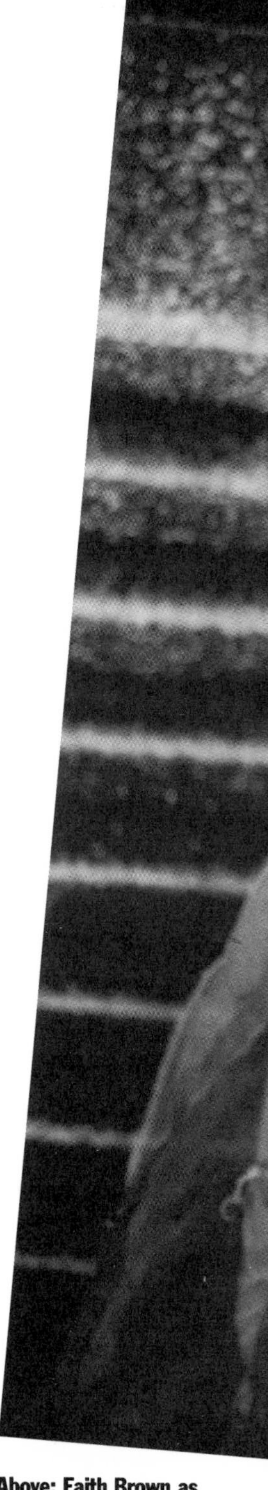

Though Maurice Denham has only infrequently had the time to watch himself on television, he had seen *Doctor Who* occasionally. 'Each of the actors brought something fresh to the series,' he said, 'which is why it has continued to fascinate people for so long. The selection of the actors has been very good, too, and I'm sure Colin Baker will make his mark. I'm a great believer in selection – both from the performer's point of view and that of the producer. As an actor I believe you must know when to turn something down.'

The start of Colin Baker's complete season in January 1985 was heralded by a considerable amount of publicity underlining the number of 'big name' actors and actresses who were to appear. In a feature-length article in the *Daily Star* of 5 January headlined 'A Who's Who Guide to the Galaxy', Geoff Baker (no relation to the new Doctor!) wrote: '*Doctor Who* is being joined by a galaxy of stars. The Time Lord doesn't just switch on the kids – he's a hit with the stars as well. "It's phenomenal," says Colin Baker. "The show has become a cult within the acting profession and well-known actors are falling over themselves to be in it."'

After listing the actors to appear in the twenty-second season, Geoff Baker continued his report with a further comment from his namesake. '"Many actors – some extremely well-known, although it wouldn't be fair of me to say who – have said that they'd like my job. They say I'm a lucky devil to have the best job on television. And it's not just because the series gives guaranteed work. There is also the appeal of having a good time while you are doing this job. It's like being a grown-up who is getting paid to play cowboys and Indians – it's great fun!"'

In the light of the subsequent unhappy ending to Colin Baker's tenure as the sixth Doctor, these comments make poignant reading.

The opening story of the season fulfilled the promise of this publicity, as well as featuring those perennial 'star' enemies, the Cybermen. They all appeared in 'Attack of the Cybermen', by Paula Moore.

There was also a return in the story for the mysterious mercenary Commander Lytton, played with such style by *Howards' Way* star Maurice Colbourne – now apparently trying to throw in his lot with the Cybermen after having been thwarted in his plotting with the Doctor's other great enemies in 'Resurrection of the Daleks'. This time, however, he was to be revealed in a very different light as the new Doctor's saviour.

Leading the opposition to the Cybermen was the well-known TV impersonator **Faith Brown**, as Flast, the leader of the Cryons. 'Playing in *Doctor Who* was perhaps my biggest success – certainly at home,' Faith joked afterwards. 'I have a daughter named Danielle who is a big fan of the series. Well, I've done *The Faith Brown Show*, *The Faith Brown Special*, even *The Faith Brown Series* – but because I've been on *Doctor Who* she now regards me as a star!'

Also appearing as Cryons were **Sarah Greene** (as Varne) and **Sarah Berger** (as Rost). For Sarah Greene, host of the young people's

Above: Faith Brown as Flast, leader of the Cryons, in 'Attack of the Cybermen' (1985).

Opposite: Jason Connery (Jondar) in 'Vengeance on Varos' (1985).

show *Saturday SuperStore*, it was the realisation of a long-standing ambition to act in a *Doctor Who* story. 'I was on holiday in Antigua when the offer came quite literally out of the blue from London,' Sarah explained in a later interview, 'and I agreed straight away without seeing the script. I was so excited.

'On the last day of my holiday I was in the West Indies in the morning and rehearsing in west London in the afternoon. All of us, Faith, Sarah and myself wore masks which fitted very tightly over our heads and had huge lenses for eye sockets. So actually we couldn't hear, we couldn't see and we couldn't even touch because of the enormous fingernails we were wearing! And, though the Cryon women are supposed to live in temperatures below freezing, we made the episode in the middle of a heatwave!'

The other Cryon, Sarah Berger, stepped into her role after the original choice, Koo Stark, the headline-making actress and friend of royalty, had declined the part after a very public disagreement. Sarah, a Royal Shakespeare Company actress, enjoyed her participation so much that she told reporters afterwards, 'Koo missed out on a lot of fun!'

'Vengeance on Varos', Philip Martin's story (February 1985) which introduced a memorable villain in the slug-like Sil (Nabil Shaban), living on a world controlled by the television screen, also featured young **Jason Connery**, son of James Bond star Sean Connery, as Jondar, the leader of a band of rebels fighting the repressive system.

The following story, 'Mark of The Rani'

Below: Eleanor Bron (Kara) in 'Revelation of the Daleks' (1985).

by Pip and Jane Baker (February 1985), introduced a new adversary for the Doctor who may well prove to be as formidable and long-lasting as The Master – another renegade Time Lord and expert scientist, The Rani, played by the beautiful if sometimes sardonic-looking actress **Kate O'Mara**. Though well-known for her roles as *femmes fatales* in movies such as *The Desperados* (1969) and *The Horror of Frankenstein* (1970), and the Hollywood TV soap opera *Dynasty* (in which she played Joan Collins's sister, Caress), Kate is a highly accomplished Shakespearean actress and has appeared in several successful stage and television dramas.

Being cast as The Rani opposite Colin Baker provided a reunion for Kate with the sixth Doctor, because they had previously appeared together in *The Brothers*. 'I had actually been offered a role in *Doctor Who* back in 1970 when Jon Pertwee was the Doctor,' Kate recalls, 'but I took the movie *The Horror of Frankenstein* instead because I needed the money. So I was very glad when John Nathan-Turner gave me a second chance with "Mark of The Rani". I just adored the part as soon as I read the script.'

Kate sees her character as a hard and ruthless megalomaniac who wants to rule the Universe, and though she tries to make her as unpleasant as possible, she still manages to introduce just a few glimmers of humour.

Her undoubted success with viewers of all ages in 'Mark of The Rani' caused John Nathan-Turner to invite Kate back to appear in Sylvester McCoy's opening adventure, 'Time and The Rani', which was again scripted by Pip and Jane Baker (September 1987). Commenting on her second appearance, she said afterwards, 'Colin and Sylvester are very different as actors – Colin rather laid back and Sylvester all movement – and it was a fascinating challenge to work with them both. I think The Rani has now become a bit like a female Moriarty to the Doctor's Sherlock Holmes, and I hope very much for another return to the series.'

The final story of the twenty-second season, 'Revelation of the Daleks' by Eric Saward (March 1985), brought it to a resounding conclusion, with arguably the most impressive array of guest stars ever seen on *Doctor Who*. Ironically, it also heralded the 18-month absence of the programme from television screens ordered by Michael Grade.

In the role of the DJ on the planet Necros where the Daleks were plotting their latest evil scheme was the alternative comic **Alexei Sayle**, who had been such a hit in the series *The Young Ones*. Sayle, a long-time admirer of *Doctor Who*, later suggested in his weekly newspaper column in the *Sunday Mirror* after the announcement of Colin Baker's departure that he should be considered for the role of the seventh Doctor!

William Gaunt, the sorely-pressed father in the sit-com *No Place Like Home*, played Orcini, a hired assassin, who became the Doctor's unlikely ally. **Clive Swift**, another familiar television face and recently a star in the BBC classic serial *The Pickwick Papers*, appeared as Jobel. **Jenny Tomasin**, an ex *Upstairs, Downstairs* star like Jean Marsh, played Tasambeker. And as the Doctor's old friend, Professor Arthur Stengos, was **Alec Linstead**, who had appeared with two of Colin Baker's predecessors: Jon Pertwee in 'The Daemons' (1971), and in Tom Baker's opening adventure, 'Robot' (1974).

Another actor creating a little piece of Whovian history in this season-closer was **Roy Skelton**, who provided the voices of several of the Daleks. By doing so he became the first actor to have worked with all six incarnations of the Doctor – having made his debut in William Hartnell's 'The Tenth Planet', way back in September 1966!

When *Doctor Who* did at last return to the nation's television screens in September 1986, it was in the form of a season of four stories under the generic title 'The Trial of a Time Lord', in which the Doctor was literally on trial for his life (and his audience). To play the Valeyard, who conducted the Doctor's trial before his fellow Time Lords on Gallifrey, the imposing Shakespearean actor **Michael Jayston** was signed for the role.

Michael brought to the series a number of associations with its past. Firstly, he knew all the previous Doctors with the exception of William Hartnell. Secondly, he was particularly friendly with Tom Baker and had co-starred with him in the multi-million-dollar movie *Nicholas and Alexandra* (1971), in which he had played Tsar Nicholas and Baker had been the evil monk Rasputin. Thirdly, he was a fan of the show. 'It's one of those series that actors just love doing,' he confirmed. 'It's an institution, isn't it, a bit like *Coronation Street*? When I was sent the scripts and

invited to play the Valeyard I agreed right away.'

Michael has a particular love of courtroom drama and consequently entered the studio to prosecute the Doctor with considerable relish. 'The thing is, the Valeyard was a man with an obsession – to get the Doctor,' he recalls. 'But clever as he is, the Doctor is his intellectual equal and the only way that he can beat him is by using dirty tricks. I thought the denouement had exactly the right amount of mystery.'

Despite the possibility of the series being ended once and for all at the conclusion of 'The Trial of a Time Lord', Michael Jayston was impressed by all the hard work and dedication that Colin Baker brought to the programme – as well as his sense of humour, which helped everyone through what was an exhausting shooting schedule.

Similar admiration was expressed by three other guest stars who appeared in the quartet of stories which were told within the trial framework. In the first of these, Robert Holmes's 'The Mysterious Planet', the comedy actress and star of numerous *Carry On* films, **Joan Sims**, appeared as the Warrior Queen, Katryca, ruler of a feudal world which the Doctor discovers to be a post-nuclear Earth. 'I dare say many people won't recognise me,' Joan told reporters during filming of the story, 'but dressing up in a bizarre costume and wearing a long red wig was such a wonderful change from what I normally do that I couldn't turn the role down!'

Also appearing in 'The Mysterious Planet' was **Tony Selby**, playing an engaging crook named Glitz who, with his partner, Dibber (Glen Murphy), was trying to steal the Black Light Source from Queen Katryca's tribe. Selby scored such a hit with viewers that producer John Nathan-Turner pencilled him in for a return appearance later that season, with a third engagement once the Doctor had regenerated as Sylvester McCoy in Ian Briggs's story 'Dragonfire' (November–December 1987).

The second story, 'Mindwarp' by Philip Martin, introduced another larger-than-life monarch, King Yrcanos of the planet Thordon, played by the former *Z-Cars* star **Brian Blessed**, whose name had once been linked with the programme as a possible Doctor himself! In August 1983, newspaper stories around the world had announced that Brian was to be the new Doctor to follow Peter Davison. In the forefront of these were the *Daily Express* in England, and the *Sydney Morning Herald* in Australia. Not only did the Sydney newspaper confirm that Brian had got the part, but also *how* he would play it: '. . . noisier and more irascible than recent inhabitants of the role, but with a flashing,

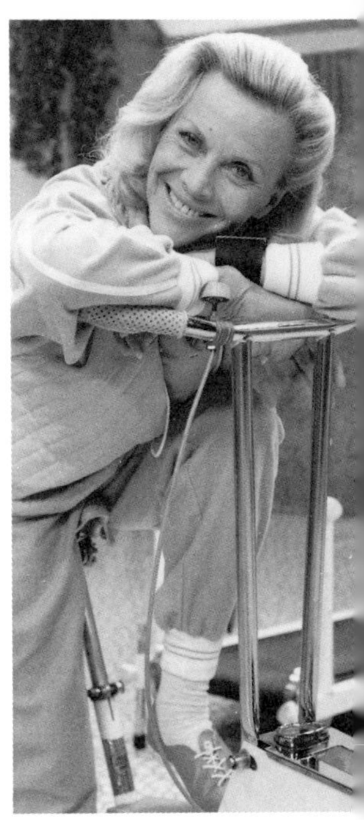

Above top: Joan Sims (Katryca) in 'The Mysterious Planet' (1986).

Above bottom: Honor Blackman as Professor Lasky in 'Terror of the Vervoids' (1986).

warming smile which will surely charm even Daleks away from extermination!'

Brian admitted during the filming of 'Mindwarp' how much he had mischievously enjoyed all these headlines – inaccurate though they were. In fact, he had made a joke about playing the Time Lord while visiting the Doctor Who Exhibition in Blackpool in the summer of 1983, and this had become the core of a rumour which had promptly flown around the world in newsprint.

'Yes, I've been an admirer of *Doctor Who* for years,' admitted Brian, 'but after getting in a rut with Fancy Smith in *Z-Cars* I'm not keen to commit myself to another long-running series. The one-off appearance in "Mindwarp" did fulfil an ambition, though.'

The penultimate adventure of the season, 'Terror of the Vervoids' by Pip and Jane Baker, had **Honor Blackman**, the unforgettable star of *The Avengers* cult TV series from 1960–3, playing the secretive Professor Lasky, an agronomist transporting some sinister alien seed pods on a space liner. 'I now have to accept that the shadow of Cathy Gale of *The Avengers* is always going to be with me, and I have resolved to come to terms with her gracefully,' Honor says. 'But it was a nice change to play someone in *Doctor Who* who wasn't quite so wondrously pure. I like the series, too, and I was very glad when the BBC decided it wasn't going to end. I'm sure it has a lot of life left yet!'

A view that the seventh Doctor, Sylvester McCoy, and all his 'Intergalactic Guest Stars' are now busy doing their best to prove accurate!

Right: Brian Blessed (King Yrcanos) in 'Mindwarp' (1986).

DOCTOR WHO AND THE MERCHANDISERS

NEWS FLASH BY MARX
A
DALEKS
HAVE INVADED TOYSHOPS!
D
B
E
C
A. Battery-operated DALEK with super mystery-action, realistic noise and flashing headlight. Behaves just like the real thing! 6½" tall (Available from Woolworths and Toy Shops). 17/11d.
B. Friction drive DALEK with flashing sparks and realistic noise. A smashing replica standing 6½" tall. 12/11d.
DALEK Construction Kit, for you to make a realistic DALEK of your own. Stands 6½" tall when complete. 6/11d.
C, D, E. DALEK ROLYKIN the miniature DALEK with the built-in movement. Fascinating rolling action! 1/-. DALEK BAGATELLES plenty of excitement in realistic DALEK surroundings. Vertical model 7/6d. Flat model available only from Woolworths 7/11d.
ALL WOULD BE DALEK OWNERS ARE ADVISED TO HURRY TO THEIR LOCAL TOYSHOP NOW!
FABULOUS FUN-FILLED TOYS BY MARX
ORIGINAL MAKERS OF 'DALEK' TOYS
LOUIS MARX & COMPANY LIMITED · SWANSEA · GLAMORGAN

TV CENTURY 21 July 31, 2065

Character merchandising has never been more important to the worlds of film and TV than it is today. Expensive blockbusters such as *Return of the Jedi*, aimed at teenage and sub-teenage audiences, devise their budgets around the huge estimated returns from products based on characters and hardware conceived for the film. Conversely, at the other end of the scale, films orientated for older age groups, including even sci-fi giants such as *Aliens*, are required to prune their budgets, in the knowledge that they cannot hope to recoup money from the sale of toys, model kits and games, simply because the vast bulk of the toy- and memorabilia-buying age group will never see that film because of its censorship rating.

The same applies to television, although rarely are the production costs of a show dependent on selling its merchandise rights. Of late, however, a tendency has emerged for enterprising toy manufacturers to produce children's TV shows – for example *He-Man and the Masters of the Universe*, based entirely around a range of toys the company intends to market, thereby transforming the actual programmes into little more than free half-hour commercials for the products. But to date, this practice is still the exception rather than the rule.

Although seldom recognised as such, *Doctor Who* was one of the pioneer programmes of TV character merchandising in this country, says **Jeremy Bentham**, an expert on the show. This is a reluctantly admitted accolade only recently acknowledged by a corporation at the time almost embarrassed at having to deal with the economic realities of the supply and demand retail industry.

ITV, in the form of its many subsidiaries and bodies of independent production groups, had, of course, been on the bandwagon for years; well, since 1956 anyway. Learning much of their craft from their US role models, the commercial companies either handled their own merchandise and publications directly, or made use of established publishing outlets and manufacturers by issuing glossy character marketing brochures inviting tenders for products based on shows such as *No Hiding Place*, *Thank Your Lucky Stars* and even *Sunday Night at the London Palladium* (yes, there really was a 'Beat the Clock' board game).

Right from the start, children's television was the front runner in the granting of licences. Much as your grandmother might have liked Richard Greene in *The Adventures of Robin Hood*, she was unlikely to have rushed out and bought a stand-up plastic figure of him. But to an impressionable six-year-old, pilot Mike Mercury in *Supercar* was a different matter. Youngsters growing up in the 'sixties, even the early 'sixties before the 'pop explosion' heralded by The Beatles, had a degree of spending power, in the form of pocket money from parents at last beginning to taste affluence after a decade of post-war austerity.

Independent producer Gerry Anderson always kept a finger firmly on the pulse of character merchandising. Even with his formative shows, such as *Torchy* and *Four Feather Falls*, he saw the revenue from inexpensive glove puppets and children's games as useful funding towards his future projects – projects that ultimately became *Thunderbirds* and *Captain Scarlet*.

What essentially helped to keep the price of these items down to a level affordable by children with just pocket-money incomes was Britain's connection with Hong Kong. At the dawn of the 1960s Hong Kong enjoyed dominion status and was a member of the Commonwealth, but it was still, effectively, a crown colony with a low standard of living. That meant that entrepreneurs opening factories in Hong Kong could get away with paying near pittance wages to an inexhaustible supply of cheap labour, thus enabling them to undercut British manufacturing costs and supply items to the UK for less. With no trade restrictions on Hong Kong imports, merchandise licence-holders in Britain found it cheaper to go over there for the actual manufacturing of their goods. And the lower the production costs, the lower the shop retail price could be.

Before *Doctor Who*, the BBC saw no real need to dabble in the field of product merchandising. They saw themselves as vested with the divine right to broadcast, and consequently their output was peculiarly devoid of shows aimed at teenagers and those in the halfway-house sub-teenage bracket. 'Children's Hour' was in existence, but above that it was almost as if Corporation chiefs wanted viewers to jump straight from childhood to adulthood with as little time as possible spent in the then socially stigmatic condition of being a teenager.

Children's TV, however, had generated a demand for character merchandising, with 'personality-based toys' such as Captain Pugwash, Pinky and Perky, Muffin the Mule and Andy Pandy keenly sought after by parents to give as Christmas or birthday presents. With no merchandising arm of its own (BBC Enterprises existed solely to sell programmes to overseas broadcasters), the BBC was quite happy to allow New Zealand-born entrepreneur Walter Tuckwell to handle the selling of their products.

Tuckwell, a keen businessman with a wide knowledge of the toy business, along with his partner Peter Barker, regularly agreed contracts with the BBC allowing them exclusive marketing rights on characters in return for five per cent of the wholesale price payable to the BBC. Up until 1964, the 'Sooty' glove puppet was the highest-selling BBC-based product with children, although ironically, Tuckwell had already begun to harvest profits from the sub-teenage spending bracket by signing up rights to *Dixon of Dock Green*, when *Doctor Who*'s Daleks came on to the scene.

Tuckwell recognised a winner instantly with the Daleks. Technology was on the march, and all forms of gadgetry were appealing to the young and to the young-at-heart. And the Daleks were perfect gadgets, with their flashing lid-lights, rotatable heads, extendable suction-cup arms, firing weaponry and grating voices. How could they fail?

THRILLS GALORE!
FULL SIZE REAL LIFE
DALEK
Playsuit
FROM THE BBC tv SERIAL 'DR WHO'
ONLY 66/6
AT 9/6 MONTHLY
A MARSHALL WARD 'BEST BUY'
Send No Money for 7 days free trial of this true-to-life Dalek suit. Excitement all day long as your child plays 'Dr. Who and the Daleks'. Completely safe, sturdily made. Including realistic sucker arm and gun.
Colour: Red/White/Silver. Height: 3' 11". Diameter at dome 15½".
After Free Approval, 7 monthly payments of **9/6. Total 66/6.** Credit over 21 in U.K. (ex. N.I.). Send for **FREE** Autumn Catalogue, that contains everything for the home and family, all items on easy credit terms.
MARSHALL WARD LTD
DEPT. F 52, BRIDGEWATER PLACE, MANCHESTER, X.

Eagerly Tuckwell phoned his contacts at the BBC, only to be told, 'Forget it. *Doctor Who* is going to finish them off after six episodes and then he is off to China with Marco Polo.' That might well have been the end of the matter had it not been for the groundswell of enthusiasm generated by the Daleks in every playground and classroom in Britain. 'Daleks Dead but won't Lie Down' screamed a

headline in the *Daily Mail*, quickly alive to the tremendous interest these robots were causing. A trickle soon became a flood of letters to the *Doctor Who* office, all asking, 'Where are the Daleks?', 'When are the Daleks coming back?', 'What is the next story with them in?'

Initially, Producer Verity Lambert spoke the truth when she replied, via the newspapers, that there were no plans to bring them back. And as if to prove her words, two of the Dalek machines were given saturation publicity when they were handed over as gifts to the orphaned children of the Doctor Barnardo's Home in Essex. But as BBC department chiefs, delighted with the ratings

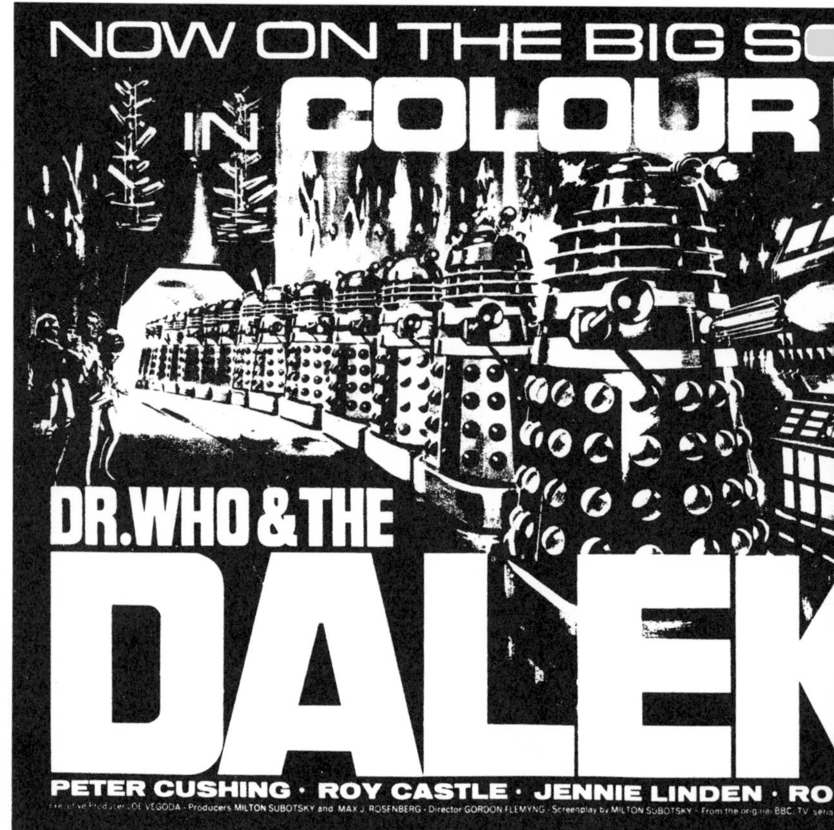

and all the publicity, renewed *Doctor Who*'s contract for a second year, it became inevitable that a Dalek sequel would be done.

Trying again some months later, Walter Tuckwell received a more favourable response, and by early summer had signed a contract allowing him exclusive merchandising rights on all Dalek toys and games. The contract was radically different to those he had signed before in that, not only did the BBC collect five per cent, but so too did Terry Nation, with a further ten per cent going to Nation's agent, the instigator of this 'new deal' for the writer/creator of the monsters. Thereafter the race was on to get Dalek toys and products into the shops in time for Christmas 1964, which also just happened to be the time during which 'The Dalek Invasion of Earth' sequel would be on television!

Tuckwell and Barker worked overtime persuading toy companies, publishing houses and souvenir manufacturers that 1964 and 1965 would be the years of the Daleks. They even produced their own glossy sales brochure with illustrations showing Daleks from every angle, drawn by artist Richard Jennings based on what few photographs the BBC had in stock. All of these photographs came originally from designer Raymond Cusick, who took them during rehearsals for the first TV Dalek serial. As a result, the rehearsal 'extras' – reels of coloured tape stuck into the waist bands, scrawled numbers on the Dalek lids to identify their operators – were clearly visible, leading Jennings to interpret them, respectively, as speaker grills and Dalek recognition symbols. For this reason, Daleks in the early comic strips frequently sported speaker panels and lettering on their lids!

Companies who bought options from Tuckwell and Co. had to rush designs and costings through to their factories in Hong Kong, with time of the essence to capture the looming, but very lucrative, Christmas shopping period.

The plastics industry found problems with the shape of the Daleks. Because of the many sharp angles, features and facets on the casing, a standard two-piece injection mould was out of the question if they wanted an accurate reproduction. The only way to achieve this would be through a series of multiple-part moulds to produce different sections of the body for later assembly by factory workers, a process costly in the extreme as steel moulds, even at Hong Kong rates, were not cheap to cast.

So the manufacturers compromised. The Dalek shape was simplified and streamlined from Cusick's original design to make moulding and the subsequent removal of parts from those moulds easier. This is the sole reason why, with the exception of the vacuum-formed self-assembly 'Sevans' Daleks, no Dalek toy in the 'sixties, 'seventies or 'eighties ever managed accuracy to the version seen on television in the *Doctor Who* series.

The winner of the race to get a Dalek toy into the shops was the Welsh-based Louis Marx company with their silver-grey, six-inch tall, battery-operated 'mystery action' toy which retailed at 17/11d (about 90p). Sales were phenomenal. The first shipload from Hong Kong completely sold out nationwide in under a fortnight. So did the next batch, and the next batch after that. Even Hamleys, the largest toyshop in the world in 1964, gave up trying to cope with irate parents demanding Daleks, and started issuing Dalek photographs instead, backed with gift vouchers, which shoppers could redeem for Dalek toys when eventually stocks were available – which for some items was not until the New Year.

The Marx company was ecstatic with its success, although the massive demand meant staff working round the clock to process and distribute orders. The resulting prosperity from such record sales enabled Marx to expand their manufacturing ability and to buy a five-floor factory in Hong Kong, which was instantly turned over, not surprisingly, to the making of more Dalek toys. The grey 'tricky-action' Dalek was followed by a black-liveried version (the concept of a Black Dalek Supreme having been introduced in 'The Dalek Invasion of Earth') and thence by assorted friction-drive Daleks, Dalek bagatelles, Dalek construction kits (unassembled versions of the 'tricky-action' model without any internal mechanics) and even little miniature 'Rolykin' Daleks – one-inch high toys that rolled along on a metal ball-bearing, costing just one shilling (5p) each. These tiny Daleks, easily within any child's budget, contributed a further round of record sales to Marx, with more than a million being sold in under six months. Alan Morris, Marx's Marketing Director, summed it up best: 'People have just gone Dalek mad.'

Marx, of course, was not the only company leasing rights from Alan Tuckwell. There were push-along Daleks from Herts Plastic Moulders (who were based in England), Dalek sweet-cigarette cards from Cadet Sweets, 'Tempo' cowboy-sized Daleks from Cherilea Toys, Dalek paint-by-number sets from Peter Pan Toys, a whole range of Dalek jigsaws from Woolworths, and even a Dalek nursery toy from Selcol Ltd: a soft-edged polythene toy aimed at toddlers who might otherwise break a battery toy or swallow a 'Rolykin', although what the thinking was behind a toy for children not even old enough to watch *Doctor Who* it is difficult to imagine.

Most of the items generated during the 'Dalekmania' boom between 1964 and 1966 were reputable in origin, but there were a few that could be classed under the heading of blatant rip-off. A classic case was the 'Anti-Dalek Rocket Gun' from Lone Star Toys. Basically a spring-loaded sucker-dart gun, this toy was released first in 1962 as Steve Zodiac's ray gun from *Fireball XL5*. With no change to the product whatsoever, it was re-released in 1965, only this time bearing a Dalek logo on its packaging. Even more eyebrow-raising was the 'Anti-Dalek Fluid Neutraliser', a toy with an even older parentage, known to less pretentious generations as a common or garden water pistol!

Another area where quality gave way to quantity was records. In 1965 a hastily assembled band of session musicians released a single called *Landing of the Daleks*, which was almost immediately banned by every radio station in Britain for illegally using the Morse code for 'S.O.S.' on the soundtrack. It was released again minus the offending signals, but thankfully it died an equally ignominious death. Another candidate for execution ought to have been the record released by Polydor Records called *Who's Who*, which was sung by Roberta Tovey (Susan in the two 'Amicus' Dalek films) in a Shirley Temple voice, with 'Glee Club' backing to match.

However, bad though both of these offerings undoubtedly were, neither plumbed the depths of musical misery inflicted by The Go-Gos on their December 1964 novelty disc, *I'm Going to Spend my Christmas with a Dalek*. With a picture sleeve depicting a Dalek photograph clumsily pasted into a shot of the group, the record began:

'I'm going to spend my Christmas with a Dalek,
And hang him underneath the mistletoe.

And if he's very nice,
I'll feed him sugar spice,
And hang a Christmas stocking from his big left toe'

. . . and went rapidly downhill from thereon, sung in tones akin to Beryl Reid's notorious *All I Want for Christmas is my Two Front Teeth* and accompanied by the worst attempt at a Dalek voice imaginable. It was not a hit.

Only one Dalek record was truly worth placing on a collector's shelf, and that was the 1965-released Century 21 EP entitled simply *The Daleks*. Running twenty minutes in total, the disc was a rearrangement of the soundtrack from episode six of 'The Chase' (the third TV Dalek story). Punctuated by voice-over narration to explain the more visual scenes, the record featured William Hartnell, William Russell, Jacqueline Hill, Maureen O'Brien, Peter Purves, the Daleks (Peter Hawkins and David Graham) and the Mechonoids (David Graham). Coming out in an era still more than ten years away from the launch of domestic video recorders, it was a valuable memento of one of *Doctor Who*'s classic episodes.

Not all the tales of Dalek merchandising in the 'sixties had happy endings. The Northants-based firm of Scorpion Automotives seemed to have the biggest winner of all on their hands when they unveiled their five-foot Dalek playsuit just in time for Christmas 1964. Constructed in hardboard with a vinyl skirt, a metal hooped base, an extendable plastic arm and a battery-operated light/buzzer gun, the playsuit, in a box cunningly resembling a police box, sold for nearly £9, a princely sum in 1964, reflecting the quality and the cost of its workmanship. Nevertheless, despite this daunting price, every playsuit was sold by Christmas Day, promising high hopes for the company in 1965.

But in April of that year a disastrous fire gutted the factory, destroying all the tools and components needed to make the playsuits. Insurance money paid for the factory refurbishing, and the firm continued for several years thereafter importing a range of inflatable Dalek punching bags and a simplified 'kiddies' playsuit, but they were never able to recoup funds sufficient to restart manufacture of the big suits, which remain today one of the most sought-after Dalek collectables.

Amidst this glut of Dalek items, onlookers could be forgiven for wondering about the rest of *Doctor Who*. Was there merchandising life beyond the Daleks? To begin with, not much. Indeed, the very first non-Dalek product to catch the eyes of collectors was not even truly a *Doctor Who* toy.

Some years earlier, Dinky Toys, the internationally famed makers of die-cast metal cars, had produced a gift set containing one red GPO phone kiosk and a blue police public call box, both to scale with their model cars. Ironically, Dinky Toys were just in the process of phasing this gift set out when *Doctor Who* arrived, although eagle-eyed fans of the series were still able to pick one up at toy shops even years later.

More obviously a TARDIS was the Plaston rigid polythene money-box released in 1965 with a photograph of William Hartnell's Doctor on the packaging. This photograph had to be there to satisfy the BBC, who were unhappy at first with the firm's insistence that they didn't need to pay copyright on the shape of a police box, which was hardly a BBC design. For years thereafter sharp-moving companies were able to market china money-boxes, bubble-bath containers, etc. without any payment at all to the Corporation, provided they did not mention the words 'Doctor Who' or 'TARDIS'. This practice finally ceased only in 1983 when BBC Enterprises paid a sum to the Metropolitan Police Force to secure exclusive rights to the police-box design.

One major *Doctor Who* product that didn't rely totally on the Daleks was the Give-a-Show projector set from Chad Valley Toys that actually gave top billing to William Hartnell, for a change. A handsomely presented toy, it comprised a rudimentary projector through which card-mounted acetate artwork slides could be moved. Each slide depicted part of a story, the idea being to move the slides through the projector, one at a time, and narrate the story on the slides to an enthralled audience. At 29/11d (nearly £1.50p) it was an expensive toy for its day, but good value for young *Doctor Who* fans. Not only did the slides feature the Doctor and the Daleks, but also Ian and Barbara, the Voord, the Sensorites, the Menoptra and the Zarbi.

Bill Strutton's giant ant-like Zarbi never really took off with merchandisers, despite hefty promotion by the BBC. Their appearance in the Give-a-Show projector set was one of only two entries into the toy field, the other being as part of a badge set in 3-D moulded plastic. Those aside, the only other appearances of the Zarbi were in books and comic strips, responsibility for which lay with BBC Publications.

Well established long before *Doctor Who*'s whirlwind birth, BBC Publications were known to demand high standards from all would-be licensees, with the result that nearly all of *Doctor Who*'s ventures into the literary media have been notable for their quality and

faithfulness to the series. Grey areas such as colouring books and join-up-the-dots type publications tended to be farmed out to Tuckwell's team, but everything else, from the *TV Comic* and *TV 21* comic strips, through the many Dalek and *Doctor Who* annuals, to the original serial novelisations in hardback, came under the aegis of BBC Publications in those early days.

Later, in the mid 'sixties, as the BBC woke up to the revenue it was losing letting others act as its agents and established BBC Merchandising as a division of BBC Enterprises, comic strips crossed over to come under the wing of Merchandising. The rules, however, stayed the same, and the prime rule was to allow only one licence per product. This meant that if someone approached the BBC to sell, for instance, *Doctor Who* sweet-cigarette cards, and the BBC approved the product, then that person would get the *sole* licence to sell *Doctor Who* sweet-cigarette cards. No one else was allowed to market a rival set of cards until that original manufacturer elected not to renew his licence.

The likenesses of the Doctor (in whichever body) and the TARDIS are the basic commodities for which a licensee applies. If a company then decides it wants to merchandise a monster, or even one of the regular characters or companions, then very often a separate clause in the contract has to be negotiated with the writer who created that monster, regular character or companion.

This happened with the Mechonoids, the large, spherical, fire-blasting robots that Terry Nation wrote into the last episodes of 'The Chase'. 'The Mechonoids will be as big as the Daleks', promised Nation's agent to Walter Tuckwell, who accordingly invited tenders from the many licensed Dalek manufacturers he had on his books. There were some takers, notably Cherilea, Herts Plastic Moulders and the publishers of the *TV 21* Dalek comic strip, from which the best product to emerge was a seven-inch tall, push-along Mechonoid, complete with fold-out arms and swivelling flame gun.

However, 'Mechonoidmania' was not to be. As always, Raymond Cusick had come up with a stunning design for the Mechonoids, and the ensuing press hype for their launch, photographed in their city with flame guns ablaze, did foster a lot of interest. But the problem with the Mechonoids was the limited size of the BBC studios in which *Doctor Who* was recorded in those days. Whereas a Dalek occupied scarcely more space than William Hartnell in a cape, a Mechonoid was enormous, almost the size of a small car. To get all three robots into the tiny studios at Lime Grove, and have room for other actors, sets and the cameras, was a near impossibility. Despite a magnetic appeal to children, their first appearance was decreed their last, and the casings were junked shortly after 'The Chase' was completed.

'Dalekmania' tailed off during 1966 as fad interest in gadgetry moved on to embrace Batman's 'Batmobile', *Man From U.N.C.L.E.* spy pens and the many *Thunderbirds* vehicles. A big nail in the coffin was a feature

25 GLORIOUS YEARS

in *The Observer Colour Supplement* over Christmas 1966, which showed a photograph of two Daleks with their 'lids' off. There, for all the world to see, was the truth: no intricate electronics, no dazzling arrays of mechanical wizardry, not even a pulsating, alien monstrosity once described as 'too horrific to picture'. Just two rather bored actors smoking cigarettes in between rehearsals for 'Power of the Daleks'.

That Dalek story launched Patrick Troughton's era as the Doctor, an era notable for generating very little in the way of *Doctor Who* merchandise, mostly at the request of Troughton himself, who didn't want to tempt the spectre of typecasting by getting too closely identified with the part.

The comic strip and the children's Christmas annuals continued along their merry way, but apart from these, the only Troughton merchandised item of note was a series of sweet-cigarette-sized trading cards given away free, one with every purchase of 'Sky Ray' ice lollies.

Kit Pedler and Gerry Davis tried to interest manufacturers in toy Cybermats, so too did Mervyn Haisman and Henry Lincoln with their Quark robots, but all to no avail. Frazer Hines, popular as Jamie in the series, tried his hand as a pop singer, recording a single in 1968 called *Who is Doctor Who*, but, like other 'sixties attempts to commit *Doctor Who* to the music industry, it was no better than its title suggests, hardly even meriting air-play on Ed Stewart's *Junior Choice* on Radio 1. Effectively, *Doctor Who* merchandising was dead until the early 'seventies.

The all-new, all-colour, action-based programmes starring Jon Pertwee revitalised public interest in *Doctor Who*. Unlike his predecessor, Jon Pertwee was very keen to get his face known as the Doctor and keenly sought every opportunity to do so.

An early, though unlikely, taker was Kellogg's Sugar Smacks breakfast cereal. Their 1966 campaign promoting *Daleks – Invasion Earth 2150 AD* film had boosted sales markedly, so in 1971 they tried again, using Jon Pertwee's likeness. For their money, punters were given free with every box a metal lapel badge depicting either the Doctor, the Brigadier, Jo Grant, The Master, 'Bessie' or the UNIT emblem. Plans were discussed with BBC Enterprises for a second promotion, offering, in exchange for several packet tops and a postal order, self-assembly model kits of the 'Bessie' car, but these came to nought, presumably due to the high capital costs involved in the kit's manufacture. By 1972 Hong Kong was no longer the centre of cheap manufacturing it had been, a fact that was to lead to the overall collapse of the toy industry in Britain during the next decade.

Another failed 'first' was the 1972 *Doctor Who* wall poster. Brought out at the height of 'poster-mania' in the early 'seventies, this full-colour item was a photographic blow-up of a scene from 'Colony in Space', showing the Doctor menaced by a giant claw. In a rare move, Jon Pertwee himself asked for the poster to be withdrawn because it showed the Doctor with an expression of fear on his face – a quality he felt was wrong in identifying his character. BBC Enterprises

agreed, and the poster was banned from sale shortly afterwards.

By the time Jon Pertwee gave way to Tom Baker, *Doctor Who* merchandising was into a new phase of ascendancy. Games and jigsaws were selling well, so too were comics, special publications and even novelisations of the serials in paperback form from Target Books. The Daleks, too, came back in vogue with 'Genesis of the Daleks' sparking off the serialisation of a new Terry Nation Dalek storyline in the *London Evening News*, a talking Dalek from Palitoy, and the reappearance, after nearly ten years, of the *Dalek Annual* in time for Christmas 1975.

Tom Baker's phenomenal popularity as the Doctor fostered many products and promotions. His face, along with other characters from the series, helped to sell Weetabix breakfast serial (in 1977 as well as 1975), Ty-Phoo tea and Nestlés milk chocolate bars, as well as two poster magazines and whole sets of birthday cards, playing cards, jigsaws, badges, note-pads and, surprise surprise, an 'official' *Doctor Who* woollen scarf from Today Promotions, available in long or extra long versions.

The last flurries from Britain's dying home-grown toy industry produced a superb set of Action Man scaled figures featuring the Giant Robot, a Cyberman, a Dalek, the TARDIS, K9, Tom Baker's Doctor and Leela, all faithful to their TV counterparts, except that Louise Jameson later admitted lying about her chest measurement to the Denys Fisher company. The K9 doll produced by Denys Fisher in 1978 was later complemented by a larger, even more detailed talking version from Palitoy in 1979, complete with an interchangeable voice disc recorded by John Leeson.

By the turn of the 'eighties, however, toy production in Britain had become a dying art. Apart from publications and jigsaws, the only items from major manufacturers during the Peter Davison era were a TARDIS play-tent in soft vinyl from Dekker Ltd and a set of Viewmaster reels from the GAF corporation of Davison's opening story, 'Castrovalva'.

Yet even as foreign-dominated toy companies deserted *Doctor Who* in the 'eighties, so their places were taken by smaller arts and crafts businesses, many of them founded by people who had begun as fans of the TV series: photographs from John McElroy's 'Whomobilia', videoed interviews with *Doctor Who* stars from Keith Barnfather's Reeltime Pictures, construction kits from Stuart Evans and promotional goods from sweatshirts to enamelled badges from Ron Katz's Doctor Who Fan Club of America.

Indeed, it almost looks as though the impetus for future *Doctor Who* products will come more from the USA than from the UK. Having witnessed the country take the series so much to its heart, American businessmen are acutely aware of the marketing potential offered by a show sold to more than 200 Public Broadcasting Service stations nationwide. And if a big deal is struck with just one of the massive toy giants operating globally, the royalties to the BBC could well surpass the entire production costs of a *Doctor Who* series – conclusive proof that nothing succeeds like excess.

THE DOCTOR IN THE COMICS

'In the year 2003, all was peaceful on Skaro. Then the Daleks discovered pure cobalt in the mountains which became known as The Radiation Range. From this precious ore the Daleks were able to manufacture a mighty Neutron Bomb. In the remote region of Darren, the Daleks perfected their terrible weapon until War Minister Zolfian was satisfied . . .' So began one of the finest illustrated sagas ever to grace the pages of a British comic, claims **Jeremy Bentham**. The strip was entitled simply 'The Daleks' and was a regular single-page feature for two years in a pioneering children's paper called *TV 21*.

As the name suggests, *TV 21* was all about television, and specifically about the television series and serials most watched by children in the mid 1960s: programmes such as *Stingray*, *My Favourite Martian*, *The Munsters*, *Fireball XL5* and later, of course, *Thunderbirds*. But unlike other comics of its day, *TV 21* did not talk down to its readership, nor did it attempt to simplify storylines and feature articles just to cater for younger children. As with *The Eagle* and *Look and Learn*, *TV 21* was pitched directly at the older comic-buying age group.

In its first few years of life, *TV 21* was phenomenally successful. Under the editorship of Alan Fennell, the magazine not only achieved its target readership but went on to capture readers above and below their anticipated thresholds until, at its peak, *TV 21* was selling more than a million copies each week.

There are many reasons behind such record sales. Partly, *TV 21* rode a wave of being the right product at the right time. The technology-obsessed 'sixties was producing a whole generation of very technically aware children whose closest proximity to the bright worlds of the future, promised by researchers and politicians alike, were the super-science TV shows of Gerry Anderson. *TV 21* was an offshoot of Anderson's spreading commercial empire, and so a good 60 per cent of the comic's content was devoted entirely to publicising the many puppet series he had been making since 1960.

Artistically, *TV 21* was also streets ahead of anything else on the market, including the slick *Marvel* and *DC* comic book outpourings from America. Each issue was laid out by skilled Fleet Street designers and printed on glossy paper using the most expensive colour printing process of the time, photogravure. The magazine employed artists whose names are now legendary among the profession – names such as Roland Turner, Mike Noble, Richard Jennings and the late, great Franks, Bellamy and Hampson. It also broke with tradition by commissioning story scripts from writers outside the somewhat closed-shop environment of comic publishing, which was how *Doctor Who* Script Editor David Whitaker came to work for *TV 21*.

With a projected launch date of January 1965, *TV 21* went into its planning stages during the summer and autumn of 1964, just in time to be present at the onrush of 'Dalekmania'. *TV 21* was going to be all about gadgetry and super-science, and so what better example of both than Terry Nation's

Daleks, reasoned Fennell and his publishers, City Magazines. Naturally, as creator of the Daleks, Nation was accorded first refusal to write the strip, but declined due to pressure of other work, recommending instead the man with whom he had worked so closely in developing their narrative roots, David Whitaker.

If anything, Whitaker's imagination had been more fired by the concept of the Daleks than had Nation's, and he jumped at the opportunity to expand and visualise their mythology, unfettered by *Doctor Who*'s TV budgetary constraints. Using Nation's original Dalek TV script as source reference, Whitaker's first script for *TV 21* was a three-part serial showing how the Daleks came into being: literally 'Genesis of the Daleks', some twenty years in advance of the TV counterpart.

In association with artist Richard Jennings, Whitaker portrayed the Daleks as a race of short, blue-skinned humanoids (not unlike Dan Dare's infamous Mekon), tremendously skilled in the fields of science and engineering, but politically dominated by war-hungry rulers anxious to stamp out Skaro's other indigenous race, the Thals. Urged on by War Minister Zolfian, two types of weapon were developed by Chief Scientist Yarvelling for the impending war. Firstly, a stockpile of neutron bombs, powerful thermonuclear devices that would kill as much from the release of deadly radiation as from the blast itself. Secondly, conical-shaped robot fighting machines that would enter the Thal cities and other war zones after the holocaust and exterminate any survivors.

But then disaster struck. A rogue storm of fiery meteorites rained down on the factories housing the nuclear stockpile. Fires began, fires which quickly merged to form a raging inferno. Protective shielding melted, circuits fused and blew, and then – catastrophe! The combined explosion of the Daleks' entire nuclear arsenal almost destroyed the planet, and for years nothing moved on the surface of this decimated world. But not everything had perished. Both Zolfian and Yarvelling emerged relatively unharmed from a shelter, only to face a worse danger. Other, less well protected survivors were facing a crippling radiation sickness which attacked, mutated and atrophied its victims. Desperately seeking armour to ward off the poisoned air, these survivors had adapted Yarvelling's robot fighting machines into shielded casings to house their rotting bodies.

Encountering this new race of mechanised Daleks, Zolfian perceives them as the key to achieving all his ambitions, maybe even mastery of the Universe itself. The bodies of these survivors may be withered, but the radiation-triggered process of mutation has greatly enlarged their brains. Working against time, he and Yarvelling strive to rebuild a war factory capable of providing these creatures with power and movement. One Dalek is chosen to be Emperor of this new species, and is given a special gold casing to match his rank. As the last of the old Daleks dies, the new Emperor avows, 'We need more machines, but there are enough here to form an invasion force. We will attack and enslave

The DALEKS
THE DALEKS TAKE FLIGHT IN AN EFFORT TO THWART THE DANGER POSED TO SKARO BY THE ROGUE PLANET.
SOME TIME LATER.
DALEADER TO SKARO. WE ARE ON COURSE TOWARDS THE NEW PLANET SKARDAL.
ALTER COURSE. CIRCLE AROUND APPROACHING METEORITES IN WEST TO SOUTH WEST.
ALL SHIPS HAVE BEEN FITTED WITH MAGRAY ULTIMATE. I HAVE ORDERED THAT IT IS TO BE FIRED AT EACH METEORITE, THUS FILLING IT WITH MAGNETIC POWER.
INCREASE ANTI-MAGS BY TEN DETS, OR WE WILL BE DRAWN ALONG AFTER THE METEORITES.
THE METEORITES WILL DRAW OFF THE NEW PLANET BUT THAT IS NOT ALL...
SKARO
SKARDAL
NOT ONLY HAVE WE TURNED THIS THREAT AWAY BUT WE HAVE USED IT AS A WEAPON OF DESTRUCTION.
THE NEW PLANET IS HEADING DIRECTLY TOWARDS OUR ENEMIES, THE MECHANOIDS. IT WILL EITHER DESTROY THEIR PLANET... OR WEAKEN THEM. DALEKS! PREPARE FOR WAR!
WAR... THE INEVITABLE OUTCOME OF THE DALEKS' POLICY. THE CHANCE TO DESTROY THE MECHANOIDS HAS PROVED TOO GREAT A TEMPTATION TO RESIST.
TO BE CONTINUED.

workers. They will obey or die.'

'The first Emperor had spoken. His word was law', read the closing caption. And Whitaker's words, too, were lore for the million plus readers who, each week, eagerly snapped up the unfolding saga of the Daleks' rise to power.

Whitaker structured his storylines very well. In the early stories the Daleks are lacking in certain technological areas and are shown gradually making those key discoveries that ultimately, in later issues, lift them out into the skies to begin their universal programme of conquest.

Heavily involved with the second TV Dalek story, 'The Dalek Invasion of Earth', Whitaker was not slow to integrate concepts from that serial into his saga. The Emperor gained a second-in-command in the form of the Black Dalek, and the Daleks' vehicles for space travel were affirmed as flying saucers although, thanks to Richard Jennings's richly textured illustrations, the Dalek saucers were less like upturned cake tins and more reminiscent of the gleaming craft seen in the 'fifties movie, *The Day the Earth Stood Still.*

Jennings and Whitaker also overcame the Daleks' principal failing – freedom of movement over rough terrain – by devising a range of one-rider flying platforms called Hoverbouts, or 'Trans-solar Discs', which were then widely adopted by artists producing illustrations for Dalek-based products (jigsaws, box-tops etc.), but which never made the transition back into the *Doctor Who* TV series as a counter to all those many jokes about staircases defeating would-be Dalek invaders.

Perhaps the cleverest aspect of Whitaker's writing was the curious morality slant he adopted towards his mechanised conquerors. The Daleks were, after all, basically villains, so to have shown them, week after week, attaining their goals of slavery and slaughter would have brought the feature up against the comic strip code of publishing which had been in existence in this country since the government ban on the 'E.C.' horror comics of the 'fifties.

So a balance was struck. Whenever the Daleks fought humanoid species with identifiable qualities of nobility, self-sacrifice, humanity, etc., they would lose – often defeated by just those 'human factor' traits that the Daleks could not understand. Often an intimation was made that if they wanted to, the Daleks could go back *en masse* and annihilate those who had successfully defeated them, but always a loophole was provided in the script as to why they should not.

The other avenue was to make the Daleks' opponents even nastier than they themselves. Placed on the defensive in such situations, Whitaker felt confident enough to give unrestricted vent to the Daleks' intuitive, but ruthless genius for war. The Monstrons, with their strange, protuberant bodies, suffered the full wrath of Dalek vengeance when they tried to conquer Skaro, and so, too, did the slave-trading Krattorians and the all-robot Mechonoids.

Richard Jennings handed over the illustration side of the comic strip after its first

WIN A REAL DALEK!!!

TV CENTURY 21

7D

ADVENTURE IN THE 21st CENTURY

No. 28 UNIVERSE EDITION

EVERY WEDNESDAY

DATELINE: July 31, 2065

DR. WHO and the DALEKS

Peter Cushing and Roberta Tovey are captured by the Daleks.

PEACEFUL THALS AMBUSHED!

DALEKS! DALEKS! TO BE WON!

"FOLLOWING attempts to make peace with the Daleks, the Thals have been viciously ambushed and a fierce battle is still being fought."

This was the first frightening news of the Daleks to it the Universe some eighteen months ago on B.B.C. elevision.

Now the exciting film, "Dr. Who and the Daleks" is on e cinema screen in glorious Technicolour. You can see at your local cinema soon.

SOLTURIAN NEWS AGENCY FLASH:—

Prince Jareth has been called in by Mirva to investigate another prophesy of Lurr. It is still not certain whether Lurr is continuing his opposition to the Daleks, or whether this new look into the future is concerned with other events.

(Full story page 20)

CORGI MODEL CLUB NEWS – EVERY WEEK PAGE 19

STOP PRESS

LONDON ANT BATTLE

Reports are coming in of fierce street fighting in the streets of London as European troops struggle to overcome massed armies of giant ants.

GHOST GALLEON SIGHTED!

Excited radio message from Lt. Phonés Sheridan of the W. A. S. P. vessel Stingray reports sighting a ghostly galleon nearing tracking station 17.

ACTOR SHOT

Actor 'Lord' Nelson was shot on the stage of the theatre during a performance of the play 'This Gun for Death'.
Captain Amos Burke is investigating.

year, taking with him his distinctive style of Dalek speech bubble lettering, whereby all the letters were squared off to give a visual impression of the harsh grating sounds heard on TV. Thus, *O*s became diamond shaped and *Z*s rather like liquid-crystal *2*s. His successors, Messrs Noble and Turner, branched away from the rigid, almost art-deco, style that Jennings had practised, and under their respective aegis, Dalek hardware and architecture became even more fanciful and grandly scaled.

The Dalek/Mechonoid war (or rather non-war, as the underlying plot rotated around keeping these two super-protagonists apart) took up six months' worth of the saga before Whitaker chose to drop the subject and leave unresolved the question of which race was the more powerful. He turned his attention instead towards developing the more fundamental paranoias of the Daleks: their inability to crush the 'human spirit', and their goal to track down the source of this incomprehensible creed.

In a turning point for the strip, Whitaker wrote a ten-part storyline showing the revival of three blue-skinned, humanoid Daleks, who had been accidentally placed in suspended animation when the neutron bombs exploded. A team of research scientists, one of their number had discovered a distant, blue-green planet, many systems from Skaro, just before the cataclysm.

Observing how ruthless and without conscience their Dalek descendants have become, the senior researcher, Lodian, predicts nothing but tragedy if ever the half-robots discover the location of this planet. For a time it looks as though one of the other scientists will betray this information to the Daleks, but choosing death before betrayal, Lodian sacrifices himself in a controlled explosion to destroy the research station and its findings. However, the Daleks are not left totally empty-handed. They have learned the name of their sought-after world – Earth.

Throughout the latter half of 1966, Whitaker kept his readers in suspense as more and more encounters with the 'human spirit' resolved the Emperor to find and crush the home of this force which was such anathema to the Dalek kind. Finally, in the very last chapter before *TV 21* dropped its option to use the Dalek comic strip, the story unfolds of an Earth space liner, *The Starmaker*, making a forced landing on Skaro. The Daleks exterminate the entire crew and passengers, but not before three of them escape in a Dalek transporter to warn Earth about the peril they face. And the peril is real. In the burnt-out wreckage of the liner the Daleks find the flight-plan memory unit intact, containing the course co-ordinates for Earth. In the closing panel, the Emperor issues a proclamation: 'The Daleks will go in search and we shall conquer. We shall conquer Earth . . .'

In an oblique fashion, and allowing for some disparity of time, David Whitaker concluded his Dalek chronicles with a lead-in to the TV 'Dalek Invasion of Earth' story, where the Daleks find and subjugate mankind, and are about to take Earth out of its orbit (thereby killing the entire population) when the Doctor turns up and ruins their plans.

But this was not the end of links between the comic strip adventures of the Daleks and their television equivalents. A prolific writer, David Whitaker had penned material for both the *Doctor Who* and the Dalek children's annuals since 1964. Paired with Richard Jennings again for the 1966-released *Dalek Outer Space Book*, he submitted a four-page story outlining the Emperor's transition from a small, mobile casing to a gigantic static unit housed in the very heart of the Dalek city on Skaro. Within a year, that same Emperor encountered his nemesis, the Doctor, during the final episodes of Whitaker's TV story 'The Evil of the Daleks', in which, not surprisingly, the Daleks were conducting studies into the nature of the 'human factor'.

So much for the Daleks. As was predominantly the case during the 'sixties, their presence constantly threatened to drown anything else the *Doctor Who* series might have produced, including spin-offs based around the good Doctor himself. The *Doctor Who* comic strip was a rare exception, appearing in print some two months before the Daleks' debut in *TV 21* and almost a year to the day from the TV serial's launch in November 1963.

Sadly, right throughout the 'sixties, the *Doctor Who* strip was a pale shadow of its Dalek co-runner. Its home was a publication very definitely aimed at younger children, called *TV Comic*. At sixpence an issue, *TV Comic* was a weekly paper from TV Publications Limited, a company which had grown up in the wake of ITV's founding in 1955. The comic itself was a combination of cheap syndicated strips from America or Europe, and home-produced stories based around shows featured in TV's 'Children's Hour'. Science fiction programmes, such as *Space Patrol* and pre-*TV 21* adventures of *Supercar* and *Fireball XL5*, had already proved their popularity to the *TV Comic* editors when the rights to a *Doctor Who* strip were tendered. Knowing they would soon be losing their Gerry Anderson shows to City Publications, they felt *Doctor Who* to be a good substitute.

The travels of William Hartnell's Doctor began on pages two and three of issue 674 of *TV Comic*, published in the week ending 14

ACROSS TIME AND SPACE TO A PEACEFUL ROAD IN ENGLAND WHERE JOHN AND GILLIAN LOOK FOR THEIR GRANDFATHER ...
NUMBER SIXTEEN— THAT'S GRANDFATHER'S NUMBER, GILLIAN!
BUT IT'S ONLY A YARD, NOT A HOUSE AT ALL!
A POLICE BOX! GRANDFATHER CAN'T LIVE IN THERE!
I'VE BEEN TOLD HE'S AN INVENTOR OR SOMETHING! ANYWAY, THE DOOR'S OPEN- I'M GOING INSIDE!
JOHN AND GILLIAN GASP IN AMAZEMENT...
BUT- BUT IT'S NOT A POLICE BOX AFTER ALL!
EXCUSE ME, WE'RE LOOKING FOR OUR GRANDFATHER — DR. WHO!
YOU MUST BE JOHN AND GILLIAN. HOW NICE TO MEET YOU!
WOW! LOOK AT THESE CONTROLS! WHAT IS THIS, GRANDFATHER?
IT IS—ER— A TIME TRAVELLING MACHINE. SEE—I CAN CHOOSE ANY YEAR IN THE PAST, OR FUTURE!
GOLLY— ISN'T IT FUN, JOHN?
GRANDFATHER— WHAT WOULD HAPPEN IF ...?
NO! DON'T TOUCH THAT BUTTON WHATEVER YOU DO!
TOO LATE! A SUDDEN RUSH OF WIND AND THE 'POLICE BOX' STARTS TO REVOLVE THEN DISAPPEARS...
YOU CLUMSY MEDDLER! THIS IS NOT A TOY— IT'S A REAL TIME MACHINE! WE'RE RUSHING HEADLONG INTO THE FUTURE — TO THE 29TH CENTURY!
THE FUTURE! JOHN, I'M FRIGHTENED! WHAT WILL WE SEE?
ON, ON INTO THE MYSTERIOUS FUTURE RUSHES THE TIME MACHINE, THEN AT LAST COMES TO A STOP...
RIGHT! I'LL OPEN THE DOORS AND WE'LL SEE WHERE WE ARE!
COME ON, GILLIAN! LET'S TAKE A LOOK OUTSIDE AT THE FUTURE!
NEVILLE MAIN
CAPTURE THEM! THEY MUST NOT ESCAPE!
JOHN — WHAT ARE THEY? HELP!
GRANDFATHER! QUICK! WE'RE IN TERRIBLE DANGER!

November 1964, where the strip replaced *Fireball XL5* and was drawn by the same artist, Neville Main. With neither the budget nor the circulation of *TV 21*, the *Doctor Who* strip was a low-key affair, printed in black and white with Main expected to script the stories as well as draw them. His simplistic line sketches, although very rudimentary in artistic terms, were quite adequate, considering the four- to ten-year-old age market at which the comic was aimed.

The copyright arrangement with the BBC covered a licence to use only the person of the doctor and the concept of his TARDIS. Other recognisable characters in the series, such as his current companions, were technically the property of the writer who created them, and so the publishers had to strike a separate deal with the BBC if they wanted, say, to have Ian Chesterton in the comic strip. *TV Comic* operated to a tight budget in 1964, and so the editor elected to design his own companions, more identifiable to their juvenile readership, a red-haired little boy in short trousers named John, and his sister, an equally young, dark-haired girl named Gillian. The opening storyline, however, did borrow a couple of ideas from the TV show's first episode.

It showed the two children visiting the home of their elderly grandfather, a mysterious inventor named 'Doctor Who'. To their surprise the address they are given leads only to a high-walled yard in a back street. Pushing open the gates, their eyes alight on the yard's only content, a police box. They venture through the doors only to find themselves inside a time travelling machine, apparently invented by their eccentrically dressed grandfather. Fascinated by the controls, John's inquisitive fingers accidentally push one of the console buttons, with startling results; 'A sudden rush of wind and the police box starts to revolve, then disappears . . .', to quote the caption.

Whatever Main's limitations as an illustrator, he was a very good storyteller, seemingly with uncanny powers of foresight. An early adventure brought the three travellers up against The Pied Piper, a wily magician who engages them in a battle of wits. Only by winning these trials of intellect and endurance will the Piper be persuaded to release the children of Hamlyn from his domain. At this time, 'The Celestial Toymaker' TV story was still more than a year away.

Another strange tale had the travellers arriving at the end of an adventure, and only by analysing the strange backwards speech of their antagonists do they realise that time, too, is rolling back and that they are heading for the beginning of the adventure, which will reunite them with the TARDIS. During his year as *Doctor Who*'s Script Editor, Christopher Bidmead investigated just such a story on TV before abandoning the idea as unworkable.

Strangest of all, though, was Main's 1965 three-part script in which the Doctor encounters the first American astronauts to land on the Moon. He predicted the date of landing as 20 July 1970 – exactly one year and one day out from the actual moment in history.

The *Doctor Who* strip proved a very popular addition to *TV comic*'s repertoire, its readership rising after a six-week experiment using licensed strip rights to the Zarbi and the Menoptra. Recognising the strip's worth, the publishers promoted it to the centre pages for a year, where it went into colour and gained new artists. Bill Mevin handled the chores for six months before handing over to John Canning, whose heavy use of dark tones and shading gave the strip a distinctly gothic look.

Canning devised the Trods as opponents for the good Doctor. Basically heavily armed, upturned conical robots that moved about on caterpillar treads, their similarity to the Daleks was impossible to ignore. Nevertheless, it got *TV Comic* round the problem of incorporating Daleks in everything but name in their strip while rights to the Daleks themselves remained with *TV 21*. The Trods made two appearances with Hartnell's Doctor, as well as turning up in the 1966 *TV Comic* annual. The strip briefly returned to black and white during the closing months of 1966, during which period the Doctor's face changed, without explanation, to that of Patrick Troughton.

The big relaunch came exactly one week after the Daleks were taken out of *TV 21* in January 1967. Accompanied by a 15-second TV advertisement featuring the Dalek film, *TV Comic* celebrated its acquisition of Dalek rights by blasting them on to the cover of issue 788, with free gifts as well for the next few weeks of sticky-backed photographs featuring TV and pop stars, plus an album in which to stick them.

As well as on the front page in colour, the *Doctor Who* strip (retitled 'Doctor Who and the Daleks' even though the metal monsters did not appear in every adventure) also extended on to pages two and three in black and white, the first time ever *TV Comic* had given more than two pages to a strip. John Canning remained the artist, a post he would hold throughout the entire Troughton era, and to mark the arrival of the Daleks, he succumbed to the perhaps irresistible temptation of putting them up against his own creation, the Trods. The result? Daleks won: Trods nil.

The scripting of the Daleks was nowhere near as inventive as it had been in *TV 21*, although Canning did at least adopt the idiosyncratic speech lettering devised by Richard Jennings. Visually the Daleks upheld the liveries and hierarchies of those seen in the two Dalek feature films – the rank and file were grey and blue, the commanders were red, and the Dalek Supreme was black. Of the golden Emperor, however, there was no sign.

Terry Nation's decision to take his Dalek rights for hopeful resale to a US TV network in mid 1967 brought an abrupt end to their inclusion in the *TV Comic* feature, and as from issue 810 the strip reverted to just two pages in black and white with the title once more purely 'Doctor Who'.

This setback proved only temporary, however. Before the end of 1967 it was back in colour as *TV Comic* negotiated permission to use the television show's latest rising-star monsters, the Cybermen. Throughout 1968, and not counting their numerous appearances in annuals and summer special publications, the Cybermen made five appearances in the *Doctor Who* strip, but always with one failing. No one thought to update the reference photographs Canning was given by the BBC. Consequently, while the Cybermen on air went through their many and varied costume and head-piece changes, the versions tackled by the comic-strip Troughton remained steadfastly the cloth-faced kind as seen with William Hartnell in 'The Tenth Planet'.

No such errors were made with the Quarks. Widely publicised by the BBC as the next 'biggies' after the Daleks and the Cybermen, they made their inaugural appearance in strip form just a fortnight after episode one of 'The Dominators' had gone out on TV.

The commencement of *Doctor Who*'s sixth season on television saw the *TV Comic* strip developing some extraordinary links with its broadcast counterpart. The first element was the introduction of a TV-seen companion. Frazer Hines as Jamie had been so well received by the British public that the BBC felt confident enough to release separate exploitation rights, making him the first non-monster character from *Doctor Who* offered under licence.

Jamie replaced John and Gillian, who had been depicted steadily growing up during their travels with the Doctor (an oddity for comic-strip creations), to a point where he felt that it was time to despatch them to life at a university. The Doctor and Jamie travelled together for six months in comic form, fighting everything from Quarks to mad American business tycoons, even Father Time himself, until without warning, the young Scot vanished with no word of explanation at the end of a story called 'Robot Reign of Terror'.

In television terms, episode ten of 'The War Games' had been screened in June 1969, wherein the Time Lords caught and exiled to Earth their errant peer, promising him a

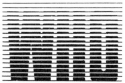

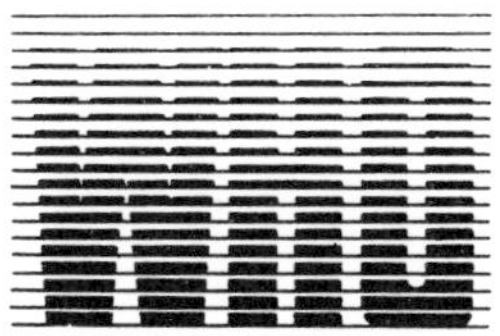

APPEARING on a TV panel game 'Explain My Mystery',. Dr. Who and a spellbound audience, listen to farmer Glenlock-Hogan tell of the mysterious 'night-walks' taken by his scarecrows. The programme's jolly compere tries to laugh off Hogan's claims but Dr. Who realises they are not to be scoffed at and visits Hogan for a weekend. Late one night they see the scarecrows walk!

THE STRANGE, LIFE-CHARGED SCARE-CROWS PAUSE IN A SMALL CLEARING...
THEY'VE STOPPED IN THEIR TRACKS!
...COULD BE THEY'VE SENSED OUR PRESENCE!

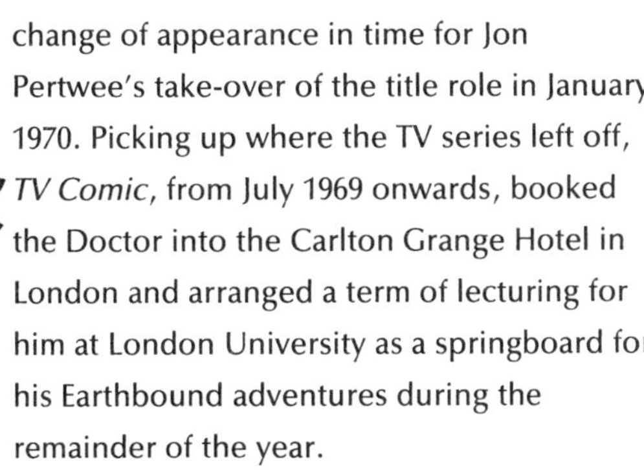

change of appearance in time for Jon Pertwee's take-over of the title role in January 1970. Picking up where the TV series left off, *TV Comic*, from July 1969 onwards, booked the Doctor into the Carlton Grange Hotel in London and arranged a term of lecturing for him at London University as a springboard for his Earthbound adventures during the remainder of the year.

Troughton's last strip adventure forged an interesting link with Jon Pertwee's first TV serial. In the strip, servants of the Time Lords, disguised as scarecrows, ambush the Doctor in a rural English field. They drag him aboard his TARDIS where they complete the Time Lords' sentence upon him by triggering his regeneration. Considering that 'Spearhead from Space' began with a very groggy new Doctor stumbling from the ship, John Canning's invention came very close to tying up an otherwise aggravating loose end between two television serials.

Jon Pertwee's earliest outings into strip form were far from complementary to the strides being made by the revamped, all-colour TV series. With little in the way of pre-season reference material to go on, John Canning played up Pertwee's renown as a comedian and depicted him as an affected fop, foiling such dastardly deeds as a schoolboy's plot to release an anarchy gas that would change children into rampaging hooligans. It was not an auspicious start, even the presence of the Brigadier and Liz Shaw adding little to raise the strip's level above the juvenile.

Things improved dramatically, however, when TV Publications Ltd completed their merger with City Publications to form Polystyle, a much larger publishing house aiming to challenge the output of their principal rival, IPC. The result was *TV Comic* continuing for younger children, while older readers were offered *Countdown*.

Viewed with hindsight, *Countdown* was the last children's paper to be launched using the expensive photogravure printing process. Transferring in time for issue one, 'Doctor Who' immediately went into full colour, gaining vastly upgraded scripts and a succession of highly talented artists, including Harry Lindfield, Frank Langford and Gerry Haylock.

Launched in February 1971, *Countdown* lasted just over a year before it became apparent that sales were not going to attain the heights of *TV 21* at its best. The dwindling market for escapist science fiction in the early to mid 'seventies, and the exorbitant costs of colour printing, fuelled by spiralling inflation, heralded a rapid rethink by Polystyle's editors to come up with a new and cheaper vehicle.

Countdown ended with issue 62, relaunching the following week as *TV Action*, a smaller, matte-paper printed comic magazine with an emphasis towards TV adventure series such as *Hawaii Five-O, The Persuaders* and *Cannon*. The *Doctor Who* strip survived this transition, partly because of its rising ratings on television, and partly because of Editor Dennis Hooper's great enthusiasm for the series. But even he could not stop the declining sales experienced right throughout the British comic industry as readerships turned towards America for newer breeds of heroes. Marvel and DC Comics were on the ascendancy and after just over one year on the market, *TV Action* was merged back into *TV Comic*, losing most of its older age-group strips along the way.

As always, however, *Doctor Who* survived, continuing its high standard of presentation under the capable hands of Gerry Haylock. Haylock stayed with the strip up until issue 1214 of *TV Comic* in March 1974, by which time he had overseen the strip transformation of Jon Pertwee into Tom Baker. Baker was a much harder likeness than Pertwee for Haylock to handle, and after completing one story he handed over the art reins for six months to an uncredited artist, believed to be Martin Asbury. Finally, in a case almost of

turning full circle, issue 1232 saw responsibility for the weekly two-page strip returning under the ever-patient wing of John Canning, where it stayed for the remainder of *Doctor Who*'s life with *TV Comic*.

That life lasted until spring 1979, by which time the 15-year-old strip was in dire straits. Further economies had reduced the number of comic-strip panels per page to between four and eight, a sure sign that the artist was not being required (or paid) to do more. In September 1976, further paring led *TV Comic* to become *Mighty TV Comic*, a tabloid-newspaper-shaped publication with an accent on using syndicated reprints. 'Doctor Who' appeared as a single-page feature, although by printing it vertically rather than horizontally, the feature spread across two physical pages when the comic was folded in half for sale.

But surely the ultimate indignity foisted upon Tom Baker's Doctor was the sight of old Patrick Troughton and Jon Pertwee strips being rehashed with just Baker's face, hat and scarf painted over either Pertwee's ruffled shirts or Troughton's baggy coat, which occurred with ever-increasing frequency as *TV Comic* lurched unsteadily towards 1979. Eventually, *TV Comic* regained its original size and format, but by then interest in its *Doctor Who* feature was negligible and the strip was dropped in the spring of that year.

For over six months, no *Doctor Who* comic strip appeared anywhere, but when it did return it was from one of the publishing house stables that had done so much damage encroaching into the sales of *TV Comic*, *TV Action* and *Countdown* during the 'seventies: Marvel Comics. The new magazine was *Doctor Who Weekly*, and hailed from Britain's division of Marvel based in London. Inspiration for this product had come from Marvel's then Editorial Director, Dez Skinn. A previous venture of his, *House of Hammer* had proved the worth of a publication based around one subject (in that case, the films of Hammer Studios) using a mixture of related comic-strip, photographs and text features.

The notion of a purely *Doctor Who*-based magazine was first discussed when Skinn met actor Tom Baker and *Doctor Who* Producer Graham Williams at the 1979 World Science-Fiction Convention in Brighton. For years, British Marvel's mainstay had been the reprinting of American strips. Now was an ideal time, he argued, with *Doctor Who* going down so well in the USA, for comic-book length *Doctor Who* strips to be generated in Britain and then repackaged and reprinted in the States. BBC Enterprises agreed the deal, and on 10 October 1979, issue number one hit the news-stands.

Two in-house strips unfolded each week at the outset, one based around characters and monsters seen in the show, the other an eight-page strip of the Doctor's own adventures.

As with their American comic-book counterparts, the scripting and art chores were split. Initially, Marvel commissioned *The Eagle* award-winning writing team of Mills and Wagner to pen some highly sophisticated storylines for the new strip, with other luminaries such as Steve Moore and Steve

Parkhouse quick to follow in their footsteps. To provide the artwork, the *Doctor Who* strip saw the skilled pen of Dave Gibbons predominantly being wielded between 1979 and 1982, before his talents were poached by the DC Corporation in America for a much greater salary than Britain could afford.

The budget for *Doctor Who Weekly*, and for *Doctor Who Monthly* as it became from issue 44, was, however, sufficient for Marvel to license other characters and monsters from the series as well as the current face of the Doctor. Grim-faced Sontarans challenged the Mongol empires of the East from a Tibetan monastery, K9 blasted Daleks to smithereens in confrontations forbidden on TV, and in one epic-length saga, 'The Tides of Time', the Doctor was brought before the father of all Time Lords, Rassilon, in a momentous encounter far more awe-striking than its counterpart in 'The Five Doctors'.

The art direction foundered awhile after the departure of Dave Gibbons, partly hampered by the strict dictates of Peter Davison's agent about achieving a good likeness of his client. Matters improved sharply with the arrival of John Ridgway on issue 88, in time to take over the strip at the outset of Colin Baker's era. Nicola Bryant's Peri joined him on his journeys soon after, but even her and the sixth Doctor's effusive personalities were inadequate to upstage the other companion on these voyages – Frobisher.

Created to begin with as a shape-changing alien purely for one or two stories, the editors, writers and artists alike were agog at the enthusiastic reception Frobisher got from readers once his shape became more or less permanently locked into that of a penguin. Since then, laconically cynical and a born coward, Frobisher's booming popularity has outlasted Colin Baker to become a resident aboard Sylvester McCoy's ship.

Present Producer John Nathan-Turner's answers have been pertinently blunt at suggestions that Frobisher should be incorporated into the TV series, but other elements from the comic strip have had more considerable influence – notably the Doctor's multi-coloured umbrella.

Colin Baker's photocall, at which his costume was first unveiled to the press, was on a day of torrential rain, and so to protect this valuable outfit, an equally colourful umbrella was hastily passed to him by an enterprising assistant. Thus, when the photographs appeared, John Ridgway used them for reference and introduced the umbrella permanently into the strip, where it became a recognised part of the Doctor's ensemble. The umbrella was eventually used on TV by Colin Baker, and then finally was deemed an ideal trademark for Sylvester McCoy's Doctor, both in the strip and on TV.

The almost unbroken twenty-four-year run of the *Doctor Who* strip makes it one of the longest in British comic-strip history, with only *The Dandy* and *The Beano* able to provide characters of such longevity. And with *Doctor Who Monthly* now retailed virtually wherever *Doctor Who* is shown, there is little doubt that as long as the television series survives, so, somewhere, will its word-ballooned companion.

THE LOST STORIES OF DOCTOR WHO

25 GLORIOUS YEARS

Above: Four episodes of the Hartnell story 'The Reign of Terror' have been recovered leaving two still missing.

Unlike other famous cult science fiction and fantasy series such as *Thunderbirds*, *Star Trek* and *Blake's 7*, the television history of *Doctor Who* is, sadly, far from complete. For, as a direct result of BBC policy in the early 1970s to 'junk' selected old programmes, a considerable number of the Doctor's early adventures were destroyed, never to be seen again.

In particular, it was the black-and-white stories of William Hartnell and Patrick Troughton which suffered this fate, as a result of a decision the Corporation now admits it regrets. But all is not quite lost – for thanks to some amazing rediscoveries and the dedicated hunting of archivists and fans, a considerable number of apparently 'lost' episodes have come to light once again. But although this may seem encouraging, as of January 1988 just over 115 episodes – all those from the show's first six years – are still unaccounted for. How this happened, and why, is something that **Jeremy Bentham** has been investigating for some years. To understand this tragic circumstance, he says, it is first necessary to look at the way the BBC works as a television programme producing body.

The BBC's TV service began in earnest shortly after the end of World War II. At that time television was basically about a camera capturing an image from a studio set, converting it into an electrical signal, and then beaming it out to the few homes in Britain equipped with the bulky receivers with their tiny seven-inch screens. It was very much a one-to-one process. Actors spoke their lines and were viewed simultaneously by their audience. No recording facilities whatsoever existed.

Then in 1947, an experimental facility was tried out in time for Princess Elizabeth's wedding to Prince Philip. This was tele-recording, in which a 16mm film camera was pointed at an expensive flat-screened television receiver so that, using a complicated system to match the scan-time of a television picture (the time it takes for the cathode beam to replenish all the lines on a TV screen) to the speed of each film frame passing through the camera's shutter-gate, a good quality negative of the programme being broadcast could be captured on film. And from that negative, numerous positive prints could be made. Thus it became possible to record a programme and make duplicate copies of it, either for storage or for distribution throughout the world.

As tele-recording became more prolific during the 'fifties, so the BBC's various film and, later, video libraries came into being to store the steadily accumulating cans of processed film and their associated negatives. Repeats of popular programmes became possible by the reverse principle of projecting the recorded film on to a screen and having a studio camera shoot it and transmit the picture across the airwaves. Later, this whole system became much easier as videotape machines ushered in the era of electronic recording, editing and duplicating. By this time, the various premises had expanded to comprise several large and spacious warehouses, all supplied with costly air-

conditioning and humidifying equipment to keep the stored cans at the optimum 55° Fahrenheit temperature. The archives at Brentford, Middlesex, was a flourishing concern, providing contemporary historians with an invaluable source of material on British society in the 'fifties and 'sixties.

However, this long-term storage facility was, in essence, a luxury, and a very expensive luxury to maintain. Nowhere in the BBC's Charter (its mandate from the government to operate in return for the public's licence money) is there provision for it to act as an archival body. *If* material were being stored then it could be useful to historians, but no legally binding covenant meant that the BBC *had* to provide this service.

Three other factors also made the existence of a BBC archive ostensibly redundant, and even undesirable, to anyone other than historians and researchers. Firstly, the agreements with various unions and performing rights' associations: in the eyes of such bodies, repeats were bad news because, in a theoretical extreme case, it would be possible for a future generation of TV broadcasters to fill their air-time with unending processions of stored repeats, thus putting actors, producers and technicians out of work. So settlements were reached permitting only a certain proportion of repeats per year, and even then allowing a programme to be reshown only within three years. For anything older, they argued, substantial negotiations would be needed, coupled with complicated scales of residual payments. The upshot was BBC policy not to rescreen a programme after its three-year retention period had expired.

A second prevailing factor was the development of colour broadcasting. As the 1970s dawned, the push for colour programming went into overdrive, fuelled by the BBC's expertise in this field, and by record sales of colour televisions throughout the UK. Up and down the country, black and white sets were being shipped to the rubbish dumps in droves as people rushed to buy new receivers now that all three channels were broadcasting in full colour.

And allied to both these elements was the related field of overseas sales. Through contracts arranged by BBC Enterprises, the Corporation recouped some of its programming outlay by selling productions to buyers in other countries. With union approval, shows could be syndicated for overseas broadcast, but again, within certain time limits and subject to varying scales of payment.

Throughout the early 'seventies black-and-white shows continued to be marketed, but the trend was inexorably downwards as other countries took on colour systems and began buying the BBC's more recent, rather than older, offerings. Thus the stage was set for the tragic destruction of many thousands of old black-and-white TV programmes in the mid 'seventies. A vast swathe of *Doctor Who* episodes were on that list, but so, too, were classic episodes of *Steptoe and Son*, *Hancock's Half Hour*, *Compact*, *Top of the Pops*, *The Troubleshooters*, even episodes of

Above: Some frames from 'The Daleks' Master Plan', which was found in a Mormon Church hall.

Till Death Us Do Part, rich in social comment about life in Britain during the 1960s.

As with all crucial acts in history, however, there had to be one main trigger. And in this case it was something as simple as a fire inspection. Lack of 'proper funding' at the libraries meant that most of the premises were substantially overcrowded by the end of 1972. With most of the storage racks jammed to capacity, cans of film and tape were being shipped in daily, frequently stored in great piles without proper indexing, wherever space for them could be found. Consequently, when insurance officers carried out their inspection, their subsequent report condemned the warehouses under just about every listable aspect of safety. Drastic measures were required to resolve the problem or else, they warned, insurance cover would not be renewed. The answer was simple – a purge on any lower graded stock that was either out of sale date, or beyond the three-year repeat threshold.

(On the subject of grading, it is worth mentioning that the BBC applies a retention classification to every programme it holds, so as to simplify the task of nominating what to junk and what to keep. Top of the list are the 'A' listed programmes: important documentaries, or plays by such luminaries as Dennis Potter, David Rudkin or Alan Bleasdale which are considered prestige television and are thus to be kept forever. At the other end of the scale, an imported series of black-and-white Spanish language instruction programmes, for example, would be 'J' listed – in other words, the first to go.)

In 1972, the pre-1970 *Doctor Who*'s were 'C' listed, meaning 'retain certain selected examples for posterity but otherwise junk as necessary' And in 1973, it became necessary . . .

Fortunately, human nature and human inefficiency came to the rescue of *Doctor Who*. Between 1973 and 1977 the vast bulk of William Hartnell and Patrick Troughton episodes were listed for junking. Cans were opened, labels removed and the films inside consigned to furnaces or dumped on to rubbish skips. A few episodes, such as part two of 'Space Pirates', were selected, probably on a random basis, for preservation as 'examples of the genre'. Others, such as 'The Dominators' and 'The War Games', were offered to the British Film Institute arts body for storage in the National Film Archive. But in the main, the purging was carried out with relentless drive.

However, accidents were not unknown during this mass purging period. When the 1968 Cybermen story 'The Invasion' was scheduled for destruction, the person in charge, cross-referencing the card file, by mistake destroyed episode one of the colour Jon Pertwee serial 'Invasion of the Dinosaurs', just because it also bore the one-word title 'Invasion' so that no one would guess the presence of the dinosaurs so early in the story.

Another calamity occurred as the 1965 'Galaxy Four' story was being negotiated for rescreening by the Doctor Who Appreciation Society at their very first convention in August 1977. The BBC had agreed to allow the Society

to hire out the film prints subject to copyright approvals being first obtained in writing. But a month later, representatives of the Society armed with the necessary paperwork, discovered that in the interim the prints and the negatives had all been destroyed!

Even more spectacular was the destruction of episodes that had been used just a few months earlier by a current production team. In April 1977, BBC 2 broadcast a special documentary in the *Lively Arts* series called 'Who's Doctor Who', an hour-long programme examining the show's massive popularity, with reference to clips from episodes such as 'Galaxy Four' and 'The Daleks' Master Plan'. Shortly after that programme was completed, those episodes were gone.

The process of junking *en masse* wound down in early 1978, partly because the operation had achieved its purpose, but also partly because a new consideration had entered the equation – domestic video recorders. Just as the British public had gone overboard for colour televisions in the early 'seventies, so the late 'seventies witnessed a similar boom in the purchase and rent of domestic VCRs. And hand in glove with the demand for machines was demand for films and programmes to play on them. It was the era of piracy and vast profits for unscrupulous dealers, with stolen copies of new films fetching small fortunes on the black market. Soon, bills were passing before Parliament to crack down on the pirates, but despite this the legitimate film and TV makers were forced to recognise that either they made their products available legally to the public, or the public would seek illegal ways of obtaining them.

Despite its six years of mass junking, the BBC still held one of the foremost television archives in the world, which in this new video age spelled potential profit for the Corporation, or at least for its commercial wing, BBC Enterprises.

About this time, too, *Doctor Who* was discovered by the United States, where the insatiable thirst for material saw bigger and bigger deals being struck for an ever-increasing market. In short, networks in the States agreed to buy whatever *Doctor Who* shows the BBC would sell them. But was there much they *could* sell pre-Jon Pertwee? For the answer, it is necessary to take into account the elements of human nature and human inefficiency.

Theoretically, the junking process should have destroyed all Hartnell and Troughton material, barring a select few episodes. In reality, much was missed by the employees entrusted to destroy the cans. Once they had signed the record card saying, for example, that 'The Sensorites' had been junked, they stopped looking for cans marked 'The Sensorites'. If any episodes turned up subsequently, say through accidental storage in a wrongly labelled can, chances were they would be put back on a shelf and ignored by the finder. Additionally, the junking team did not always check every single repository of programmes in the BBC, and by this omission they overlooked one of the largest bodies

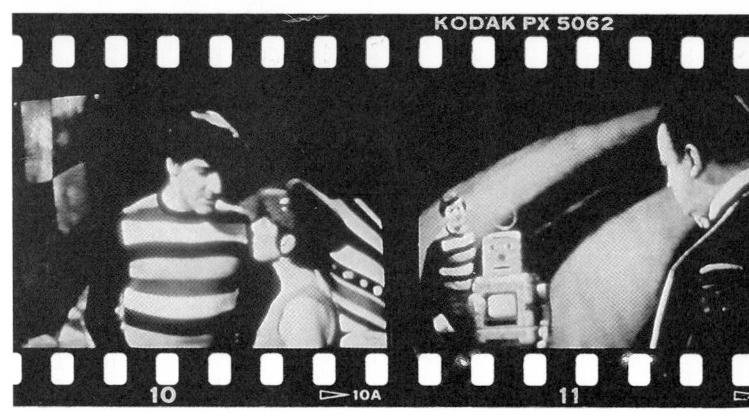

Above: Episode 4 of 'The Celestial Toymaker', which came to light in Australia.

holding film reels and negatives, BBC Enterprises.

Thirdly, for whatever motives by the persons concerned, not all the programmes consigned for junking went into the fires or on to the scrap heaps. A great deal of material 'accidentally' fell into briefcases, or mysteriously disappeared from racks marked 'For Destruction'. Many programmes found their way, by surreptitious means, into the hands of collectors, others were saved because the person responsible could not bring himself to destroy something he had perhaps watched and admired. The most famously reported incident was of the man who, years later, returned the very first episode of *Z-Cars* to the BBC, having preserved it for so long because '. . . the kids like the show so much'.

And lastly, while the BBC could clean out its own house, it could not be thorough in cleaning out other people's. In their contracts, BBC Overseas Sales stipulate that once a sold programme has reached its expiry date for broadcasting, it should be returned or destroyed. But that clause presupposes infallible efficiency on behalf of the overseas buyer. And as events were to prove, such was rarely the case.

A new name came on to the scene in 1978 – Sue Malden, a young woman selected by the BBC to be the Film Library's first Archive Selector. As the job title implies, her role was to examine and grade all material in, and coming into, the Library and to pick out, more carefully than had been done before purely by the librarians, programmes for long-term retention. Coming in on the dawn of the video sales era, Sue Malden expanded her brief by taking on the task of seeking out lost episodes of old programmes that could once more prove commercially viable in the light of BBC wishes to renegotiate their repeat rights with the unions.

An early success was finding virtually the entire first two seasons of William Hartnell's Doctor intact, in pristine negative form, at the back of a dust-laden vault at BBC Enterprises. Overlooked by the purging team, the excellent quality footage was brought back to Brentford where a top-notch print of the first story, 'An Unearthly Child', was struck in 1981 for rerunning on BBC 2 as part of its 'Five Faces of Doctor Who' season.

Often, Sue Malden's work involved the less glamorous task of individually opening every can of film, to check its contents against the label on the side, and to cross-reference with the record cards held by the Library; painstaking work, but frequently with unexpected rewards. One historic find was a spuriously labelled can containing the never-screened pilot episode of *Doctor Who*: the original version of the 'Unearthly Child' episode, complete with all the crashing cameras, line fluffs and falling props that had driven Sydney Newman into authorising a full remount of the entire production.

Another bit of luck was finding part one of 'The Web of Fear', the Douglas Camfield-directed Yeti classic set on the London Underground. That entire story had been long gone from the archives when Sue Malden happened, one afternoon, to pass a

stack of film cans newly returned from an overseas TV station. Curious, she inspected the contents and was delighted to find the missing episode, clips of which have subsequently made appearances in programmes as far afield as ITV's *The South Bank Show*, for which one clip was used to introduce a programme about the London Underground.

Some of the episodes Sue Malden found were 'slash prints'. A slash print is a rough edit of an episode, with the music and sound effects track missing, often with silences at the beginnings and endings of a scene which would be taken out during later editing sessions. These rough edits were made when an episode needed too many edits to be done on video, so they were transferred to film for the editing to take place.

These days, raw edits of *Doctor Who* episodes are sent along on VHS video complete with viewdata- inserted timecode (rather like a CEEFAX clock display), but in the 'sixties such material could only be supplied on black-and-white film. Part six of 'The Wheel in Space' was found in slash print form, rendering it unsuitable for rebroadcasting, but nevertheless one more recovered episode.

A few years ago, Sue Malden was succeeded by Steve Bryant, who came into the department just as BBC drama and comedy series were beginning to be sold on commercial videotape. Within a year or two BBC Enterprises's output was competing with film distributors such as CBS and Twentieth Century Fox for places in the top ten video sales charts, and not just with recent productions. Vindicating the practice of retaining old television has been the unqualified success of the entire *Forsyte Saga* and a whole range of *Hancock's Half Hour* compilations. Even one of the lesser Jon Pertwee *Doctor Who* stories, 'Death to the Daleks', defied pundits' predictions by shooting up to the top of the budget video chart within a week of its release.

The USA, however, continues to be the main outlet for old black-and-white *Doctor Who* shows. With over 400 Public Broadcasting Service stations showing *Doctor Who* throughout the States, BBC Enterprises scored one of their biggest sales ever in the mid 1980s when they sold prints of every full Hartnell and Troughton story held in the archives to the distribution company Lionheart, a deal worth millions of dollars involving some 106 episodes, all of them at one time thought to be lost forever.

It would be wrong, though, to attribute all the praise for finding these episodes to staff working at the BBC. Of equal importance in this saga have been the efforts of a small number of earnest fans who, since 1977, have applied themselves to the task of hunting down and returning lost *Doctor Who* episodes to the BBC.

A valued adviser to these early film hunters was show-business personality Bob Monkhouse, whose own collection of comedy films and TV productions is considered second to none in the UK. Monkhouse's help was given in two ways. He was able to provide from his own extensive

Above: Part 3 of 'The Wheel in Space' was returned by a film collector.

records names and addresses of suggested contacts in the many 16mm film clubs operating countrywide. These in turn led to dialogue with other collectors, and from that stemmed the return of some half-dozen episodes, including part two of 'The Abominable Snowman', episode six of 'The Reign of Terror' and a replacement copy of 'Invasion of the Dinosaurs' part one, albeit as a black-and-white film print only.

Indirectly, Bob Monkhouse was also able to answer some of the hunters' queries about copyright. Sued at one time by a major film company for holding and showing copies of 'their' films to his friends, Monkhouse won the case by proving he was doing so without thought of financial gain in the privacy of his own home. The legal precedent established by this case helped to clarify one of the grey areas brought about by the evolution of domestic video recorders. Effectively it meant that people could hold copyright material in their homes without seeking the approval of the copyright holders, provided the playing back of such material was only for domestic pleasure, that no financial transactions were involved (save perhaps the cost of blank tapes), and that no fees were charged to the public for subsequent playbacks. The law on copyright is still intensely complex and convoluted, but the Monkhouse verdict did at least allay fears of those searching for lost episodes, for whom possession of a copy of a found print is their only reward.

Leads to tracing old *Doctor Who* material have often proved fruitless, and the problem has invariably been to separate third-generation rumours from fact, if not from the downright criminal. In 1979, a strong rumour surfaced that an episode of 'Power of the Daleks' existed in Australia, the owner of which was prepared to trade for copies of more recent episodes shown in England. To substantiate his claim, the trader circulated photographs, taken off screen, showing the 'Dalek production line' sequence from episode four or five. The ensuing rush to arrange swaps was of tidal wave proportions, with batches of English videotaped episodes being sent out at great expense to a post office box somewhere in New South Wales. Too late, the would-be traders in England discovered they had been fooled. The off-screen photographs supporting the existence of the episode were, in fact, from a clip in a schools programme called *C for Computer*. By the time that was verified, a good many fans in England had lost money, and the hirer of the post office box had long disappeared, presumably with large quantities of video tapes under his arm. Fortunately, instances such as this have been rare and never perpetrated to the same degree. The three per cent (on average) of leads that have yielded positive results over the last eleven years have more than made up for the 97 per cent of leads stemming from nothing more substantial than fantasy and imagination.

An opposite case to the criminal deception noted above was an occurrence in Brighton during the summer of 1985 at the Doctor Who Appreciation Society's annual convention. A group of outsiders turned up claiming to represent a private collector owning two lost

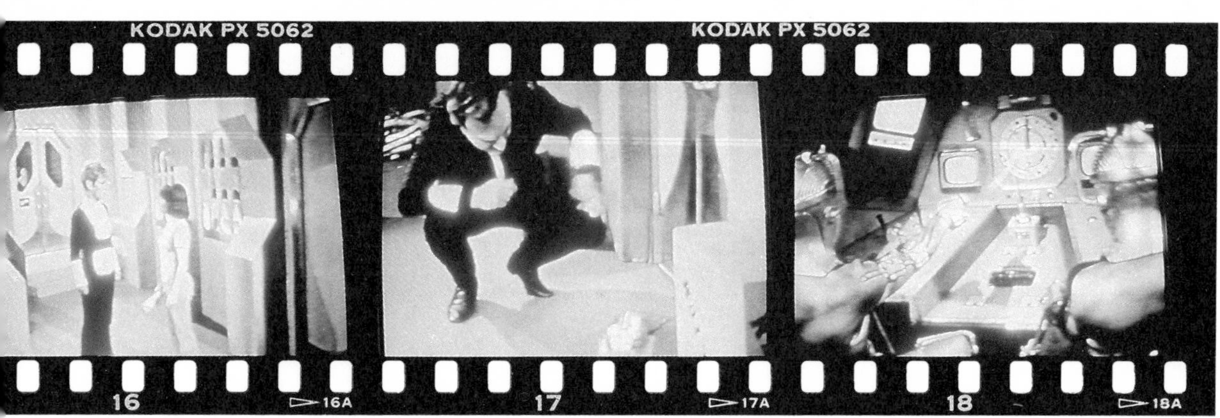

episodes. Their offer was to hire out a cinema in Brighton and show the episodes to fans at a late-night private screening in return for admission money only. Armed with several 'laundry-style' raffle books, the group asked permission to enter the convention to sell their tickets. They were bluntly told to leave the convention by the organisers, to whom the whole set-up rang of fraud. This they did, but it took over two years for the truth to emerge that the group had been genuine in their claim. They had made approaches to a Brighton cinema club to arrange a screening. They were going to charge admission price only. And, most importantly, they did have with them 16mm prints of 'The Faceless Ones' part three, and the classic second episode of 'The Evil of the Daleks'.

No less remarkable was the return of 'The Curse of Peladon' to the BBC from TV Ontario in Canada. Although not technically a lost story, it was nevertheless untransmittable in its original form as only a black-and-white copy of part two survived at the BBC.

In a burst of initiative, one of the *Doctor Who* episode hunters, on a free afternoon during a business trip to Canada, decided to call in at the TV Ontario station on the off-chance they might still have a few old episodes left, even though they were technically outside the broadcasting expiry date. Sure enough, the company still possessed 525-line full-colour prints of 'The Curse of Peladon' and 'The Time Monster'. A few phone calls to London later, and agreement was reached to return them.

That was not quite the end of the story, however. The quality of the 525-line tape had deteriorated noticeably over the years, causing heads on the playback machine to 'gunge-up' every few minutes whenever an attempt was made to view the reel. Nevertheless, in his own time a BBC technician lavished hours of effort transferring the 525-line NTSC format recordings on to British-viewable 625-line PAL master tapes, diligently stopping to disassemble, clean, reassemble and rethread the Canadian recordings every couple of minutes as the shed quantities of oxide built up. By timely coincidence, this full-colour copy of 'The Curse of Peladon' was borrowed from the Library within a year, when it was used to launch a season of *Doctor Who* repeats on BBC 1 in summer 1981.

The possibility of unclassified episodes existing abroad surfaced again in 1984 when a TV development specialist, assisting in the set-up of a satellite education/communications system in Africa, was interviewed on Radio 2. Discussing the problems of working in the Third World, he happened to mention as an example that the TV company operating in Nigeria was so behind the times that they were still showing *Doctor Who* episodes with Patrick Troughton as the Doctor. Following up this lead, innumerable phone calls were made to Nigerian Television to try to substantiate this observation, which proved no mean feat in itself. Because of its sheer size, the company has no less than 32 stations dotted about the country, some literally just prefabricated tin sheds in the middle of the desert.

25 GLORIOUS YEARS

Above: Two frames from the elusive Jon Pertwee story 'The Mind of Evil'. No colour print of this now exists at the BBC.

Nevertheless, patience (and a hefty phone bill) prevailed, and within a couple of months, persistent enquiries yielded two full, and previously incomplete, William Hartnell stories, 'The Time Meddler' and 'The War Machines', both of which, after lengthy customs hold-ups, eventually found their way back to Brentford, to become part of the big package of Hartnell/Troughton serials sold to the USA in the mid 'eighties.

This remarkable story of recovery finally stirred BBC Enterprises into spending some of their money in telexing every single TV company ever to have bought *Doctor Who*, no matter how many years ago, for a list of anything they might still hold. The replies were a mixed bag of responses. Some politely regretted that they had nothing to offer. A company in Crete, on the other hand, unearthed parts one, two and three of 'The Reign of Terror' for a welcome trip back to England. Only Iran was less than helpful. In a curt note back to BBC Enterprises they demanded to know, 'Who in the name of Allah are you talking about?'

Surely the most unexpected find of all, though, had to be parts five and ten of 'The Daleks' Master Plan', which turned up in summer 1983. Sitting at his desk at the BBC one morning, Steve Bryant took a phone call from his secretary asking if he would like to speak to representatives of the Mormon Unification Church of Great Britain. Wary of being sold a subscription for a series of religious publications, Bryant took the call. To his amazement he found himself speaking to one of the Church leaders who was phoning from their newest temple in Clapham, south London. Apparently, having just acquired this previously long-derelict church, the Mormon disciples were busy cleaning out the basement when they came across an old crate in one corner marked 'BBC Property'. Opening it, they discovered inside a dozen or so cans of 16mm film, again emblazoned with the BBC logo. Did the BBC want them back? His curiosity aroused, Bryant went to visit the Mormon temple, and was staggered to find the two missing episodes of *Doctor Who* in the crate, nestling alongside some children's programmes and an early edition of the drama series *Warship*, among others. All the episodes were safely restored to the Library, but to this day no one is any the nearer solving the mystery of just how the crate came to be in that church basement.

As the show passes its twenty-fifth anniversary, it seems improbable that any more bulk finds from abroad will be made, now that all the TV companies ever to have been sold *Doctor Who* have, presumably, checked their records. The future for episode recovery is therefore likely to stay in the hands of the lone episode hunters, patiently coupling hope with instinct and the tenacity to follow leads no matter how slender or tenuous.

The possibility of restoring *Doctor Who*'s full history seems very slim, but it would be unwise ever to dismiss the possibilities of further episode finds. The truth, as always, will remain stranger than even *Doctor Who*'s unique brand of fiction.

BBC-TV: 35mm. MINIATURES AND SPECIAL EFFECTS for: "DR WHO" ~ "CURSE of SEPHIROTH": BRAY FILM STUDIOS: 8th.9th.10th. MAY: 79. PROD-NO: 1148/3723

FIRST SEQUENCE: 48.f.p.s.

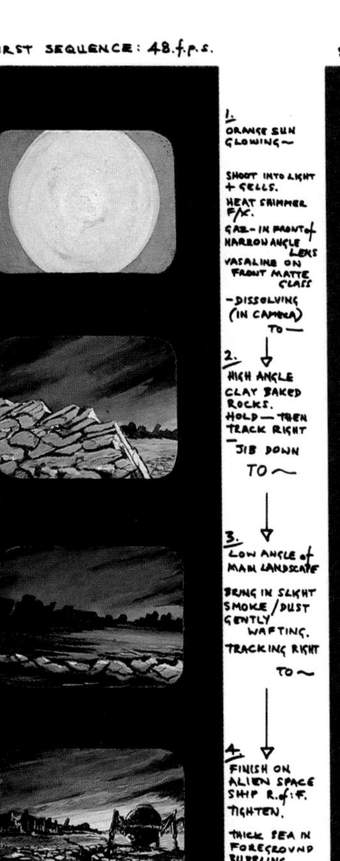

1.
ORANGE SUN GLOWING ~
SHOOT INTO LIGHT + GELS.
HEAT SHIMMER F/X.
GAS-IN FRONT of NARROW ANGLE LENS
VASALINE ON FRONT MATTE GLASS
-DISSOLVING (IN CAMERA) TO ~
2.
HIGH ANGLE CLAY BAKED ROCKS.
HOLD - THEN TRACK RIGHT
JIB DOWN
TO ~
3.
LOW ANGLE of MAIN LANDSCAPE
BRING IN SLIGHT SMOKE/DUST GENTLY WAFTING.
TRACKING RIGHT
TO ~
4.
FINISH ON ALIEN SPACE SHIP R. of F. TIGHTEN.
THICK SEA IN FOREGROUND BUBBLING WITH DRY ICE.

SECOND SEQUENCE: 48.f.p.s.

THIRD SEQUENCE: 48/72. f.p.s.

AGAINST BLACK VELVET ON PEDISTAL

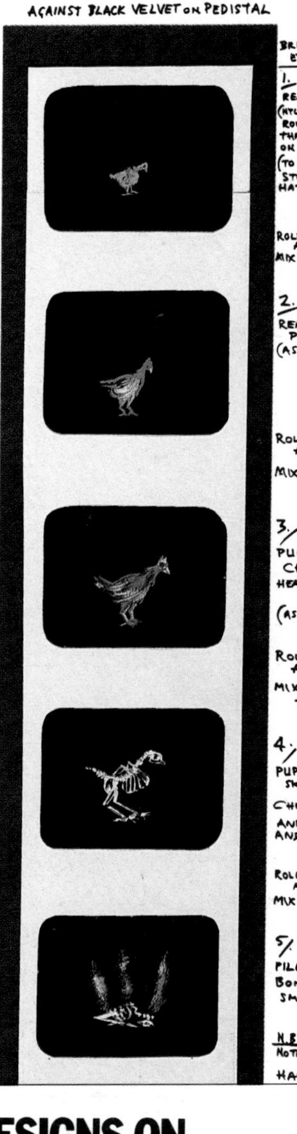

BRING UP EXPOSURE
1.
REAL CHICK (NYLON LINE ROUND ANKLES THROUGH HOLE ON PLATFORM. (TO CUT INTO STOP FRAME HATCHING SHOT)
ROLL BACK AND MIX DISSOLVE TO ~
2.
REAL PULLET (AS BEFORE).
ROLL BACK AND MIX DISSOLVE TO ~
3/.
PUPPET CHICKEN HEAD MOVES. (AS BEFORE)
ROLL BACK AND MIX DISSOLVE TO: ~
4/.
PUPPET SKELETON of CHICKEN. ANIMATE IT AND COLLAPSE
ROLL BACK AND MIX DISSOLVE TO ~
5/.
PILE of BONES. SMOKING! DUST.
N.B. NOTE TO EDITOR HAVE A

DESIGNS ON Doctor WHO

Special effects, ranging from alien worlds to space-craft, have been one of the most impressive features of Doctor Who during its 25 years. One of the many talented designers who has worked on the show is Ian Scoones, photographed left preparing a model scene prior to filming 'City of Death', the storyboard for which is shown above. Reproduced on the following pages are Ian's original storyboard designs for the impressive visual effects used in the 1977 story 'The Invisible Enemy', in which the Doctor battled with a space virus on an earth-shuttle craft.

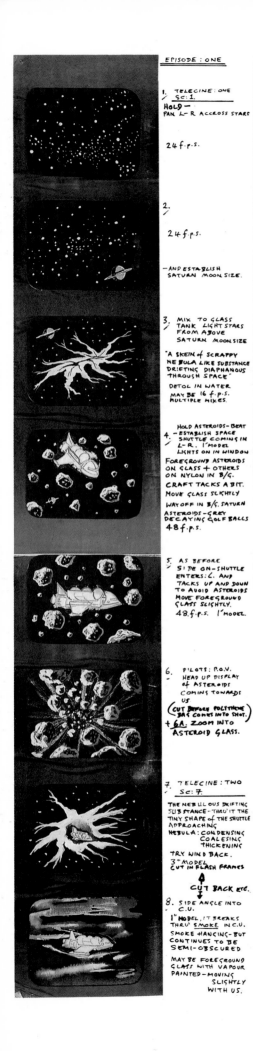

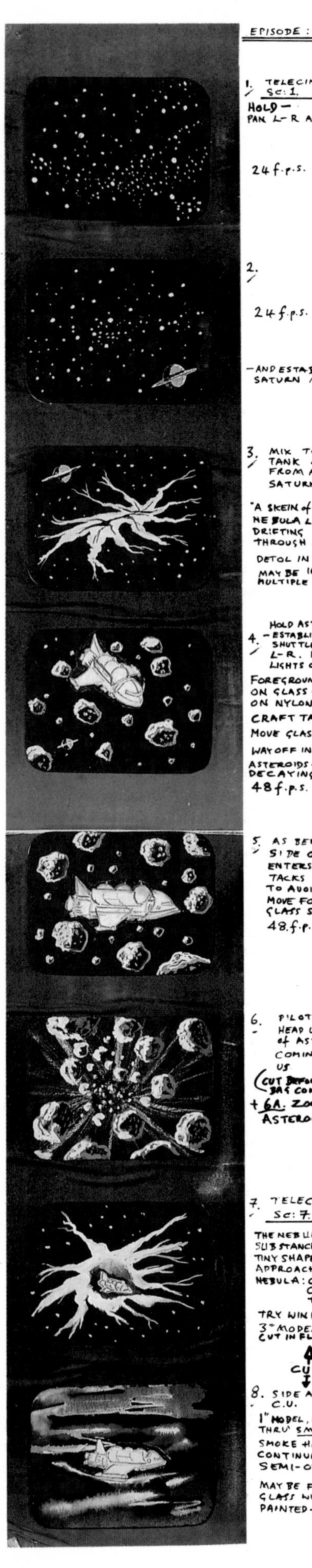

EPISODE : ONE

1. TELECINE : ONE
Sc: 1.

HOLD —
PAN L–R ACCROSS STARS

24 f.p.s.

2.

24 f.p.s.

— AND ESTABLISH
SATURN MOON SIZE.

3. MIX TO GLASS
TANK LIGHT STARS
FROM ABOVE
SATURN MOON SIZE

"A SKEIN of SCRAPPY
NEBULA LIKE SUBSTANCE
DRIFTING DIAPHANOUS
THROUGH SPACE"

DETOL IN WATER
MAY BE 16 f.p.s.
MULTIPLE MIXES.

4. HOLD ASTEROIDS – BEAT
– ESTABLISH SPACE
SHUTTLE COMING IN
L–R. 1" MODEL
LIGHTS ON IN WINDOW

FOREGROUND ASTEROIDS
ON GLASS + OTHERS
ON NYLON IN B/G.

CRAFT TACKS A BIT.

MOVE GLASS SLIGHTLY

WAY OFF IN B/G. SATURN

ASTEROIDS – GREY
DECAYING GOLF BALLS
48 f.p.s.

5. AS BEFORE
SIDE ON – SHUTTLE
ENTERS: L. AND
TACKS UP AND DOWN
TO AVOID ASTEROIDS
MOVE FOREGROUND
GLASS SLIGHTLY.
48.f.p.s. 1" MODEL.

6. PILOTS: P.O.V.
HEAD UP DISPLAY
of ASTEROIDS
COMING TOWARDS
US
(CUT BEFORE POLYTHENE
BAG COMES INTO SHOT.)
+ 6A. ZOOM INTO
ASTEROID GLASS.

7. TELECINE : TWO
Sc: 7.

THE NEBULLOUS DRIFTING
SUBSTANCE – THRU' IT THE
TINY SHAPE of THE SHUTTLE
APPROACHING
NEBULA: CONDENSING
COALESING
THICKENING

TRY WIND BACK.
3" MODEL
CUT IN FLASH FRAMES

CUT BACK ETC.

8. SIDE ANGLE INTO
C.U.

1" MODEL, IT BREAKS
THRU' SMOKE IN C.U.

SMOKE HANGING – BUT
CONTINUES TO BE
SEMI-OBSCURED

MAY BE FOREGROUND
GLASS WITH VAPOUR
PAINTED – MOVING
SLIGHTLY
WITH US.

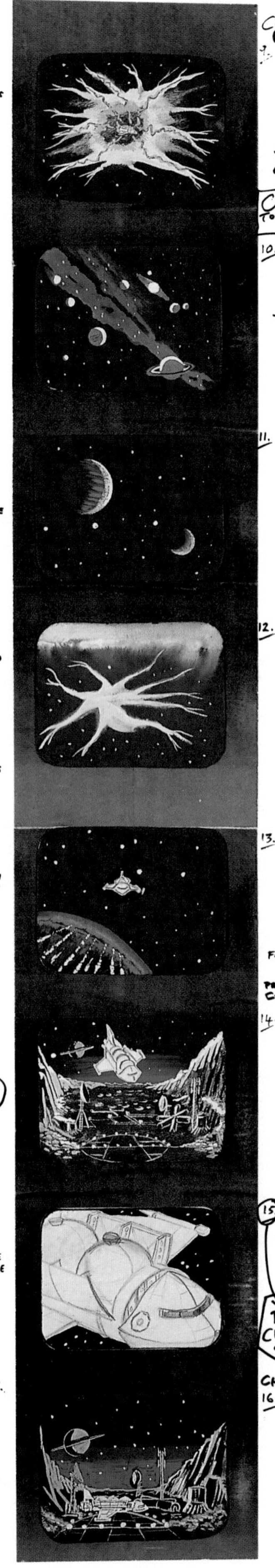

CUT IN HAND SHOT
PILOTS CONTROL
STUDIO.

9. TELECINE: THREE
(PAGE: 9).

SNAKY LIGHTENING
HITS SHUTTLE – TINY
BY COMPARISON
TO CLOUD – CRAFT
VEERS AWAY.

CUT OUT CERTAIN
FLASHES TO MINIMUM
CUT IN FLASH
FRAMES

CUT IN VIEW POINT
TO MAKE IT WORK.

10. PAGE 11/12 INT TARDIS
DR LOOKS AT SCREEN
"THE SOLAR SYSTEM
JUPITER AND SATURN"

– GOES IN AND OUT
of FOCUS

SUN FLARES.

11.

RE-FOCUS – TIGHTER
SHOT.
"NR. JUPITER
AND ASTEROID BELT"

12. TELECINE: FOUR
Sc: 14.

THE NEBULOUS CLOUD
HANGING — SHIFTING
SHAPE

MAY BE FOREGROUND
TOP SMOKE ON GLASS

13. TELECINE: FOUR: A.
Sc: 16.

SHUTTLE COMES IN
OVER TITAN

TILT CAMERA · WIDE
ANGLE LENS – BACK
LIGHT – WATCH FALL
OFF IN FOREGROUND,
DOESN'T GIVE IT AWAY!
FAIRLY HIGH ANGLE TO
HELP IT!

PRINT-UP. TO LIGHTEN.
CHOOSE: T/K.1. – EDITOR.
HIGH ANGLE:

14. SHUTTLE COMES IN
OVER TITAN BASE
COCOA BROWN SANDY
COLOUR WITH SALT
FOR SNOW LIGHTLY
COVERING MOUNTAINS
SUGGESTION of ICE
(CLEAR RESIN) SKY
DARK BLUE – GOING TO
BLACK
RINGS OF SATURN
ARE SEEN ALMOST
EDGE ON – SMALL
"RHEA" ON LEFT.
LITTLE ATMOSPHERE
USE STAR FILTER
ON LANDING PAD
LIGHTS. 72.f.p.s.

15. B.C.U. SHUTTLE
TURNS
1" MODEL

BEFORE THIS
CUT TO
STUDIO CONTROLS

CHOOSE: T/K.2. EDITOR.

16. LIGHT JETEX
MOTORS – SHUTTLE
LANDS ON PAD
– FULLERS EARTH
DUST
72 f.p.s.
1" MODEL

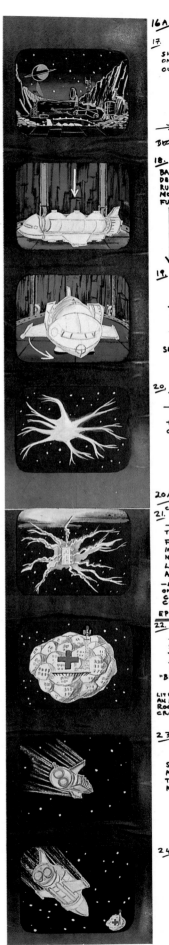

16A – HIGH ANGLE
of CRAFT DRO

17. SHUTTLE DOCK
ON BASE – PRO
OUT-of-VIEW

→ STUDIO
CUT-IN.
BECAUSE of LACK
SK

18. REVERSE ANG
BASE WITH CRA
DECENDS ON
RUNNERS – JETE
MOTORS AND
FULLER'S EARTH
LEADING TO.

19. BASE WITH
CRAFT
REVOLVES T
NOSE HEAD
– BASE IN T
CRAFT TOWA

SEE EXTRA S

20. TELECINE: 5
EP: 1. Sc: 27

THE NEBULOUS
CLOUD
QUIESCENT

20A. TARDIS IN S
CUT IN FLASH F
CUT OUT A FEW LIGH

21. TELECINE: 6.
EP: 1. Sc: 3

TARDIS MATERIA
FOREGROUND – G
INTO CENTRE O
NEBULOUS – SNA
LIGHTENING HIT
AND IT DE-MATE

– LIGHTS ON AND O
ON SMOKE (CONS
CUT IN FLASH F
CUT OUT LIGHTENI

EPISODE : TWO

22. TELECINE: 2.
EP: 2. PAGE

SLIGHT BACK LIG
TO GIVE SEPERA
HOLD IN L/S –
ZOOM TO ESTA
"BI-AL FOUNDAT
"K.406

LIT WINDOWS EMBED
AN IMMENCE CLIF
ROCK – LARGE R
CROSS AND LANDIN

23. TELECINE:
EP: 2.

SHUTTLE FALL
AWAY FROM U
TUMBLING TOW
K.4067

24. ANOTHER
ANGLE
"TARGET"
SIGHT IN

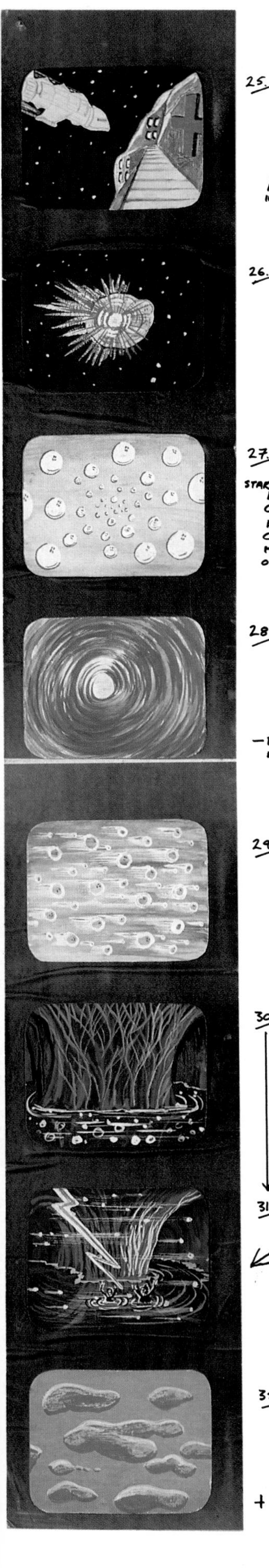

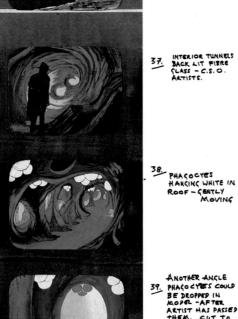

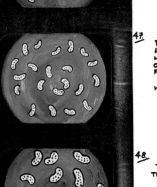

25. SHUTTLE CRASHES ONTO MIDDLE of RED CROSS
"SUPER SILENT EXPLOSION AND DEBRIS"
CUT ON EXPLOSION AS CRAFT-STILL IN SHOT TO:

26. WIDE ANGLE L/S OF "SUPER SILENT BANG" – TITANIUM.
2ND TAKE.

27. TELECINE: 5
EP: 2. P. 58.
START OUT OF FOCUS.
LOOKING DOWN CONE OF LIQUID
MULTIPLE BUBBLES COMING UP AT US
MAYBE WIND BACK ON CAMERA FOR MULTIPLES!

28. START TO SWIRL VORTEX - RED AND BLUE DYE
– GIVE TUNNEL F/X LIKE OPENING TITLES
MAYBE ADD GLITTER
– NOW FOR END of EPISODE (DIRECTOR'S WISHES!)

29. TELECINE: 5
EP: 2. CONTINUED
BUBBLES RUSHING SIDEWAYS L-R.
RED/BLUE B/G.

30. PLAY MULTI-COLOURED LIGHT ONTO WATER
HOSE F/X ROUND TANK
PULL BACK TO SHOW:
"BODIES of LEELA AND DR. BEING RUSHED ALONG A MULTICOLOURED STREAM-LIKE OBJECTS CAUGHT IN RAPPIDS.
– AWAY THEY GO FLOUNDERING AND FIGHTING THE CURRENT-BEARING ON 'THRU' THE SPINAL CORD UP IN THE BRAIN

31. LIGHTENING FLASH
FOREGROUND TANK OF BUBBLES
(STUDIO SCENE IS PINK/BLUE AFTER THIS)
ARTISTS IN C.S.O. TIGHTS

32. B/G PLATE FOR C.S.O.
"NORDIC ASTRA LAMP ON SIDE (– CAMERA?)
12. f. p. s.
LOOP.
L-R.

+ 32.A. AS ABOVE UP & DOWN.

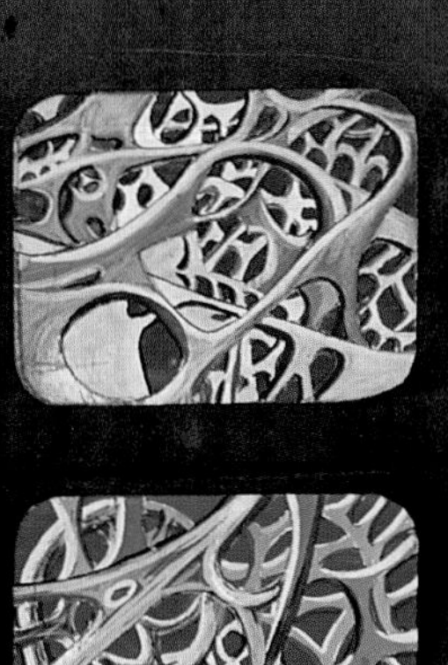

33. BRAIN
FOREGROUND GLASS AND MODEL
C.S.O. B/G.
GREY FEELING
ESTABLISH SMALL ARTISTS ON BRIDGE
SIDE ANGLE
(USE CINEMOID 39. PRIMARY GREEN.)

34. ANOTHER VIEW
HIGH ANGLE
ARTISTS ON SLOPE
(MAYBE WALKING ON FOAM RUBBER).
THIS LEADS TO:

35. BRIDGE SHOT
OCASIONAL SYNAPTIC ELECTRIC FLASH (MAGNESIUM FLASH BULB)
"THEY TURN A CORNER AND ARE ON THE EDGE OF A CHASM.
A PERILOUS NARROW BRIDGE OF TISSUE ARCHES OUT INTO SPACE AND ENDS IN THE MIDDLE IN TOTAL BLACKNESS

36. C.S.O. ARTISTS.
REVERSE ANGLE OR ALTERNATIVE VIEW POINT.

37. INTERIOR TUNNELS
BACK LIT FIBRE GLASS – C.S.O. ARTISTS.

38. PHAGOCYES HANGING WHITE IN ROOF – GENTLY MOVING

39. ANOTHER ANGLE
PHAGOCYTES COULD BE DROPPED IN MODEL – AFTER ARTIST HAS PASSED THEM. CUT TO STUDIO

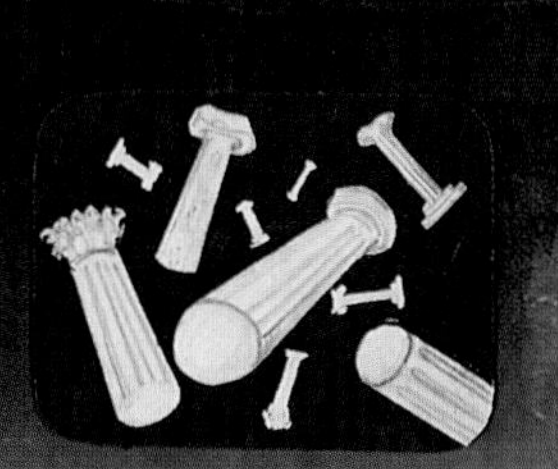

1. STRAIGHT SHOT + MULTIPLE EXPOSURE

40. EPISODE THREE
EP: 3. P. 30
"THEY EMERGE INTO A VAST CAVE – THE WALLS ARE BLACK AND SHINY LIKE COAL.
THERE ARE PILLARS – CLASSICAL AND SILVER FLOATING IN IMPOSIBLE PERSPECTIVE – SOME SOLID – SOME REAL
– ON WIRES: C.S.O.
ALSO: DROP TO/AWAY

EPISODE FOUR:

41. TELECINE: 4.
EP: 4.
ZOOM INTO K. 4067.
RED CROSS IN CLIFF IS BROKEN
DIFFERENT SHUTTLE ON LANDING STAGE WITH RE-DRESSED 'TANKS' IN ITS HOLD.
ALSO HAS RED CROSS ON WINGS.

(NON TIGHT GAS SETS)

42. BIG C.U. GAS JETS BLASTING AWAY
BECAUSE of GAS CUT A FEW FRONT FRAMES WITHOUT GAS ONTO END.
TO CUT TO

43. "UP AND AWAY"
– LEFT.

44.

PAN WITH MODEL

45. SHUTTLE COMES INTO FRAME
WE ESTABLISH SATURN (USE MODEL PLANET.
– AND OUT R.

ORANGE/RED
(NEED COLOUR OVER)

46. P. 10. EPISODE: 3.
INLARGE 3 TIMES
INHIDOSOL AND COPPER/SILVER AEROSOL PAINT IN FILM CAN
HEAT – FILL TO THE TOP
ADD COLOUR WITH GELL.

47. PERSPEX SHAPES LIKE PEANUTS WITH POPPYSEEDS ON THEM – MOVING FLOATING.
MAYBE CAMPHOR WOULD HELP.

48. THIS IS LEELA'S TISSUE

TELECINE 4. CONT.

49. INSERT LEELA'S P.O.V. P.14. EP:4.

"SPECIMENS ON SLIDE NOW HAVE A FISH HOOK SHAPED ANTI-BODY

GO FOR FULL SHOT NOT C.U.'S

50. TELECINE 3. EP:4.

USE PORRAGE
GREEN FOOD DYE
SWAFFEAGER
DRY-ICE.
POLYSTYRENE BALLS
GAS RING UNDER SET.
EGGS GET BIGGER
SHOOT L/S-3 TIMES.

51.

ANOTHER ANGLE — LITTLE SCALE TO HELP EXT. TANK

52. BIG C.U. EGGS BUBBLING IN MIXTURE — STEAM: F.K.

53. TELECINE: 3. SC: 32. PAGE: 51.

TITAN SHOWS A ROSE of FLAME - IT BURSTS INTO A HUGE EXPLOSION

GAS FLAME
IGNIGHTED
FISH TAIL.
CAPSOLATED
PETROL

(FLAME N.G. TO CUT TO 54) - SO USE SHOT 54. ONLY.

54. HUGE EXPLOSION (SET of 3) IN SUCCESSION
FIT MORTAR IN PIT - PEAT
COLRON,
GUNPOWDER
MAGNESIUM

BRING LIGHT UP ON SKY (WHITE/ORANGE)
PLASTIC DEBRIS

55. INT. TARDIS SCANNER L/S TITAN
ZOOM OUT AS IT GLOWS BRIGHTER — SPARKS SHOOTING OUT TOWARDS US (ARC-WELDER)
(MANY TAKES AT DIFFERENT SPEEDS)

56. SMOKELESS WHITE TITANIUM EXPLOSION
(NOW NO NEED AS 55- COVERS THIS)

CUT BACK TO DR + LEELA.

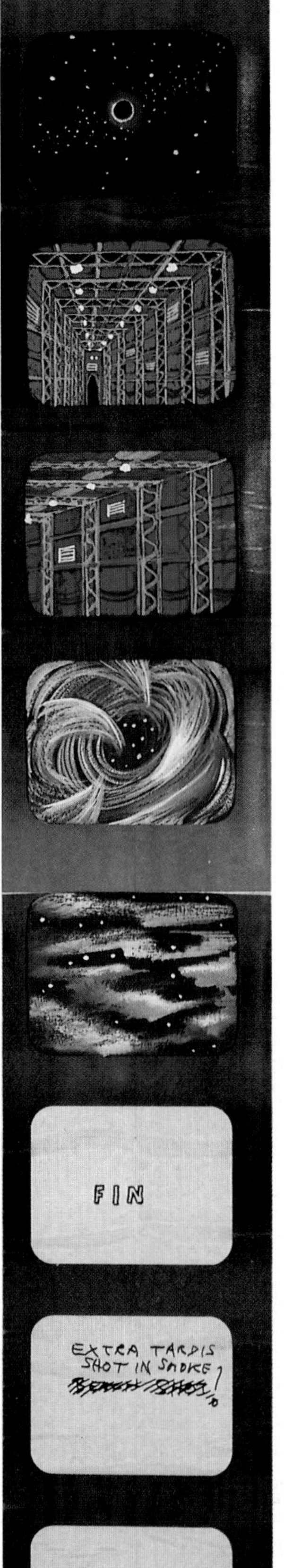

"DR WHO" - INVISIBLE ENEMY. PROJECT NO: 02347/2204

743·8000 X 3865 VISUAL EFFECTS BBC-TV

IAN SCOONES

57.

LONG SHOT - TARDIS VIEW POINT
TITAN RE-MAINS - NOW WITHOUT ATMOSPHERE - LOOKING ALMOST LIKE A "BLACK HOLE" (BACK LIGHT)
PICK UP ON PULL-OUT - HOLD TILL END of ZOOM.

58. EXTRA SHOT FOR BARRY
LOW ANGLE: TRACK INTO AIR LOCK CORRIDOOR FOR C.S.O. CRAFT'S P.O.V.
SHOT: 19A. EPISODE: ONE.
GIRDERS - ROCK - LIGHTS.
SHOOT UP "CINEMASCOPE" WIZE BECAUSE of CUT OFF IN C.S.O. STUDIO.

59. SIDE WINDOW OF CRAFT'S P.O.V. TRACK ALONG R-L.
L. ANGLE:
LIGHTS IN ROOF.

59.A. SIDE ON TRACK R-L.

60. SHOT: 9 A. EPISODE ONE:
C.S.O. PILOT'S P.O.V.
SWIRLING SMOKE HEAD ON IT CLEARS TO STARS BEHIND - ARC LIGHTENING TO BACK LIGHT SMOKE INTERMITTENTLY.
CAMERA ON BUNGY TO SWING ABOUT.

61. STATIC SMOKE
CAMERA ON BUNGY.
PILOTS: P.O.V. FOR C.S.O.
SHOT: 9 B.
SMOKE CLEARS.
LEAVE STARS - STATIC.

61.A. SMOKE R.-L. } CLEARING TO STARS. PILOTS P.O.V.
61.B. " L.-R. }

62.

63.

64.

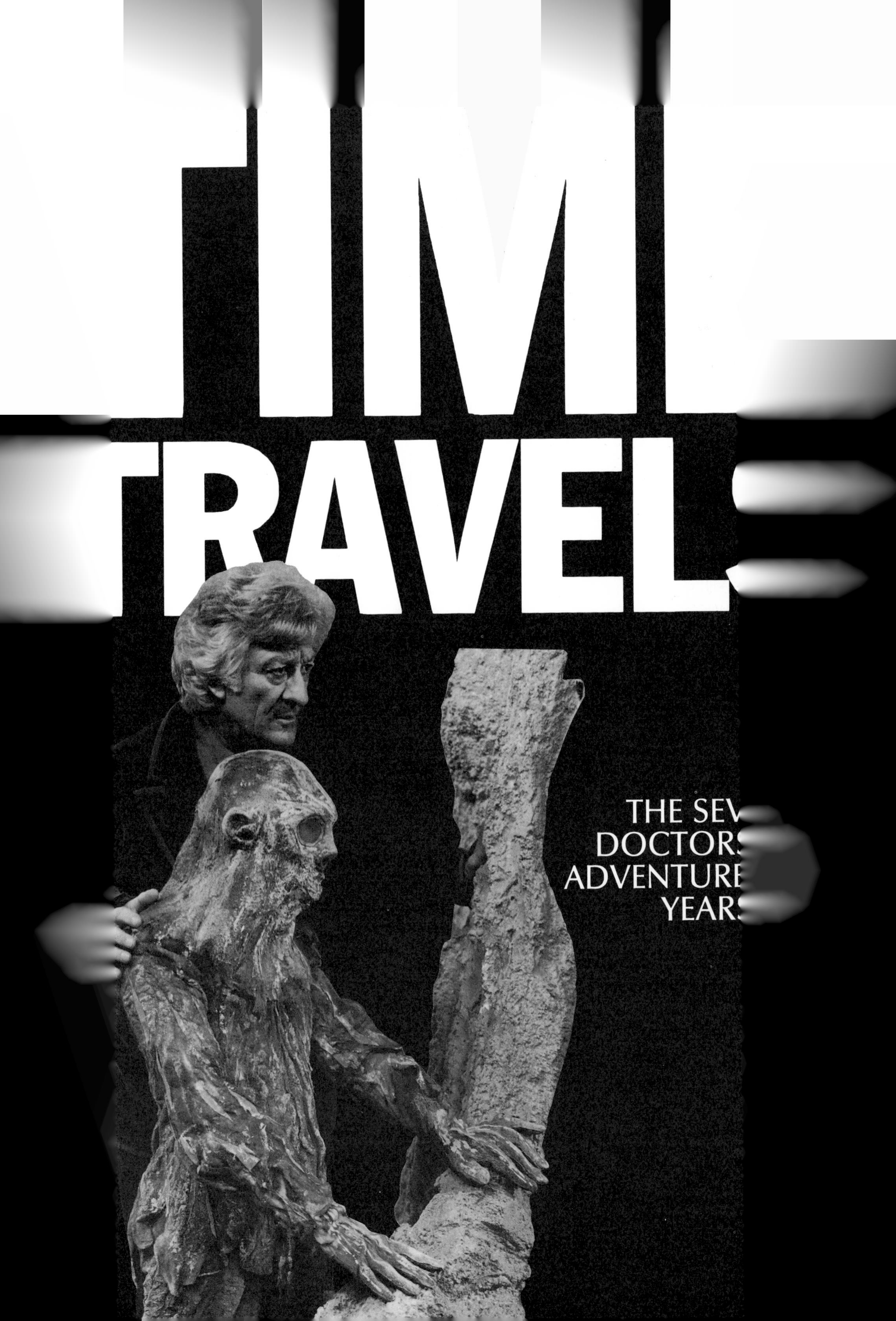
TIM
TRAVEL
THE SEV
DOCTORS
ADVENTURE
YEARS

I WILLIAM HARTNELL

FIRST SEASON

(Producers: Verity Lambert and Mervyn Pinfield)

1 An Unearthly Child by Anthony Coburn and C. E. Webber (4 episodes).
Directed by Waris Hussein.
Guest stars: Derek Newark (Za), Alethea Charlton (Hur).
Screened: 23 November–14 December 1963.

2 The Daleks by Terry Nation (7 episodes).
Directed by Christopher Barry and Richard Martin.
Guest stars: Alan Wheatley (Temmosus), Philip Bond (Ganatus), Virginia Wetherell (Dyoni).
Screened: 21 December 1963–1 February 1964.

3 The Edge of Destruction by David Whitaker (2 episodes).
Directed by Richard Martin and Frank Cox.
Guest stars: None.
Screened: 8 February–15 February 1964.

4 Marco Polo by John Lucarotti (7 episodes).
Directed by Waris Hussein and John Crockett.
Guest stars: Mark Eden (Marco Polo), Derren Nesbitt (Tegana), Tutte Lemkow (Kui-Ju).
Screened: 22 February–4 April 1964.

5 The Keys of Marinus by Terry Nation (6 episodes).
Directed by John Gorrie.
Guest stars: George Coulouris (Arbitan), Raf de la Torre (Senior Judge), Donald Pickering (Eyesen).
Screened: 11 April–16 May 1964.

6 The Aztecs by John Lucarotti (4 episodes).
Directed by John Crockett.
Guest stars: Keith Pyott (Autloc), John Ringham (Tlotoxl).
Screened: 23 May–13 June 1964.

7 The Sensorites by Peter R. Newman (6 episodes).
Directed by Mervyn Pinfield and Frank Cox.
Guest stars: Stephen Dartnell (John), Ilona Rodgers (Carol), Peter Glaze (Sensorite).
Screened: 20 June–1 August 1964.

8 The Reign of Terror by Dennis Spooner (6 episodes).
Directed by Henric Hirsch.
Guest stars: Neville Smith (d'Argenson), Keith Anderson (Robespierre), Ronald Pickup (Physician).
Screened: 8 August–12 September 1964.

SECOND SEASON

(Producers: Verity Lambert and Mervyn Pinfield)

9 Planet of Giants by Louis Marks (3 episodes).
Directed by Mervyn Pinfield and Douglas Camfield.
Guest stars: Alan Tilvern (Forester), Frank Crawshaw (Farrow).
Screened: 31 October–14 November 1964.

10 The Dalek Invasion of Earth by Terry Nation (6 episodes).
Directed by Richard Martin.
Guest stars: Bernard Kay (Carl Tyler), Peter Fraser (David Campbell).
Screened: 21 November–26 December 1964.

11 The Rescue by David Whitaker (2 episodes).
Directed by Christopher Barry.

Guest stars: Ray Barrett (Bennett/Koquillion), Tom Sheridan (Captain).
Screened: 2 January–9 January 1965.
12 The Romans by Dennis Spooner (4 episodes).
Directed by Christopher Barry.
Guest stars: Derek Francis (Nero), Kay Patrick (Poppea), Barry Jackson (Ascaris).
Screened: 16 January–6 February 1965.

(Producer: Verity Lambert)

13 The Web Planet by Bill Strutton (6 episodes).
Directed by Richard Martin.
Guest stars: Roslyn de Winter (Vrestin), Arne Gordon (Hrostar), Martin Jarvis (Captain Hilio).
Screened: 13 February–20 March 1965.
14 The Crusade by David Whitaker (4 episodes).
Directed by Douglas Camfield.
Guest stars: Julian Glover (Richard the Lionheart), Walter Randall (El Akir), Tutte Lemkow (Ibrahim), Jean Marsh (Joanna).
Screened: 27 March–17 April 1965.
15 The Space Museum by Glyn Jones (4 episodes).
Directed by Mervyn Pinfield.
Guest stars: Peter Craze (Dako), Jeremy Bulloch (Tor).
Screened: 24 April–15 May 1965.
16 The Chase by Terry Nation (6 episodes).
Directed by Richard Martin.
Guest stars: Hywel Bennett (Rynian), Peter Purves (Morton Dill), Roslyn de Winter (Grey Lady).
Screened: 22 May–26 June 1965.
17 The Time Meddler by Dennis Spooner (4 episodes).
Directed by Douglas Camfield.
Guest stars: Peter Butterworth (Monk), Alethea Charlton (Edith).
Screened: 3 July–24 July 1965.

THIRD SEASON

(Producer: Verity Lambert)

18 Galaxy Four by William Emms (4 episodes).
Directed by Derek Martinus.
Guest stars: Stephanie Bidmead (Maaga), Barry Jackson (Garvey).
Screened: 11 September–2 October 1965.
19 Mission to the Unknown by Terry Nation (1 episode).
Directed by Derek Martinus.
Guest stars: Edward de Souza (Marc Cory), Jeremy Young (Gordon Lowery).
Screened: 9 October 1965.

(Producer: John Wiles)

20 The Myth Makers by Donald Cotton (4 episodes).
Directed by Michael Leeston-Smith.
Guest stars: Max Adrian (Priam), Francis de Wolff (Agamemnon), Tutte Lemkow (Cyclops).
Screened: 16 October–6 November 1965.
21 The Daleks' Master Plan by Terry Nation and Dennis Spooner (12 episodes).
Directed by Douglas Camfield.
Guest stars: Brian Cant (Kert Gantry), Nicholas Courtney (Bret Vyon), Kevin Stoney (Mavic Chen), Peter Butterworth (Monk).

Screened: 13 November 1965–29 January 1966.

22 The Massacre by John Lucarotti (4 episodes).

Directed by Paddy Russell.

Guest stars: Eric Thompson (Gaston), Andre Morell (Tavannes), Leonard Sachs (Admiral de Coligny).

Screened: 5 February–26 February 1966.

23 The Ark by Paul Erickson and Lesley Scott (4 episodes).

Directed by Michael Imison.

Guest stars: Eric Elliott (Commander), Inigo Jackson (Zentos).

Screened: 5 March–26 March 1966.

(Producer: Innes Lloyd)

24 The Celestial Toymaker by Brian Hayles (4 episodes).

Directed by Bill Sellars.

Guest stars: Michael Gough (The Toymaker), Campbell Singer (Joey), Carmen Silvera (Clara).

Screened: 2 April–23 April 1966.

25 The Gunfighters by Donald Cotton (4 episodes).

Directed by Rex Tucker.

Guest stars: William Hurndell (Ike Clanton), Laurence Payne (Johnny Ringo), Sheena Marshe (Kate).

Screened: 30 April–21 May 1966.

26 The Savages by Ian Stuart Black (4 episodes).

Directed by Christopher Barry.

Guest stars: Ewen Solon (Chal), Frederick Jaeger (Jano), Kay Patrick (Flower).

Screened: 28 May–18 June 1966.

27 The War Machines by Ian Stuart Black (4 episodes).

Directed by Michael Ferguson.

Guest stars: William Mervyn (Sir Charles Summer), Alan Curtis (Major Green), Kenneth Kendall (Newsreader).

Screened: 25 June–16 July 1966.

FOURTH SEASON

(Producer: Innes Lloyd)

28 The Smugglers by Brian Hayles (4 episodes).

Directed by Julia Smith.

Guest stars: Terence de Marney (Churchwarden), George A. Cooper (Cherub) Paul Whitsun-Jones (Squire).

Screened: 10 September–1 October 1966.

29 The Tenth Planet by Kit Pedler and Gerry Davis (4 episodes).

Directed by Derek Martinus.

Guest stars: Robert Beatty (General Cutler), Dudley Jones (Dyson).

Screened: 8 October–29 October 1966.

II PATRICK TROUGHTON

(Producer: Innes Lloyd)

30 Power of the Daleks by David Whitaker (6 episodes).

Directed by Christopher Barry

Guest stars: Bernard Archard (Bragen), Pamela Ann Davy (Janley), Edward Kelsey (Resno).

Screened: 5 November–10 December 1966.

31 The Highlanders by Gerry Davis and Elwyn Jones (4 episodes).

Directed by Hugh David.

Guest stars: Hannah Gordon (Kirsty), William

Dysart (Alexander), Donald Bisset (Laird).
Screened: 17 December 1966–7 January 1967.

32 The Underwater Menace by Geoffrey Orme (4 episodes).
Directed by Julia Smith.
Guest stars: Joseph Furst (Professor Zaroff), Colin Jeavons (Damon), Catherine Howe (Ara).
Screened: 14 January–4 February 1967.

33 The Moonbase by Kit Pedler (4 episodes).
Directed by Morris Barry.
Guest stars: Patrick Barr (Hobson), Andre Maranne (Benoit).
Screened: 11 February–4 March 1967.

34 The Macra Terror by Ian Stuart Black (4 episodes).
Directed by John Davies.
Guest stars: Peter Jeffrey (Pilot), Gertan Klauber (Ola).
Screened: 11 March–1 April 1967.

(Producers: Innes Lloyd and Peter Bryant)

35 The Faceless Ones by David Ellis and Malcolm Hulke (6 episodes).
Directed by Gerry Mill.
Guest stars: Wanda Ventham (Jean Rock), Pauline Collins (Samantha Briggs), Donald Pickering (Blade).
Screened: 8 April–13 May 1967.

(Producer: Innes Lloyd)

36 The Evil of the Daleks by David Whitaker (7 episodes).
Directed by Derek Martinus.
Guest stars: Marius Goring (Theodore Maxtible), Windsor Davies (Toby), Geoffrey Colville (Perry).
Screened: 20 May–1 July 1967.

FIFTH SEASON

(Producer: Peter Bryant)

37 The Tomb of the Cybermen by Kit Pedler and Gerry Davis (4 episodes).
Directed by Morris Barry.
Guest stars: Cyril Shaps (Viner), Clive Merrison (Callum), Shirley Cooklin (Kaftan), George Pastell (Klieg).
Screened: 2 September–23 September 1967.

(Producer: Innes Lloyd)

38 The Abominable Snowmen by Mervyn Haisman and Henry Lincoln (6 episodes).
Directed by Gerald Blake.
Guest stars: Jack Watling (Professor Travers), Norman Jones (Khrisong).
Screened: 30 September–4 November 1967.

39 The Ice Warriors by Brian Hayles (6 episodes).
Directed by Derek Martinus.
Guest stars: Peter Barkworth (Clent), Peter Sallis (Penley), Bernard Bresslaw (Varga).
Screened: 11 November–16 December 1967.

40 The Enemy of the World by David Whitaker (6 episodes).
Directed by Barry Letts.
Guest stars: Bill Kerr (Kent), George Pravda (Denes), Milton Johns (Benik).
Screened: 23 December 1967–27 January 1968.

(Producer: Peter Bryant)

41 The Web of Fear by Mervyn Haisman and Henry Lincoln (6 episodes).
Directed by Douglas Camfield.
Guest stars: Nicholas Courtney (Colonel Lethbridge-Stewart), Jack Watling (Professor Travers), Jack Woolgar (Sergeant Arnold).

Screened: 3 February–9 March 1968.

42 Fury from the Deep by Victor Pemberton (6 episodes).
Directed by Hugh David.
Guest stars: Victor Maddern (Robson), Margaret John (Megan Jones).
Screened: 16 March–20 April 1968.

43 The Wheel in Space by David Whitaker and Kit Pedler (6 episodes).
Directed by Tristan de Vere Cole.
Guest stars: Donald Sumpter (Enrico Casali), Anne Ridler (Dr Corwyn).
Screened: 27 April–1 June 1968.

SIXTH SEASON

(Producer: Peter Bryant)

44 The Dominators by Norman Ashby (5 episodes).
Directed by Morris Barry.
Guest stars: Ronald Allen (Rago), Kenneth Ives (Toba), Brian Cant (Tensa).
Screened: 10 August–7 September 1968.

45 The Mind Robber by Peter Ling and Derrick Sherwin (5 episodes).
Directed by David Maloney.
Guest stars: Emrys Jones (Master of the Land), Bernard Horsfall (Gulliver), Christopher Robbie (Karkus).
Screened: 14 September–12 October 1968.

46 The Invasion by Derrick Sherwin and Kit Pedler (8 episodes).
Directed by Douglas Camfield.
Guest stars: Nicholas Courtney (Brigadier Lethbridge-Stewart), John Levene (Benton), Kevin Stoney (Tobias Vaughn).
Screened: 2 November–21 December 1968.

47 The Krotons by Robert Holmes (4 episodes).
Directed by David Maloney.
Guest stars: Philip Madoc (Eelek), James Copeland (Selris).
Screened: 28 December 1968–18 January 1969.

48 The Seeds of Death by Brian Hayles (6 episodes).
Directed by Michael Ferguson.
Guest stars: Alan Bennion (Slaar), Harry Towb (Osgood), Hugh Morton (Sir James Gregson).
Screened: 25 January–1 March 1969.

49 The Space Pirates by Robert Holmes (6 episodes).
Directed by Michael Hart.
Guest stars: Dudley Foster (Caven), Donald Gee (Warne), George Layton (Penn), Lisa Daniely (Madeleine).
Screened: 8 March–12 April 1969.

(Producer: Derrick Sherwin)

50 The War Games by Malcolm Hulke and Terrance Dicks (10 episodes).
Directed by David Maloney.
Guest stars: Philip Madoc (War Lord), Bernard Horsfall (Time Lord), Trevor Martin (Time Lord).
Screened 19 April–21 June 1969.

III JON PERTWEE

SEVENTH SEASON

(Producer: Derrick Sherwin)

51 Spearhead from Space by Robert Holmes (4 episodes).

Directed by Derek Martinus.
Guest stars: Hugh Burden (Channing), Derek Smee (Ransome).
Screened: 3 January–24 January 1970.

(Producer: Barry Letts)

52 Doctor Who and the Silurians by Malcolm Hulke (7 episodes).
Directed by Timothy Combe.
Guest stars: Bill Matthews (Davis), Fulton Mackay (Dr Quinn), Geoffrey Palmer (Masters), Paul Darrow (Hawkins).
Screened: 31 January–14 March 1970.

53 The Ambassadors of Death by David Whitaker and Malcolm Hulke (7 episodes).
Directed by Michael Ferguson.
Guest stars: Ronald Allen (Ralph Cornish), John Abineri (Carrington), Cyril Shaps (Lennox).
Screened: 21 March–2 May 1970.

54 Inferno by Don Houghton (7 episodes).
Directed by Douglas Camfield and Barry Letts.
Guest stars: Olaf Pooley (Stahlman), Sheila Dunn (Petra Williams), Derek Newark (Greg Sutton).
Screened: 9 May–20 June 1970.

EIGHTH SEASON

(Producer: Barry Letts)

55 Terror of the Autons by Robert Holmes (4 episodes).
Directed by Barry Letts.
Guest stars: Roger Delgado (The Master), Richard Franklin (Captain Yates), Harry Towb (McDermott).
Screened 2 January–23 January 1971.

56 The Mind of Evil by Don Houghton (6 episodes).
Directed by Timothy Combe.
Guest stars: Simon Lack (Professor Kettering), Michael Sheard (Dr Summers).
Screened: 30 January–6 March 1971.

57 The Claws of Axos by Bob Baker and Dave Martin (4 episodes).
Directed by Michael Ferguson.
Guest stars: Tim Pigott-Smith (Harker), Peter Bathurst (Chinn), Donald Hewlett (Sir George Hardiman).
Screened: 13 March–3 April 1971.

58 Colony in Space by Malcolm Hulke (6 episodes).
Directed by Michael Briant.
Guest stars: David Webb (Leeson), Sheila Grant (Jane), Nicholas Pennell (Winton).
Screened: 10 April–15 May 1971.

59 The Daemons by Guy Leopold (5 episodes).
Directed by Christopher Barry.
Guest stars: Eric Hillyard (Doctor Reeves), Stephen Thorne (Azal), Damans Hayman (Olive Hawthorne).
Screened: 22 May–19 June 1971.

NINTH SEASON

(Producer: Barry Letts)

60 The Day of the Daleks by Louis Marks (4 episodes).
Directed by Paul Bernard.
Guest stars: Wilfred Carter (Sir Reginald Styles), Aubrey Woods (Controller).
Screened: 1 January–22 January 1972.

61 The Curse of Peladon by Brian Hayles (4 episodes).

Directed by Lennie Mayne.
Guest stars: Geoffrey Toone (Hepesh), David Troughton (Peladon).
Screened: 29 January–19 February 1972.

62 The Sea Devils by Malcolm Hulke (6 episodes).
Directed by Michael Briant.
Guest stars: Clive Morton (Trenchard), Edwin Richfield (Hart)
Screened: 26 February–1 April 1972.

63 The Mutants by Bob Baker and Dave Martin (6 episodes).
Directed by Christopher Barry.
Guest stars: Paul Whitsun-Jones (Marshal), Geoffrey Palmer (Administrator), George Pravda (Jaeger).
Screened: 8 April–13 May 1972.

64 The Time Monster by Robert Sloman (6 episodes).
Directed by Paul Bernard.
Guest stars: Ingrid Pitt (Galleia), Susan Penhaligon (Lakis), Dave Prowse (Minotaur).
Screened: 20 May–24 June 1972.

TENTH SEASON

(Producer: Barry Letts)

65 The Three Doctors by Bob Baker and Dave Martin (4 episodes).
Directed by Lennie Mayne.
Guest stars: William Hartnell (First Doctor), Patrick Troughton (Second Doctor), Roy Purcell (President).
Screened: 30 December 1972–20 January 1973.

66 Carnival of Monsters by Robert Holmes (4 episodes).
Directed by Barry Letts.
Guest stars: Leslie Dwyer (Vorg), Tenniel Evans (Major Daly).
Screened: 27 January–17 February 1973.

67 Frontier in Space by Malcolm Hulke (6 episodes).
Directed by Paul Bernard.
Guest stars: James Culliford (Stewart), Vera Fusek (President).
Screened: 24 February–31 March 1973.

68 Planet of the Daleks by Terry Nation (6 episodes).
Directed by David Maloney.
Guest stars: Bernard Horsfall (Taron), Jane How (Rebec).
Screened: 7 April–12 May 1973.

69 The Green Death by Robert Sloman (6 episodes).
Directed by Michael Briant.
Guest stars: Stewart Bevan (Professor Jones), Jerome Willis (Stevens).
Screened: 19 May–23 June 1973.

ELEVENTH SEASON

(Producer: Barry Letts)

70 The Time Warrior by Robert Holmes (4 episodes).
Directed by Alan Bromley.
Guest stars: Kevin Lindsay (Linx), Sheila Fay (Meg), Jeremy Bulloch (Hal).
Screened: 15 December 1973–5 January 1974.

71 Invasion of the Dinosaurs by Malcolm Hulke (6 episodes).
Directed by Paddy Russell.
Guest stars: Noel Johnson (Charles Grover), Martin Jarvis (Butler), Carmen Silvera (Ruth).

Screened: 12 January–16 February 1974.

72 Death to the Daleks by Terry Nation (4 episodes).

Directed by Michael Briant.

Guest stars: Duncan Lamont (Galloway), John Abineri (Railton), Joy Harrison (Jill Tarrant).

Screened: 23 February–16 March 1974.

73 The Monster of Peladon by Brian Hayles (6 episodes).

Directed by Lennie Mayne.

Guest stars: Donald Gee (Eckersley), Nina Thomas (Queen Thalira).

Screened: 23 March–27 April 1974.

74 Planet of the Spiders by Robert Sloman (6 episodes).

Directed by Barry Letts.

Guest stars: Cyril Shaps (Professor Clegg), Kevin Lindsay (Cho-Je), Gareth Hunt (Arak).

Screened: 4 May–8 June 1974.

IV TOM BAKER

TWELFTH SEASON

(Producer: Barry Letts)

75 Robot by Terrance Dicks (4 episodes).

Directed by Christopher Barry.

Guest stars: Edward Burnham (Professor Kettlewell), Alec Linstead (Jellicoe), Patricia Maynard (Miss Winters).

Screened: 28 December 1974–18 January 1975.

(Producer: Philip Hinchcliffe)

76 The Ark in Space by Robert Holmes (4 episodes).

Directed by Rodney Bennett.

Guest stars: Kenton Moore (Noah), Wendy Williams (Vira).

Screened: 25 January–15 February 1975.

77 The Sontaran Experiment by Bob Baker and Dave Martin (2 episodes).

Directed by Rodney Bennett.

Guest stars: Kevin Lindsay (Styre), Glyn Jones (Krans).

Screened: 22 February–1 March 1975.

78 Genesis of the Daleks by Terry Nation (6 episodes).

Directed by David Maloney.

Guest stars: Michael Wisher (Davros), Dennis Chinnery (Gharman).

Screened: 8 March–12 April 1975.

79 Revenge of the Cybermen by Gerry Davis (4 episodes)

Directed by Michael Briant.

Guest stars: Alec Wallis (Warner), Kevin Stoney (Tyrum).

Screened: 19 April–10 May 1975.

THIRTEENTH SEASON

(Producer: Philip Hinchcliffe)

80 Terror of the Zygons by Robert Banks Stewart (4 episodes).

Directed by Douglas Camfield.

Guest stars: John Woodnutt (Duke of Forgill), Hugh Martin (Munro).

Screened: 30 August–20 September 1975.

81 Planet of Evil by Louis Marks (4 episodes).

Directed by David Maloney.

Guest stars: Frederick Jaeger (Sorenson), Ewen Solon (Vishinsky).

Screened: 27 September–18 October 1975.

82 Pyramids of Mars by Stephen Harris (4 episodes).

Directed by Paddy Russell.
Guest stars: Bernard Archard (Professor Marcus Scarman), Peter Mayock (Namin).
Screened: 25 October–15 November 1975.

83 The Android Invasion by Terry Nation (4 episodes).
Directed by Barry Letts.
Guest stars: Martin Friend (Styggron), Milton Johns (Guy Crayford).
Screened: 22 November–13 December 1975.

84 The Brain of Morbius by Robin Bland (4 episodes).
Directed by Christopher Barry.
Guest stars: Philip Madoc (Solon), Colin Fay (Condo).
Screened: 3 January–24 January 1976.

85 The Seeds of Doom by Robert Banks Stewart (6 episodes).
Directed by Douglas Camfield.
Guest stars: Tony Beckley (Harrison Chase), John Gleeson (Charles Winlett).
Screened: 31 January–6 March 1976.

FOURTEENTH SEASON

(Producer: Philip Hinchcliffe)

86 The Masque of Mandragora by Louis Marks (4 episodes).
Directed by Rodney Bennett.
Guest stars: Jon Laurimore (Count Frederico), Tim Pigott-Smith (Marco).
Screened: 4 September–25 September 1976.

87 The Hand of Fear by Bob Baker and Dave Martin (4 episodes).
Directed by Lennie Mayne.
Guest stars: Glyn Houston (Professor Watson), Frances Pidgeon (Miss Jackson).
Screened: 2 October–23 October 1976.

88 The Deadly Assassin by Robert Holmes (4 episodes).
Directed by David Maloney.
Guest stars: Bernard Horsfall (Chancellor Goth), George Pravda (Castellan Spandrell), Erik Chitty (Co-ordinator Engin).
Screened: 30 October–20 November 1976.

89 The Face of Evil by Chris Boucher (4 episodes).
Directed by Pennant Roberts.
Guest stars: Leslie Schofield (Calib), Victor Lucas (Andor).
Screened: 1 January–22 January 1977.

90 The Robots of Death by Chris Boucher (4 episodes).
Directed by Michael Briant.
Guest stars: Russell Hunter (Commander Uvanov), Pamela Salem (Toos).
Screened: 29 January–19 February 1977.

91 The Talons of Weng-Chiang by Robert Holmes (6 episodes).
Directed by David Maloney.
Guest stars: Deep Roy (Mr Sin), Michael Spice (Magnus Greel).
Screened: 26 February–2 April 1977.

FIFTEENTH SEASON

(Producer: Graham Williams)

92 Horror of Fang Rock by Terrance Dicks (4 episodes).
Directed by Paddy Russell.
Guest Stars: Colin Douglas (Reuben), John Abbott (Vince).

Screened: 3 September–24 September 1977.

93 The Invisible Enemy by Bob Baker and Dave Martin (4 episodes).

Directed by Derrick Goodwin.

Guest stars: Frederick Jaeger (Professor Marius), Michael Sheard (Lowe).

Screened: 1 October–22 October 1977.

94 Image of the Fendahl by Chris Boucher (4 episodes).

Directed by George Spenton-Foster.

Guest stars: Wanda Ventham (Thea Ransome), Denis Lill (Dr Fendelman).

Screened: 29 October–19 November 1977.

95 The Sun Makers by Robert Holmes (4 episodes).

Directed by Pennant Roberts

Guest stars: Richard Leech (Gatherer Hade), Henry Woolf (Collector).

Screened: 26 November–17 December 1977.

96 Underworld by Bob Baker and Dave Martin (4 episodes).

Directed by Norman Stewart.

Guest stars: James Maxwell (Jackson), Alan Lake (Herrick).

Screened: 7 January–28 January 1978.

97 The Invasion of Time by David Agnew (6 episodes).

Directed by Gerald Blake.

Guest stars: Milton Johns (Kelner), John Arnatt (Borusa).

Screened: 4 February–11 March 1978.

SIXTEENTH SEASON

(Producer: Graham Williams)

98 The Ribos Operation by Robert Holmes (4 episodes).

Directed by George Spenton-Foster.

Guest stars: Iain Cuthbertson (Garron), Nigel Plaskitt (Unstoffe), Cyril Luckham (White Guardian).

Screened: 2 September–23 September 1978.

99 The Pirate Planet by Douglas Adams (4 episodes).

Directed by Pennant Roberts.

Guest stars: Bruce Purchase (Captain), Rosalind Lloyd (Queen Xanxia).

Screened: 30 September–21 October 1978.

100 The Stones of Blood by David Fisher (4 episodes).

Directed by Darrol Blake.

Guest stars: Susan Engel (Vivien Fay), Beatrix Lehmann (Professor Rumford).

Screened: 28 October–18 November 1978.

101 The Androids of Tara by David Fisher (4 episodes).

Directed by Michael Hayes.

Guest stars: Peter Jeffrey (Count Grendel), Neville Jason (Prince Reynart).

Screened: 25 November–16 December 1978.

102 The Power of Kroll by Robert Holmes (4 episodes).

Directed by Norman Stewart.

Guest stars: Philip Madoc (Fenner), Neil McCarthy (Thawn).

Screened: 23 December 1978–13 January 1979.

103 The Armageddon Factor by Bob Baker and Dave Martin (6 episodes).

Directed by Michael Hayes.

Guest stars: Valentine Dyall (Black Guardian), John Woodvine (Marshal).

Screened: 20 January–24 February 1979.

SEVENTEENTH SEASON

(Producer: Graham Williams)

104 Destiny of the Daleks by Terry Nation (4 episodes).

Directed by Ken Grieve.

Guest stars: Peter Straker (Commander Sharrel), Suzanne Danielle (Agella).

Screened: 1 September–22 September 1979.

105 City of Death by David Agnew (4 episodes).

Directed by Michael Hayes.

Guest stars: Julian Glover (Scaroth), Catherine Schell (Countess Scarlioni), John Cleese and Eleanor Bron (Art-lovers).

Screened: 29 September–20 October 1979.

106 The Creature from the Pit by David Fisher (4 episodes).

Directed by Christopher Barry.

Guest stars: Myra Frances (Lady Adrasta), Geoffrey Bayldon (Organon).

Screened: 27 October–17 November 1979.

107 Nightmare of Eden by Bob Baker (4 episodes).

Directed by Alan Bromley.

Guest stars: Geoffrey Bateman (Dymond), Peter Craze (Costa).

Screened: 24 November–15 December 1979.

108 The Horns of Nimon by Anthony Read (4 episodes).

Directed by Kenny McBain.

Guest stars: Simon Gipps-Kent (Seth), Janet Ellis (Teka).

Screened: 22 December 1979–12 January 1980.

(Unnumbered) Shada by Douglas Adams. (6 episodes).

Directed by Pennant Roberts.

Guest stars: Denis Carey (Professor Chronotis), Christopher Neame (Skagra).

Screened: Never completed due to industrial dispute at the BBC.

EIGHTEENTH SEASON

(Executive Producer: Barry Letts)

(Producer: John Nathan-Turner)

109 The Leisure Hive by David Fisher (4 episodes).

Directed by Lovett Bickford.

Guest stars: Adrienne Corri (Mena), David Haig (Pangol), Laurence Payne (Morix).

Screened: 30 August–20 September 1980.

110 Meglos by John Flanagan and Andrew McCulloch (4 episodes).

Directed by Terence Dudley.

Guest stars: Bill Fraser (Grugger), Edward Underdown (Zastor), Jacqueline Hill (Lexa).

Screened: 27 September–18 October 1980.

111 Full Circle by Andrew Smith (4 episodes).

Directed by Peter Grimwade.

Guest stars: Richard Willis (Varsh), George Baker (Login).

Screened: 25 October–15 November 1980.

112 State of Decay by Terrance Dicks (4 episodes).

Directed by Peter Moffatt.

Guest stars: William Lindsay (Zargo), Rachel Davies (Camilla).

Screened: 22 November–13 December 1980.

113 Warriors' Gate by Steve Gallagher (4 episodes).

Directed by Paul Joyce and Graeme Harper.

Guest stars: Clifford Rose (Rorvik), Kenneth Cope (Packard).

Screened: 3 January–24 January 1981.

114 The Keeper of Traken by Johnny Byrne (4 episodes).

Directed by John Black.

Guest stars: Anthony Ainley (Tremas), Sheila Ruskin (Kassia), Geoffrey Beevers (Melkur).

Screened: 31 January–21 February 1981.

115 Logopolis by Christopher H. Bidmead (4 episodes).

Directed by Peter Grimwade.

Guest stars: John Fraser (Monitor), Dolores Whiteman (Aunt Vanessa).

Screened: 28 February–21 March 1981.

V PETER DAVISON

NINETEENTH SEASON

(Producer: John Nathan-Turner)

116 Castrovalva by Christopher H. Bidmead (4 episodes).

Directed by Fiona Cumming.

Guest stars: Frank Wylie (Ruther), Michael Sheard (Mergrave), Derek Waring (Shardovan).

Screened: 4 January–12 January 1982.

117 Four to Doomsday by Terence Dudley (4 episodes).

Directed by John Black.

Guest stars: Stratford Johns (Monarch), Annie Lambert (Enlightenment), Burt Kwouk (Lin Futu).

Screened: 18 January–26 January 1982.

118 Kinda by Christopher Bailey (4 episodes).

Directed by Peter Grimwade.

Guest stars: Richard Todd (Sanders), Nerys Hughes (Todd).

Screened: 1 February–9 February 1982.

119 The Visitation by Eric Saward (4 episodes).

Directed by Peter Moffatt.

Guest stars: John Savident (Squire John), Anthony Calf (Charles).

Screened: 15 February–23 February 1982.

120 Black Orchid by Terence Dudley (2 episodes).

Directed by Ron Jones.

Guest stars: Michael Cochrane (Lord Cranleigh), Barbara Murray (Lady Cranleigh), Moray Watson (Sir Robert Muir).

Screened: 1 March–2 March 1982.

121 Earthshock by Eric Saward (4 episodes).

Directed by Peter Grimwade.

Guest stars: Beryl Reid (Captain Briggs), James Warwick (Lieutenant Scott).

Screened: 8 March–16 March 1982.

122 Time-Flight by Peter Grimwade (4 episodes).

Directed by Ron Jones.

Guest stars: Nigel Stock (Professor Hayter), Richard Easton (Captain Stapley).

Screened: 22 March–30 March 1982.

TWENTIETH SEASON

(Producer: John Nathan-Turner)

123 Arc of Infinity by Johnny Byrne (4 episodes).

Directed by Ron Jones.
Guest stars: Michael Gough (Councillor Hedin), Colin Baker (Commander Maxil).
Screened: 3 January–12 January 1983.

124 Snakedance by Christopher Bailey (4 episodes).
Directed by Fiona Cumming.
Guest stars: Colette O'Neil (Tanha), John Carson (Ambril).
Screened: 18 January–26 January 1983.

125 Mawdryn Undead by Peter Grimwade (4 episodes).
Directed by Peter Moffatt.
Guest stars: Nicholas Courtney (The Brigadier), Valentine Dyall (The Black Guardian), David Collings (Mawdryn).
Screened: 1 February–9 February 1983.

126 Terminus by Steve Gallagher (4 episodes).
Directed by Mary Ridge.
Guest stars: Liza Goddard (Kari), Andrew Burt (Valguard).
Screened: 15 February–23 February 1983.

127 Enlightenment by Barbara Clegg (4 episodes).
Directed by Fiona Cumming.
Guest stars: Keith Barron (Captain Striker), Lynda Baron (Captain Wrack).
Screened: 1 March–9 March 1983.

128 The King's Demons by Terence Dudley (2 episodes).
Directed by Tony Virgo.
Guest stars: Gerald Flood (The King), Frank Windsor (Ranulf).
Screened: 15 March–16 March 1983.

129 The Five Doctors by Terrance Dicks (1 episode: Anniversary Special).
Directed by Peter Moffatt.
Guest stars: Richard Hurndall (First Doctor), Patrick Troughton (Second Doctor), Jon Pertwee (Third Doctor).
Screened: 25 November 1983.

TWENTY-FIRST SEASON

(Producer: John Nathan-Turner)

130 Warriors of the Deep by Johnny Byrne (4 episodes).
Directed by Pennant Roberts.
Guest stars: Tom Adams (Vorshak), Ingrid Pitt (Solow).
Screened: 5 January–13 January 1984.

131 The Awakening by Eric Pringle (2 episodes).
Directed by Michael Morris.
Guest stars: Denis Lill (Sir George Hutchinson), Polly James (Jane Hampden).
Screened: 19 January–20 January 1984.

132 Frontios by Christopher H. Bidmead (4 episodes).
Directed by Ron Jones.
Guest stars: Peter Gilmore (Brazen), Lesley Dunlop (Norna).
Screened: 26 January–3 February 1984.

133 Resurrection of the Daleks by Eric Saward (2 episodes).
Directed by Matthew Robinson.
Guest stars: Rula Lenska (Styles), Rodney Bewes (Stein), Les Grantham (Kiston).
Screened: 8 February–15 February 1984.

134 Planet of Fire by Peter Grimwade (4 episodes).
Directed by Fiona Cumming.

Guest stars: Peter Wyngarde (Timanov), Barbara Shelley (Sorasta).

Screened: 23 February–2 March 1984.

135 The Caves of Androzani by Robert Holmes (4 episodes).

Directed by Graeme Harper.

Guest stars: Maurice Roeves (Stotz), Christopher Gable (Sharaz Jek).

Screened: 8 March–16 March 1984.

VI COLIN BAKER

136 The Twin Dilemma by Anthony Steven and Eric Saward (4 episodes).

Directed by Peter Moffatt.

Guest stars: Maurice Denham (Edgeworth), Edwin Richfield (Mestor), Dennis Chinnery (Sylvest).

Screened: 22 March–30 March 1984.

TWENTY-SECOND SEASON

(Producer: John Nathan-Turner)

137 Attack of the Cybermen by Paula Moore (2 episodes).

Directed by Matthew Robinson.

Guest stars: Maurice Colbourne (Lytton), Brian Glover (Griffiths), Faith Brown (Flast).

Screened: 5 January–12 January 1985.

138 Vengeance on Varos by Philip Martin (2 episodes).

Directed by Ron Jones.

Guest stars: Jason Connery (Jondar), Martin Jarvis (The Governor).

Screened: 19 January–26 January 1985.

139 The Mark of The Rani by Pip and Jane Baker (2 episodes).

Directed by Sarah Hellings.

Guest stars: Kate O'Mara (The Rani), Terence Alexander (Lord Ravensworth).

Screened: 2 February–9 February 1985.

140 The Two Doctors by Robert Holmes (3 episodes).

Directed by Peter Moffatt.

Guest stars: Patrick Troughton (Second Doctor), Frazer Hines (Jamie), John Stratton (Shockeye), Jacqueline Pearce (Chessene), Laurence Payne (Dastari).

Screened: 16 February–2 March 1985.

141 Timelash by Glen McCoy (2 episodes).

Directed by Pennant Roberts.

Guest stars: Paul Darrow (Tekker), Denis Carey (The Old Man).

Screened: 9 March–16 March 1985.

142 Revelation of the Daleks by Eric Saward (2 episodes).

Directed by Graeme Harper.

Guest stars: Alexei Sayle (The DJ), Eleanor Bron (Kara), William Gaunt (Orcini).

Screened: 23 March–30 March 1985.

TWENTY-THIRD SEASON

(Producer: John Nathan-Turner)

THE TRIAL OF A TIME LORD

143 The Mysterious Planet by Robert Holmes (4 episodes).

Directed by Nick Mallett.

Guest stars: Michael Jayston (The Valeyard), Linda Bellingham (The Inquisitor), Joan Sims (Katryca), Tony Selby (Glitz).

Screened: 6 September–27 September 1986.

144 Mindwarp by Philip Martin (4 episodes).

Directed by Ron Jones.

Guest stars: Brian Blessed (Yrcanos), Christopher Ryan (Kiv).

Screened: 4 October–25 October 1986.

145 Terror of the Vervoids by Pip and Jane Baker (4 episodes).

Directed by Chris Clough.

Guest stars: Honor Blackman (Professor Lasky), Michael Craig (Commadore Travers).

Screened: 1 November–22 November 1986.

146 The Ultimate Foe by Robert Holmes and Pip and Jane Baker (2 episodes).

Directed by Chris Clough.

Guest stars: Geoffrey Hughes (Mr Popplewick), James Bree (The Keeper).

Screened: 29 November–6 December 1986.

VII SYLVESTER McCOY

TWENTY-FOURTH SEASON

(Producer: John Nathan-Turner)

147 Time and The Rani by Pip and Jane Baker (4 episodes).

Directed by Andrew Morgan.

Guest stars: Kate O'Mara (The Rani), Donald Pickering (Beyus), Wanda Ventham (Faroon).

Screened: 7 September–28 September 1987.

148 Paradise Towers by Stephen Wyatt (4 episodes).

Directed by Nick Mallett.

Guest stars: Richard Briers (Chief Caretaker), Clive Merrison (Deputy Chief Caretaker), Brenda Bruce (Tilda), Elizabeth Spriggs (Tabby).

Screened: 5 October–26 October 1987.

149 Delta and the Bannermen by Malcolm Kohll (3 episodes).

Directed by Chris Clough.

Guest stars: Ken Dodd (Tollmaster), Don Henderson (Gavrok), Stubby Kaye (Weismuller), Belinda Mayne (Delta), Hugh Lloyd (Goronwy).

Screened: 2 November–16 November 1987.

150 Dragonfire by Ian Briggs (4 episodes).

Directed by Chris Clough.

Guest stars: Tony Selby (Glitz), Edward Peel (Kane), Patricia Quinn (Belaz).

Screened: 23 November–14 December 1987.